國務總理段祺瑞為呈請事竊據鑲紅旗蒙古都統

軍都護使治格咨陳民國三年一月同清皇室

前往奉天熱河兩處檢取清宮歷存陳設物品

實書籍等件運送來京分置太和中和保和文

華武英各殿統計兩處古物共七十餘萬件均經分別

品類登記冊簿旋由清皇室派員約同古玩商家逐件

審定折中估價約五百餘萬元之譜尚有物極罕貴無

從擬價之件不在此數當經內務總長商明清皇室

THE LAST EMPEROR

The
Last Emperor

The Life of
the Hsüan-t'ung Emperor
Aisin-Gioro P'u-yi
1906-1967

Neville John Irons

Published by
THE HOUSE OF FANS LIMITED
London

First published in Great Britain by
The House of Fans Limited
P O Box 580, London SW1V 3QJ
September 1983

ISBN: 0 907918 12 3

Setting by A K H Wong
Designed by N J Irons
Jacket Photograph by D Frost

Printed and bound in Great Britain by
Butler & Tanner Limited, Frome & London

Contents

For Anson

Preface

Although it is only sixteen years since the Last Emperor of the Ch'ing Dynasty died, little, if anything, is known of him in the West, or for that matter, the first fifty years of this century's Chinese history in which he played so tragic a role. He ascended the Dragon Throne in 1908 at the age of three and was forced to abdicate in 1912; became Emperor again in 1917 for a brief period, and continued to hold court within the confines of the Forbidden City until 1924 when both he and the remaining members of the Imperial family were evicted at gun-point by the 'christian General'. Exile followed in the Japanese concession in Tientsin until finally he became Emperor of Manchukuo under the Japanese in 1932. At the end of the Second World War he was captured by the Soviets and imprisoned in Siberia for five years before being handed over to the Chinese Communist authorities and imprisoned for a further ten years. He was released in 1959 and returned to his former capital Peking after an absence of thirty years, he died there as recently as 1967.

History, both Chinese and Western, has all but forgotten him, yet his story is irrevocably entwined in China's 'long march' into the cold grey light of the twentieth century.

My principal sources have almost all been Chinese, many previously untranslated including P'u-yi's own writings, his father's, Prince Ch'un diaries, and the Chinese and Japanese press of the period, Court and Republic records together with many other authorities. The only reliable account in English of P'u-yi's early years is Reginald Johnston's 'Twilight in the Forbidden City', (Gollancz 1934), and although for diplomatic reasons, Johnston omits, or clouds a number of issues, his intermit knowledge of the young Emperor and his court has been invaluable. A so-called autobiography was published in China in 1964, but as this was "demanded" by the Chinese authorities while P'u-yi was still in prison as part of his "ideological re-moulding" programme, it cannot be relied upon, for it was obviously stringently edited, and so politically biased as to render most of it quite unacceptable. P'u-yi was after all at this time fighting for his life, and had been so demoralized that he would, on his own admission, have said anything to placate his gaolers.

I trust that the reader will bear with me in the early chapters of explanation and introduction for the situation was a complex one and needed much clarification so that the narrative could flow unimpeded without the need of constant analytical blockages. Chinese names and places are set in italics according to the wade-Giles system of romanization, which happily was still in force at this period, before the emergence of the new inept pin-yin crept in to confuse everyone. I have listed in the Bibliography the principal sources consulted in the research for this work.

Some may be outraged by my reading of twentieth century Chinese history, especially that concerning such notables as Sun Yat-sen and Chiang Kai-shek; my answer must be, the truth, however unpopular, it is the truth. P'u-yi has suffered too long from neglect and misrepresentation, now, if I have not wholly succeeded in vindicating him, I have at least told the truth, his truth and the interpretation of it now must be yours.

Neville John   Iröns

London 1983

"Whenever I think of my childhood my head fills with a yellow mist. The glazed tiles were yellow, my sedan-chair was yellow, my chair cushions were yellow, the linings of my hats and robes were yellow, the girdle around my waist was yellow, the dishes and bowls from which I drank and ate, the padded cover of the congee saucepan, the material in which my books were covered, the window curtains, the bridle of my horse . . . . .everything was yellow. Even in my earliest years yellow made me feel that I was unique and had a 'heavenly' nature, different and apart from all mankind.''

The Hsüan-t'ung Emperor
(Aisin-Gioro P'u-yi)
1906-1967

CHAPTER ONE

Dragon and Phoenix Ascend

"The Emperor T'ung-chih, having left no heir, is compelled to issue a Decree to the effect that as soon as a child should be born to His Majesty the Kuang-hsü Emperor, that child would be adopted as heir to the said T'ung-chih Emperor. But now His majesty the Kuang-hsü Emperor has ascended on high, dragon-born, and he has also left no heir. I am therefore, now obliged to decree that P'u-yi, son of Tsai-fêng, (Prince Ch'un), 'Prince co-operating in the government', should become heir by adoption to the T'ung-chih Emperor, and that, at the same time, he should perform joint sacrifices at the shrine of His late Majesty the Kuang-hsü Emperor."

Thus ran the decree which the Dowager Grand Empress *Tz'u-hsi* published on 13th November 1908. With one masterful stroke she silenced her many critics, satisfying all court parties, quelling all prejudices by this unprecedented, yet simple and original document. To those unacquainted with the labyrinth of Manchu court protocol and the laws of Imperial succession, this decree may seem acceptable enough, but it was in fact so *modern* that, had it been announced by anyone less masterful and determined than the Empress Grand Dowager, it would have caused a hailstorm of controversy. To make the living Emperor assume a dual personality towards two of his departed Imperial ancestors was, dynastically without precedent, and must have caused numb amazement in both court and scholarly circles. However, that was what she had decreed, and none were in any doubt that, 'Old Buddha', who had ruled the Celestial Empire for almost half a century, and whose rage on being criticized or thwarted was well known, and something to be strenuously avoided.

The following day, she rose, as was her custom at six, received the Grand Council in audience and afterwards spent some time talking to the newly appointed Regent Prince *Ch'un* and his wife, (daughter of her old intimate friend *Jung-lu*), on matters concerning the succession of their son *P'u-yi*. Arrangements were discussed regarding the elaborate ceremonies planned to celebrate the new titles, which were to be simultaneously bestowed when the proclamation appointing the new Regent was made.

At noon, she lunched as usual on a wide variety of dishes served by her ladies-in-waiting; she sat, eating alone as etiquette demanded, whilst her attendants stood poised to anticipate her every wish. Some ten days before she had been tempted by a succulent dish of crab-apples and sour cream which had severely upset her digestion, then she had been unable to resist it, now, she tried to practice more discretion. She reassured herself that this minor upset had quite passed and, perhaps because this was her main meal of the day she indulged too rashly; some few moments later she was seized by a convulsive fainting fit. This sent her ladies into concerted panic and *'Old Buddha'* was carried back to her apartments. On regaining consciousness she summoned the regent, the Empress Dowager *Lung-yu* and the members of the Grand Council to her bedside. She realized that the hour of her death was fast approaching. Speaking in calm measured tones, which she always used in transacting the business of Government, she slowly dictated the following decree:

> *"By command of the Empress Grand Dowager: Yesterday I issued an edict whereby Prince Ch'un was made Regent, and I command that the whole business of government should be in his hands, subject only to my instructions. Being now seized of a mortal sickness, and being without hope of recovery, I now order that henceforward the government of the Empire shall be entirely in the hands of the Regent. Nevertheless, should there arise any question of vital importance, in regard to which an expression of the Empress Dowager's opinion is desirable, the Regent shall apply in person to her for instructions, and act accordingly."*

The last section of this death-bed decree is not without its subtle intention; *Tz'u-hsi* was determined that her *Yehonala* Clan should not loose its authority, the new Dowager Empress was her niece and daughter by adoption whom she had well-schooled in the affairs of state, and through whom she was determined to rule, even from the tomb. As her last moments ebbed away, each minute counted by the discordant ticking of the many clocks that had been one of her abiding passions, she calmly dictated her Valedictory Mandate, which is the orthodox swan-song of all Celestial Sovereigns, observing all the classical niceties, even correcting some characters when it was presented for her approval. Then, in accordance with Chinese custom, she was asked to pronounce her last words. She stirred, her countenance clear and peaceful, her eyes deep and shining, and in a voice of *assured tranquility* she said, *"Never again allow any woman to hold the supreme power in the state. It is against the house-laws of our Dynasty and should be strictly forbidden. Be careful not to permit the eunuchs to meddle in government matters. The Ming Dynasty was brought to ruin by eunuchs, and its fate should be a warning to my people."*

Only hours before she had invested with authority a woman of her own clan; now, faced with the *great darkness*, she drew back from perpetuating a system that had made her unchallenged ruler of the Middle Kingdom for half a century.

She prepared herself for the moment of death, straightening her limbs and turning her face to the south, seemingly oblivious of the weeping of her ladies; at precisely three p.m., her soul left her body and began its long journey to the *Nine Springs*.

In her Valedictory Mandate *Tz'u-hsi's* instructions to the new Emperor were clear:

> " . . . . *The New Emperor is but an infant, just reaching the age when wise instruction is of the highest importance. The Prince Regent and all our officials must henceforth work loyally together to strengthen the foundations of our Empire. His Majesty must devote himself to studying the interests of*

5

the country and so refrain from giving way to personal grief. That he may diligently pursue his studies, and hereafter add fresh lustre to the glorious achievements of his ancestors, is now my most earnest prayer."

Tenth Moon, 23rd day.
(15th November)

At 5 p.m. the day before the death of the *Kuang-hsü* Emperor, *P'u-yi* was brought in floods of tears from his father's mansion in the old Tartar area of *Peking* to be presented to the dying Emperor and *Tz'u-hsi* in the *Forbidden City*. The Emperor, was by now unconscious and could not recognize even his closest attendants and lingered, in the great archway of death until the afternoon of 14th November. The day before he had received the news of the succession from Prince *Ch'ing* and although deeply ill had replied, *"Would it not have been better to nominate an adult? No doubt, however, the Great Empress Dowager knows best."* After this he sank into a coma and his attendants prepared for their long night of vigil. In the early hours of the next morning he stirred and awoke with the sure knowledge that his time was close, the eunuchs were all asleep and the night lanterns flickered, affording just enough light for him to write, in an almost illegible hand, his last testament which he prefaced with the following significant words:

> *"We were the second son of Prince Ch'un when the Empress Dowager selected Us for the throne. She always hated Us, but for our misery of the past ten years Yüan Shih-k'ai is responsible, and one another. . . . .* (here it is said the writing became illegible and the name of his persecutor has never been established, was it perhaps *Li Lien-ying, Tz'u-hsi's* henchman and chief eunuch?) *When the time comes I desire that Yuan be summarily beheaded."*

It is known that the Emperor's consort took possession of this document but that others witnessed it, the chief eunuch *Li Lien-ying* was undoubtedly present so that he might, as he always did, report all the happenings directly to his Imperial mistress. Later in the day a decree announced to the inhabitants of *Peking* and as was customary on such occasions, the most skillful physicians were summoned post-haste to the capital so that His Majesty's life might yet be saved. This was tantamount to an announcement of death; few were unaware of the veiled meaning behind this statement.

Yüan Shih-k'ai, named by the dying Emperor as his chief tormentor had, since the collapse of the reform movement in 1898, (for which he was almost singularly responsible), become increasingly powerful and under his direct control was the most modern army in China based at *Peiyang*. When the Regency of Prince *Ch'un* was announced and *P'u-yi* as heir-apparent, *Yuan* arrogantly advanced to the throne and haughtily put forward his own nominee, Prince *P'u-lun*, *Tz'u-hsi* turned upon him in fury, *"You think that I am old and in my dotage, but you should have learned by now that when I make up my mind nothing stops me from acting upon it. At a critical time in the nation's affairs a youthful Sovereign is no doubt a source of danger to the State, but do not forget that I shall be here to direct and assist Prince Ch'un."* Then, turning away from *Yüan* and addressing her other trembling counsellors she said, *"Draft two decrees at once, in my name, the first, appointing Tsai-feng, (Prince Ch'un) to be 'Prince co-operating in the Government', the second commanding that P'u-yi, son of Prince Ch'un, should enter the palace forthwith, to be brought up within the precincts."* With this stated, she glared defiance at the offending *Yuan* and terminated the audience.

Tz'u-hsi fully realized that she could not simply dismiss *Yüan Shih-k'ai*, his influence over the *Peiyang* army was too strong, nor could she, at one stroke, separate him from his fellow conspirator Prince *Ch'ing*. She felt ill, old and threatened and decided to retire to her bed to plan her next move, it was just a little over an hour later that she received a frightening and seemingly incredible piece of news from her faithful *Li Lien-ying*: *Yüan Shih-k'ai* was planning to have the *Kuang-hsü* Emperor murdered, and in his place to install the son of his fellow-plotter Prince *Ch'ing*. Despite Prince *Ch'ing's* skill in dealing with foreigners and his flattery to her, despite all that *Yüan* had done in the past, despite the fact that the victim of this plot was the *Reforming Emperor*, whom she deeply hated, she was keenly aware that such a plot would seriously injure her own power and that of her clan, it must not happen. Prince *Ch'ing* was dispatched on a fictitious mission away from the capital and the majority of the *Peiyang* army within *Peking* was replaced by forces loyal to her. By the time Prince *Ch'ing* returned, the succession of *P'u-yi* was secure, along with the Regency of his father.

Yüan Shih-k'ai was another matter, whether or not he succeeded in his plot to poison the Emperor, will now, never be known, but the facts speak for themselves; according to witnesses at the time, the *Kuang-hsü* Emperor was much recovered and was seen walking and reading within the confines of his apartment; his illness had been officially diagnosed as a common cold and this report further stated that his pulse was normal, yet, four hours later he was dead. The reason for his sudden death was a dose of medicine he had been sent, and the name of the benefactor must have inspired him with confidence for, ignoring the usual procedures he took the potion. The normal court practice in such cases when the Emperor was ill, was for copies of the prescriptions and diagnoses of the Grand Physicians to be given to each of the senior officials of the Imperial Household Department or, in the case of serious illness, to all the members of the Grand Council. Palace rumour had it that the sender of this *medicine* was none other than *Yüan Shih-k'ai* himself.

Some Western sources have named *Tz'u-hsi* as the *taker of the dragon's life*, but from contemporary records it is clear that she was overcome with grief at the news. Two hours before the Emperor's death *Tz'u-hsi*, though weak herself, made her way to the *Ocean Terrace* to visit the failing Emperor, he was unconscious and did not know her. An hour before the end he regained consciousness and his attendants tried to persuade him to change into the *ceremonial Robes of Longevity*, in which court etiquette prescribes that a Sovereign should die. This was considered of paramount importance for if the robes were put on after death it was thought to be most inauspicious. He refused,

Yuan Shih-k'ai wearing a Manchu dragon robe.

knowing that his gaoler for the last ten years, *Tz'u-hsi* was present, and his dismissal of an important part of Imperial usage would annoy her. He died at five o'clock.

Although the death of the Emperor cannot with certainty be laid at the feet of *Yüan Shih-k'ai*, his record speaks for itself; he betrayed the *Kuang-hsü* Emperor and the members of the reform movement in 1898, being directly responsible for the death of at least six of it members. He betrayed the *Hsüan-t'ung* Emperor in 1911 and, the so-called *Republic of China* in 1916, even trying vainly to proclaim himself Emperor of a new Dyansty. He was certainly directly accountable for at least three *assassinations* of prominent political rivals and indirectly for the increase of poverty and misery of the people, which he irresponsibly ruled as President of the Republic.

In May 1917, the year following the deserved downfall of *Yüan Shih-k'ai* an article appeared in the *Hsin Ch'ing Nien*, (New Youth) written by Professor *Ch'en Tu-hsiu* of Peking University:

> *"I do not share the prevalent optimism about the immediate future of our Republic . . . . I am not at all sure that there will be no further attempts to change the form of government . . . . I was by no means surprised that the Ch'ou-An Society suddenly began to advocate the re-establishment of the Monarchic system. Now that Yüan Shih-k'ai has come to greif and died, it is generally supposed that the republic is firmly established. But I have serious doubts. . . . . although there seems to be no general opposition to the republican idea, people's minds are still obsessed with the old monarchic notions. They have not the slightest idea of what the civilized democratic societies of Europe or America really are . . . . . . .It was no idle dream of Yüan Shih-k'ai to make himself Emperor. He knew very well that the great majority of the people of China still believed in monarchy and had no faith in a republic. Even those who opposed the recent attempt to revive the monarchy, more than half were not genuinely and fundamentally opposed to monarchic principal but merely*

to Yüan Shih-k'ai becoming Emperor . . . . Although Yüan is dead, the popular hankering after monarchy, of which he tried to make use for his own advantage, is still in existence. It seems to me that it would be easier to climb up to heaven than to establish the republic so securely that no monarchic rivals could ever take place again. If we want to stabilize our republic, there is only one thing to be done . . . . we must clear our people's minds of every trace of the antiquated monarchic ideas that still possess them."

By this date, (1917) the Chinese government had become even less republican than at its inception in 1912, the people under it had suffered from an accumulation of evils which make the worst days of Manchu rule seem like a golden age of peace and prosperity. The main trouble with the Chinese republic, was that there were no republicans! The various factions of warlords who controlled many areas of China paid lip service to the republic but little else, jealous of their own power and influence they were unprepared to surrender it to this so-called representative government.

P'u-yi was born on 7th February 1906 in the *Ch'un* family mansion situated in the old Tartar city of *Peking*. His grandfather *Yi-huan* was the seventh son of the *Tao-kuang* Emperor, (1821-1850) and the first Prince *Ch'un*. His father *Tsai-fêng*, the second Prince *Ch'un*, inherited his title although he was only the fifth son, the third and fourth having died in childhood and the second became the *Kuang-hsü* Emperor (1875-1908). *Yi-huan* was a faithful supporter of the Dynasty and at the death of the *Hsien-fêng* Emperor, (1851-1861) his devotion to the now Dowager Empress *Tz'u-hsi* brought him at last the official favours long denied him; this was really the rise of the family fortunes for, whatever else may be said about *Old Buddha*, she never forgot her true friends. In the *Ch'un* mansion there were many scrolls, some bearing his grandfather's own calligraphy and a pair which seems to have caught the boy's early attention stated:

Wealth and fortune breed more fortune
Royal favours bring more favours

These words *P'u-yi* was to remember all his life.

11

This bewildered three year-old boy, separated from his mother and nurses, plunged into the strange atmosphere of the *Great Within*, as the *Forbidden City* was called, was abandoned to the class-room and all but ignored by his father, who was vainly wrestling with the complexities of his official duties as regent. It was only during the last three years of his short reign that he even actually recognized him.

One morning as *P'u-yi* was at his studies, a eunuch announced the approach of *His Royal Highness* the Prince Regent, the tutors were in a flurry of nervousness, tidying the tables and gabbling instructions to their young student, as how he should behave in the presence of his august father.

"Stand up and wait for him and be respectful" one tutor instructed. A moment later the doors opened and a beardless stranger in full court dress entered, his peacock feather bobbing up and down, he advanced and stood stiffly before his small son. Formal greetings were exchanged and father and son sat down nervously together, *P'u-yi* opened his book and began to read as his tutor had instructed, but was so flustered that after the second line his voice and concentration faltered and he came to a mumbling halt, eyes downcast. *"Good, good, very good, your Majesty, study hard, study hard, study hard."* He rose and was gone, peacock feather still bobbing as he passed from sight. He had spent but two minutes with his lonely and nervous son. The old tutor was too overcome to speak for a moment and *P'u-yi* looked towards the door through which this stranger, who he now knew to be his father had vanished. *'So that is what he looks like'* mused the boy, *'but why does his peacock feather dance about so? Is it perhaps magic?'* This parental visit was repeated every two months and the duration of each visit was always only two minutes long. Soon *P'u-yi* knew why the feather on his father's hat shook so, he had a slight stutter and was forever nodding his head and uttering *"Good, good, good,"* in an almost indistinct voice.

Prince *Ch'un* was weighed down by the affairs of state which, he was neither strong enough to manage as *Tz'u-hsi* would have done, nor was he *without honour*, which made the advice of some of his

Prince Ch'un (Tsai-feng), Regent and father of P'u-yi.

counsellors unacceptable. *Yüan Shih-k'ai*, who he believed was responsible for his brother's death and whose summary execution had been the dying wish of the unfortunate Emperor still plagued him. As much as he wished it, this villain could not be done away with, for, there was always the shadow of his fellow conspirator the powerful Prince *Ch'ing* to contend with. This was perhaps his most serious dilemma and much of the trouble he encountered during this period stemmed from his inability to resolve this basic conflict. In retrospect Prince *Ch'un* was to realize that the three years of his Regency were the three least successful years of his entire life. Perhaps his character is best summed up in two scrolls upon which he wrote: *To have books is real wealth, to be at leisure is halfway to being an immortal.*

At a meeting between the Princes when this problem of *Yüan Shih-k'ai* was being discussed, the Regent's blood ran cold when Prince *Ch'ing* calmly said, *"Oh, there would be no problem about killing Yüan Shih-k'ai but, what would happen if the Peiyang Army mutinied?"* What little decisiveness Prince *Ch'un* possessed evaporated and it was left to the new Dowager Empress *Lung-yu* to resolve the matter; she sent *Yüan* off to his country estates to nurse a *foot ailment*, when other strategies failed.

Caught between court factions Prince *Ch'un* patiently listened to the advice of all his counsellors, agreed with first one side, then the other, and then did nothing.

Reginald Johnson who was to become *P'u-yi's* English tutor left a word portrait of the infant Emperor's father Prince *Ch'un*:

> *"Prince Ch'un was a man of some amiable qualities, free from malice and vindictiveness, sociable, as interested in Chinese drama as he was interested in politics or in the affairs of the great world. He must be given credit for being one of the two Manchu Princes,* (Tsai-hsun is the other) *who had a respectable knowledge of the Manchu language. He is well intentioned. Tries in his languid and ineffectual way to please everyone, shrinks from responsibility, is thoroughly unbusiness-like, is disastrously deficient in energy, will-power and grit, and there*

is no reason to believe that he lacks both physical and moral courage. He is helpless in an emergency, has no original ideas, and is liable to be swayed by any smooth-talker. After he became Regent, however, the flattery of sycophants tended to make him obstinately tenacious of his own opinions, which almost invariably turned out to be wrong. During several years of fairly intimate contact with Prince Ch'un I came to be so deeply impressed by his fatal tendency to do the wrong thing or choose the wrong course in matters affecting the Imperial House or the interests of the young Emperor his son, that I once made the suggestion to my colleagues in the Fobidden City that we might actually turn that tendency of his to good account by adopting the following principal: If two possible courses of action present themselves, ask Prince Ch'un which in his opinion should be followed, then follow the other!"

After the death of *Lung-yu* Dowager Empress, of whom he stood in awe, he began to develop a curious strain of vanity which manifested itself in odd ways, Johnston tells us:

". . . . . .To this day he is blissfully ignorant of any political or other short comings in himself, or of anything whatever in his career as a ruler or as a statesman that deserves censure or contempt. He has about him an air of bland self-satisfaction which seems to be the outward sign of an inward malaise and which may indeed have its defensive uses; for if that malaise were to emerge above subconsciousness it might drive him mad with shame and despair."

After Prince *Ch'un* had resigned his regency in 1911 he went straight home to his *Pei Fu* in the Tartar City and greeted his wife with, *"From today onwards, I can stay at home and hug my children"* his wife was so astonished and angry at this light-hearted statement that she burst into tears and on recovering said to *P'u-yi's* brother, *"Please do not be like your father when you grow up!"*

Once when one of *P'u-yi's* four grandmothers was suffering from an ulcer of the breast which the Chinese doctors had been unable to cure, Prince *Ch'un* called in a French doctor on his brother's advice. The doctor wanted to operate but this *barbarian* request was opposed by the whole family so the doctor prescribed an ointment which he would apply before leaving. He took out a spirit lamp from his medical bag and lit it to sterilize the instruments. This act gave Prince *Ch'un* a terrible shock and he exclaimed, *"What . . . . . . what is he doing? Is he going to burn the old lady?"* When the foreign doctor returned a few days later he was puzzled to find the old lady's condition unimproved and he asked Prince *Ch'un* for the box of ointment, dutifully the Prince disappeared and returning a few moments later with the ointment, on examining it the doctor found that the seal was still unbroken, turning to Prince *Ch'un* he asked why it had not been administered, *"Well"* replied the Prince in a clear voice, *"I thought you just meant me to keep it safe, that I have done."*

After the death of *Tz'u-hsi* and his appointment as Regent he adopted a very *modern* attitude, referring openly to himself as a reformer and a man of the twentieth century. As if to demonstrate this he was the first of the Princes to own a motor car and to install a telephone; the first to cut off his queue and to wear Western clothes, although this had its lighter side. Having decked himself out in what he considered to be the best *barbarian* fashion he confided to this son, *"Why do your shirts fit you so well where as mine are always longer than my jacket?"* On examination his son found that Prince *Ch'un* had been wearing his shirt outside his trousers and had been putting up with this discomfort for some days.

Years later *P'u-yi* was to consult his father's diaries to try to understand more about the three years of his Regency but all he found was; *"Had my hair cut short as usual . . . . Started to let my hair grow as usual."* There were various entries as to the formal dress he wore on state occasions, the fresh fruit he consumed but the bulk of the entries concerned his passion for astronomy. It is little wonder that the burden of the Regency sat so uncomfortably on his shoulders.

Prince Ch'un with his two sons, P'u-chieh on his
knees and the Emperor elect P'u-yi standing.

Before *P'u-yi* was taken to the palace the greatest influence in his life was his grandmother, who doted on him and filled his days with love and care. After his succession he saw neither his mother nor grandmother for seven years; not until his tenth birthday were they summoned to the palace. He hardly recognized them, although his loving grandmother never took her eyes from him and he recalls that they were *'glistening with tears'*. His mother was still slightly frightening and distant; *"Your Majesty must study diligently the precepts of your ancestors, ... your Majesty must not be greedy, ...your Majesty must get up early and go to bed early . . . . . . Your Majesty's body is a sacred body . . . . "*.

How this small lonely boy longed for the secure comfort of his grandmothers arms around him for *love* seemed *forbidden* in the *great within*. He begged that she might be allowed to look after him but because of her humble origins this was, *'out of the question'*.

On that fateful evening, November 13th 1908 the *Ch'un* Mansion, *Pei Fu* was in chaos. Once the Grand Dowager Empress's decree was known Prince *Ch'un* in the company of Grand Counsellors and palace eunuchs made their way through the softly falling snow to his family mansion in the Tartar City. *P'u-yi's* grandmother fainted on being told the news of his election and maids and eunuchs rushed about making ginger-tea and sending for doctors; the child Emperor elect was sobbing amid the confusion and Prince *Ch'un* vainly trying to take control of the frenzied situation only made matters worse. The Grand Counsellors and eunuchs were impatient to be on their way back to the *Forbidden City* with their new Emperor, the old lady revived and was helped into an inner room where her grandson was still volubly signifying his resistance to the Imperial edict, howling and hitting at the strange eunuchs as they tried to pick him up. The palace eunuchs forced themselves to smile while waiting for the members of the Grand Council to get the situation under control while the Grand Counsellers waited helplessly for the Prince Regent to deal with the confusion; but all the Regent could do was to nod and intone, "Good, good, good."

Had it not been for the wet-nurse who ended the infant Emperor's cries in the traditional manner, the commotion might have lasted for hours, but the child's sudden silence seemed to bring the officials to their senses, and it was agreed that she should accompany the child to the *Forbidden City*.

Even at this tender age *P'u-yi* was to recall in later years his meeting on that evening with the Dowager Empress *Tz'u-hsi*, *"the shock left a deep impression on my mind. I remember being surrounded by strangers, while before me through a gold curtain I could just see the silhouette of the Great Empress."* *P'u-yi* was again howling uncontrollably, *"Give him a string of candied haws"* the Dowager Empress soothed, but this Imperial perquisite was immediately thrown to the floor as the poor frightened child called for his grandmother, *"What a nosiy child"* *Tz'u-hsi* murmured, *"Take him away to play."*

Two days later the *Old Buddha* was dead and on December 2nd the *Great Ceremony of Enthronement* took place in the Hall of Supreme Harmony, *(Tai Ho Tien)*. This was preceeded by a ceremony in the Hall of Central Harmony, *(Chung Ho Tien)* at which the infant Emperor received the obeisance of the Commanders of the Palace Guard and the ministers of the inner court and other leading civil and military officials. It was bitterly cold and as the procession arrived at the Hall of Supreme Harmony, the protesting child was placed on the high throne with his father kneeling below supporting him, it became too much for the infant to bear.*"I want my nanny. . . . .I don't like it here. . . . . I want to go home. . . . . I want to go home!"* Even with the bitter cold Prince *Ch'un* was in a lather of perspiration, as succeeding rows of officials came forward and performed the time-honoured *kowtow*, the infant Emperor's cries grew even louder. *"Don't cry, don't cry . . . . . it will all soon be over"* whispered his distracted father.

When the ceremony was finally over, the officials gathered in small groups, *"What did he say? It will all be over soon?"*, *"A bad omen"* murmured another, *"I want to go home . . . . .is that what his Majesty said?. . . . . . . but this is his home."*

19

Outside the night closed in and the snow flurries of the afternoon turned into ghostly grey cloaks suspended from a leaden sky, nervous whispers were carried on the cold night-wind throughout *Peking*. The murmurings of revolution that had persisted during the closing years of *Kuang-hsü's* reign were now becoming more vociferous and disquieting. Within, there was still *Yüan Shih-k'ai* to contend with; the rebels without, and *Yüan* within; this was surely the most ill-omened reign in the long history of the *Da Ch'ing* Dynasty.

On his accession to the Dragon Throne his personal name, *P'u-yi* was tabooed, and his reign title *Hsüan-t'ung* succeeded it, although he was referred to by the Chinese equivalent of 'His Imperial Majesty', *(hung shang)*. Even after the death of an Emperor his personal name is never used nor his reign title, *(nien-hao)* both are supplanted by a *miao-hao* or temple name under which sacrifices are offered in accordance with the rites of ancestor-worship. With the fall of the Dynasty this dignity was denied *P'u-yi* the *Hsüan-t'ung* Emperor, officially that is, although no recorded temple name was accorded him, the author has sure knowledge that this necessary last honour was given him in private, and that the incense of remembrance ascends each year in his temple name.

During the three years leading up to the *revolution* of 1911, life continued much as usual for the lonely boy Emperor, shut off from the outside world in the *Purple Forbidden City*. Lessons occupied most of his time, occasionally to be interrupted when his father Prince *Ch'un* would nurse 'The Son of Heaven' on his knee at audience seated on the Dragon Throne. Unknown to him at this time the dark clouds of national unrest were gathering, heralding a storm of such devastating intensity which was to enveloped the Middle Kingdom for almost forty years.

As previously stated, one of the first acts of the Prince Regent and his *adviser* the Dowager Empress *Lung-yu* was to banish *Yüan Shih-k'ai*, stripping him of all his posts and sending home to nurse an *imaginary leg ailment*. It should be remembered that *Yüan* had palyed a principal part in the Reform Movement of 1898, betraying his Emperor and all those who had placed confidence in him. After this betrayal, which really amounted to treason, he naturally stood high in *Tz'u-hsi's* favour, for it gave her the opportunity she had been waiting for to regain power, discredit the Emperor, whom she virtually imprisoned for the next ten years. He was Viceroy of the Metropolitan Province in 1901, Minister of the Army Reorganization Council in 1903, President of the Board of Foreign Affairs in 1907 and was made a Grand Councillor in the same year. The continuance of his highly prosperous official life, not to mention his physical life, depended totally on the maintenance of his patroness's power, which was seriously undermined by the Boxer disturbances; he used all his influence with the *foreigners* to make sure she resumed the Regency and that the *Kuang-hsü* Emperor, whom he had betrayed, stayed under restraint. His actions were always those of a completely selfish opportunist, readily adapting his principals and loyalty to whatever the circumstances should demand. There was no possibility of a reconciliation between *Yüan* and his Emperor and certainly not with the survivors of the reform movement. Chief among these survivors was *K'ang Yu-wei*, whose deep and bitter hatred of *Yüan* was well known and respected, and of all men it was probably *K'ang's* vengeance that *Yüan* most feared. Even after that *Boxer Fiasco* when *Tz'u-hsi* was forced into a reform movement of her own, having only two years earlier ruthlessly destroyed the Emperor's Reform party. *K'ang Yu-wei* and his friends were neither forgiven nor invited to take part, *Yüan* saw to that.

Had Prince *Ch'un* not vacillated over the dying wish of his brother an had ordered *Yüan's* execution he would have saved both himself and the Empire from the 'thousand cuts' *Yüan* was to inflict in the years to come. Even in the last decade of the dynasty, and Imperial Command was enough to send the most powerful official in the Empire back to his country estate, stripped of all his high offices with all the *loss of face* this implied, without apparently a murmur. Had this occurred ten or even twenty years later under the so called *republic*, it would, no doubt has resulted in a declaration of independence on *Yüan's* part, to be followed by yet another ruinous civil war. But the Dragon Throne was still to be obeyed in all things and the Emperor, even if he was only a child of three, ruled China. *Yüan's* influence in army circles at this time was enormous but he dared not use this against 'the Son of Heaven', for armies had not yet become the personal playthings of their commanders to be used for their private ambitions and aggrandizement, this evil was still a little time off, but when that time did finally arrive, China was to be subjected to a blood-bath unparalleled in its long history.

That Prince *Ch'un* was unequal to his task as Regent, is something of an understatement, but history should not condemn him too harshly, he was merely the wrong man in the wrong position at the wrong time. Apart from all the inherited problems, every day heaped more upon this *private* man, nor was his task made light by his appointed *advisor* Dowager Empress *Lung-yu*, who was not only the widow of the late Emperor, but the *adopted* mother of the present sovereign and a niece and daughter by adoption of *Tz'u-hsi*. As the edict had clearly stated: Prince *Ch'un* must take her instruction in all matters of importance, and as far as she was concerned *All* matters were of importance. As far as the court was concerned she had rights and privileges by mere virtue of her relationship with the late Emperor, added to this was her relationship with the present Emperor, she was his aunt by marriage and his adopted mother, but most important of all, she was *Tz'u-hsi's* niece, and a member of the *Yehonala* clan and that same indomitable blood flowed in her veins. Poor Prince *Ch'un* was literally faced with a *New Buddha*, who seem determined to emulate her aunt and adoptive Mother in every particular.

The seeds of reform that *Kuang-hsü* had courageously planted and which *Tz'u-hsi* had so ruthlessly dug up, then in the face of *foreign* pressure, had half-heartedly replanted, were inherited by Prince *Ch'un*, he had become nominally *head-gardener* with *Lung-yu* as his ambitious assistant. The task was beyond them both for, instead of cultivating and tending these delicate seedlings in unison they gardened the same plot independently, undoing each other's labours and forgetting the most important rule of all, to weed regularly. However, the movement towards constitutional reform, if somewhat hapharzard, continued to grow. Early in 1909 a decree was issued stating that the court was completely committed to establishing a constitutional government; some ultra-conservative officials who opposed these changes were dismissed or punished in an effort to show the Throne's sincere commitment to national reform.

One of the Emperor's uncles *Tsai-hsün*, was sent to England at the head of a mission that was to investigate naval affairs in preparation for the building of a *Modern* Chinese Navy; he was received with courtesy at King Edwards' Court, as his brother *Tsai-t'ao* was by Kaiser Wilhem, *t'ao* having been sent as head of a similar mission to Germany to study military affairs. Both men were deeply impressed by their receptions in Europe and remained life-long friends of these two nations.

Whether these costly missions were merely intended as good propaganda proclaiming China's new reformed image, or as serious attempts to modernize was not made clear, but given the rather naive virtues of Prince *Ch'un* who became *modern* himself simply by acquiring a motor car, telephone and Western clothing, perhaps the latter was the only *serious* intention.

Meanwhile, petitions were arriving in Peking in an ever increasing number, all pressing for an early opening of the much promised parliament and the establishment of a responsible and representative cabinet, the great majority of which originated in the South. In a effort to reassure this growing clamour an edict was issued on 4th November 1910 stating that the parliament would be duly opened in the fifth year of the reign of the *Hsüan-t'ung* Emperor (1913); it also stated that all the necessary preparations, rules and conditions governing the selection of members of the upper and lower houses together with all matters appertaining to constitutional reform would be ready to be put into force before the said opening of parliament. During the same year an assassination attempt was made on the life of Prince *Ch'un* by one *Wang Ching-wei* a follower of *Sun Yat-sen*, who was perhaps the first 'professional revolutionary' of modern times and who subsequently emerged from the blood-soaked pages of Chinese history as only slightly less inept than his intended victim. Even in the face of this savage attempt on his life Prince *Ch'un* remained as conciliatory as ever and commuted the deserved death sentence to one of life imprisonment. Had he but known that his pardoned assassin would emerge from prison to become a leading member of the *Kuo-min tang* and of the Nationalist Government at *Nanking* he may well have overcome his human scruples. But, knowing something of his character, perhaps not. In the following year, 1911 an edict was issued in the name of the Dowager Empress *Lung-yu*, which was to have far-reaching personal implication for the six-year old Emperor; it announced that the little Emperor was to commence his formal education in the *Yu-ch'ing kung*, which for many years past had always been the Imperial school-room of the *Forbidden City*. Three Imperial tutors were to be appointed (who would be joined some time later by the blue-eyed Scot Reginald Johnston, who was to become perhaps *P'u-yi's* only true and intimate friend).

Meanwhile during the fateful year of 1911 the murmurings of provincial discontent became louder, in the main they emanated from *Kwangtung*, which had traditionally been the breeding ground of revolt, here had been fertilized the sporn that grew into the Taiping rebellion which devastated China in the mid-nineteenth century. At this moment in history, *Sun Yat-sen* and his followers compared with the Taipings, who had been murderously drunk on the heady wine of pseudo-christianity, these new *revolutionaries* were suffering from severe political-indigestion brought about by the over-hasty consumption of *half-baked* theories. Had the *Sunites* emerged earlier in the Dynasty they would surely have been little more than a nine-days-wonder, but now with the weakened state of Imperial government and the scent of Imperial confusion in their nostrils, their spark of courage flamed, fanned by the prevailing wind of ineptitude.

A serious revolt broke out at this time in Canton lead by *Huang-hsing* who was later to become a *revolutionary War-Lord*; the headquarters of the Viceroy were completely destroyed, but the local army and military quelled the uprising and *Huang* fled, like so many revolutionaries both before and after him, to *Hong Kong*, to take refuge under the British flag from where he continued his

Prince Ch'un's Household, (from right to left), Prince Ch'un, his mother, his secondary mother and his wife, P'u-yi's mother.

activities against the Dynasty. It was at this time that Prince *Ch'un* tried to placate his political enemies by appointing a cabinet based more or less on the Western model, but nothing seemed to satisfy them; *'This cabinet has too many Manchu Princes!'* , this was true but, contrary to the then common assumption, not all were avaricious or degenerate, it contained some extremely able and honest men, the real reason for the dissatisfaction was that the tradition of placing members of the Imperial family in key positions, for which many were unqualified and, who had progressively brought discredit on the Throne by either their avarice or incompetence or both. It was fast becoming a hopeless situation, whatever concessions the Dynasty put forward were unacceptable, although the *revolutionaries* had no suggestions of their own, or rather none that they could agree upon amongst themselves.

The gun-powder was crammed in the keg, the protagonists were all loudly proclaiming their intention to ignite it, shouting each other down in an effort to achieve at least vocal superiority. The fatal spark was supplied by an almost unrelated incident; some time before plans had been put in hand for the unification of the Chinese railway system under a central control, implementation of these plans, if only tentatively, caused a storm of opposition from the various embryo-war-lords, who saw this as a direct threat to their existence and a means whereby Imperial troops could, if necessary be swiftly moved throughout the Empire. Actual hostilities did occur in *Ssu-ch'uan* in September and *Wu-Ch'ang* in October, 1911 but were really only a minor reptition of what had already occurred in several other centres, however, because of the confusion, not to mention the discovery of an *anti-Sun* conspiracy *Wu-ch'ang* became the headquarters of the revolutionary movement and almost by accident, *Li Yuan-hung* its reluctant commander-in-chief.

To say that the government in *Peking* at this time was panic striken would be a gross understatement, it was in a state bordering on imbecility; the arrogant Dowager Empress and the complacent Prince Regent were frozen with fear. Of all the serious blunders Prince *Ch'un* had committed in his short regency, his next action was by far the most ill-advised. He decided, or was prevailed upon, to recall his most treacherous adversary, *Yüan Shih-k'ai,* whom he had humiliated and degraded three years earlier. There is no doubt that some case, however flimsy, could be made out for *Yüan's* recall; he still exercised influence over the rank and file of the best trained army in China, his influence was also not inconsiderable in many political circles; no-one could doubt that he was a capable leader, if not a completely level-headed stateman; he was, as far as anyone could know, still loyal to the dynasty; and perhaps most important of all, his stock stood high with the *foreigners* particularly those representatives in the *Peking* Legations and elsewhere throughout China. This last, though seemingly lesser reason, was in fact paramount; if the rebellion was to be successfully suppressed it would cost a great deal of money and this could not be raised internally amid the present chaos, it would have to come from *foreign* sources and *Yüan's* name would almost certainly guarantee this. The year before The Times had published an article, " . . . . . . *an excellent, if gloomy, description of the plight in which China found herself, together with a plea for the recall of Yüan Shih-k'ai as the only man able to save the situation.*" This was the view prevalent among *foreigners*, but Prince *Ch'un* should have known better, even if they did not. Foreign interests were wholly pecuniary, Dynasty or so-called *republic*, all was one, as long as the four hundred million Chinese were peaceful and reasonably prosperous and could afford the Western imports, and work for a pittance in the foreign owned factories, as indeed many now did in the Treaty Ports. All seemed to welcome the *new republic*, whatever it was, profit, or perhaps even a bigger slice of the Chinese mainland might well be forthcoming under this new *enlightened* regime. Had anyone paused to really think, they might have realized that the recall of *Yüan Shih-k'ai* was destined not to advance any of these *rosy* theories, merely his own, and that boded ill for Chinese and foreigner.

In reply to the first Imperial summons from *Peking, Yüan* sent a message heavily laced with sarcasm and innunendo; he was sorry to learn of the thrones apparent inability to deal with the present situation but, he could not respond in person because of the *leg injury* he had been sent home to nurse three years earlier, it was still giving him some trouble. This had the direct result of driving the already wretched Prince *Ch'un* to even deeper depths of despair, which were not lessened by the hysterical rantings of the

Dowager Empress and the shaking heads of the Grand Council. Needless to say, *Yüan* soon, with a little more presuasion finally deigned to come to *Peking* and, on arrival quickly summed up the trembling situation and turned it swiftly to his own advantage. Realizing that he could now impose his own terms on the government he quickly demanded the immediate resignation of several Imperial Princes; was confirmed as Viceroy of Hukuang, Commander-in-Chief of the Imperial forces and Premier in the newly formed cabinet. This accomplished, without a voice raised against him, he took the entire stratagem into his own hands. Within weeks he turned the tide of battle against the revolutionaries in the middle *Yangtse*; *Hankow* and *Hanyang* on the northern banks of the river opposite the rebel headquarters were recaptured, which was designed to show them forcibly that any final settlement of the *revolutionary* question must respect his views. It soon became evident, even to Prince *Ch'un* that *Yüan* was pursuing his own policy, he could easily have followed up his initial victories and completely subdued the rebels, but he did not, what he did do was to write his own name in large letters for all to read, *Yüan Shih-k'ai all powerful opportunist*. What upset the court even more was that this man was Chinese not Manchu, and one of his 'conditions' in taking command was that an amnesty be offered to the offending revolutionaries.

The central control of the railway network which was credited with the 'spark' that really set the revolt in motion, was more anti-foreign than anti-Manchu; a four-power consortium had been set up in 1908 by British, French, German and American banks to invest in the Chinese railway, providing loans, negotiations were set in motion to buy out all local interests. This was fiercely resisted and as a direct consequence the fighting that *Yüan* had quelled, resulted.

The revolutionary delegates were already arriving in *Nanking* for their first assembly, a city which ironically had been the 'heavenly capital' of the Taiping rebels some sixty years earlier. The obvious military forbearance that *Yüan Shih-k'ai* had demonstrated against the rebel forces now bore fruit, it was suggested that he should join them in *Nanking* and become the first President of the New

Chinese Republic, that is, after he had abandoned the Dynasty of course. Nor was *Yüan* kept in any ignorance of this possibility for, during the planned lull in fighting the two sides were regularly in touch. When the news of the the *Nanking* assembly reached *Sun Yat-sen* he hurriedly made plans to return to China. He had been born in 1866 of peasant-stock not far from Canton and at the age of twelve he left the South China Coast to join his brother in Hawaii where he received his education in a mission school and later studied medicine in Hong Kong. Having spent so much of his life outside China he was in many ways ignorant of the deeper feelings and aspirations of his fellow-countrymen and this, coupled with the anti-Manchu upbringing of his early days, which were always prevalent in both *Kwangtung* and *Fuhkien*, created the lack of balance in his thinking. Even as far back as 1894, he had formed a secret anti-Dynastic society which in the following year attempted, at his insistence, an ill-advised rising in Canton; the plot was discovered and *Sun* was forced to flee Canton with a price on his head. This reward was almost collected in 1896 when *Sun*, who was then in London, was recognized and forcibly bundled into the Chinese Embassy where he was held prisoner to await extradition to China where certain death awaited him. He was only saved at the eleventh hour by the intervention of his old medical professor who prevailed upon the British Government to intercede on his behalf. After his lucky escape he continued his travels concentrating on areas with large overseas-Chinese populations where he tried to win adherents to his dream of a Chinese Republic, but where more importantly he was able to raise the necessary finance to keep both himself and his plans alive. It was this overseas-Chinese lable that he was never able to shake off, and his countrymen had a term which was applied to such people, the Cantonese colloquiualism *herng jue*, (which literally means banana. . . . . . yellow outside but white inside) and it was *Sun's* lot to remain to many of his fellows as a *herng jue*.

Japan, after her sensational victory over the Russians in 1905 had become the model for all *modern* Orientals, and *Sun Yat-sen* was no exception. In that same year he formed in Tokyo his revolutionary society called the *T'ung-meng-hui* and for the very first time declared his political programme. This was a rather vague document, for apart from proclaiming its intention to overthrow the *Ch'ing* Dynasty and establish in its place a *republic*, there was very little else, and taken as a whole it demonstrated *Sun's* out-of-touch conception of what the actual problems that confronted China were.

To the mass of *Sun's* overseas-Chinese followers in Japan at this time, none seemed to notice either the transparency of *Sun's* unrealistic attitude implicit in this document. Among the *Sunites* were a number of young officers from the various regional Chinese armies who were undergoing military training along Japanese lines, and who were kept busy by the *T'ung-meng-hui* in the usual revolutionary fashion, with armed attacks on government offices and the statutory amount of bomb-throwing. What these young men demanded was action, theories could wait, which for *Sun* was just as well, for he really had none. One young officer stood out, not only possessing military skill and courage but a more than usual amount of political know-how, his name was *Chiang Kai-shek*, who made himself as indispensible to *Dr Sun* as possible, but rather than being his disciple, history has shown that if he was anyone's disciple, it was probably of *Yüan Shih-k'ai*. When the news reached *Sun Yat-sen* in Tokyo of the assembly in *Nanking* and the revolutionary victories, such as they were, he made all haste to China and arrived on Christmas day ready and eager to take up his post as provisional President of the republic; he might really have saved himself the journey, for he was informed that, yes, he could be sworn in as the provisional President but the assembly had already negotiated with, and offered the presidency to .. *Yüan Shih-k'ai*. *Sun* was staggered at the news, but quickly regaining his poise he accepted the situation, and agreed to stand down in *Yüan's* favour. This was a shock from which he was never fully to recover, not only was it a severe blow to his ego and expectations, but to have to move aside for a man like *Yüan?* That was even a deeper wound, did they not realize that this *opportunist* could, and had, changed allegiances at a moment's notice? Did they not realize that this man could not be trusted? These *truths* did not improve the situation, for it was openly assumed by most, that this was a severe attack of *sour grapes* on *Sun's* part, and not doubt *Yüan* was aware, or was soon made aware, of his rivals feelings.

Yüan was again in the ascendant, he saw himself as *master* of China but the three years he had suffered nursing his *leg ailment* were not forgotten. He had received huge amounts of money from the Imperial treasury to finance his military expeditions, he was almost President of the *New Republic*, all that was now necessary was to deliver the *coup de grace* to the tottering *Da Ch'ing* Dynasty.

He took the *arrow's flight* of the moment and informed the Court that if the Dynasty was to be saved it could only be achieved by surrendering all its powers to the *New Republic*. The Emperor must abdicate, although he would be permitted to retain his reign title and his state within the confines of the *Forbidden City* which would be supported by a generous yearly allowance from the *Republic*, all the members of the Imperial family would be confirmed in their rights of property.

Had this amazing compromise been arrived at in any other country then China, it may well have been considered too fantastic to merit serious consideration. A Republican form of government was to be established by Imperial degree; the Emperor was to announce his own abdication; in return for his willingness to grant the *alleged* wishes of the people the *Republic* would guarantee the continuance of various privileges including the retention of his full Imperial title, confirming the ownership of his own property plus a large annual grant for the maintenance of the Imperial Family and their palaces.

The six year old Emperor recorded in his diary some years later his recollections of *Yüan Shih-k'ai's* meeting with the Dowager Empress *Lung-yu*, the following is a translation:

> *"One incident of those days stands out clearly in my memory;*
> *The Empress Lung-yu was seated in a side room of the Mind*
> *Nurture Palace, (Yang Hsin Tien) wiping her eyes with a*
> *handkerchief while a fat old man knelt on a red cushion in*
> *front of her, tears too were rolling down his face. I was*
> *seated at the right of the Dowager feeling rather bewildered*
> *and wondering why the two adults were weeping. There was*
> *no one in the room besides the three of us and it was very*

quiet; the fat man was sniffing loudly while he talked and I could not understand him. Later I learnt that this fat man was Yüan Shih-k'ai. This was the only time I ever saw him and it was his last meeting with the Dowager Empress. If what I have been told is right, this was the occasion on which Yüan brought up the question of my abdication. After this meeting Yüan made the excuse that an attempt had been made on his life not to come to the court again."

Once more *Yüan Shih-k'ai* had betrayed the Dragon Throne.

CHAPTER TWO

Dynastic Twilight

"The whole nation is now inclined towards a republican form of government. The southern and central provinces first gave clear evidence of this inclination, and the military leaders have since promised their support to the same cause. By observing the nature of the people's aspirations we learn the Will of Heaven (T'ien-ming). It is not fitting that we should withstand the desires of the nation merely for the sake of the glorification of Our own house. We recognize the signs of the age, and We have tested the trend of popular opinion; and We now, with the Emperor at our side, invest the nation with Sovereign power, and decree the establishment of a constitutional government on a republican basis. In coming to this decision, We are actuated not only by a hope to bring solace to Our subjects, who long for the cessation of political tumult, but also by a desire to follow the precepts of the sages of old who taught that political sovereignity rests ultimately with the poeple."

Issued by the *Lung-yu* Empress Dowager.
February 12th, 1912.

The consternation and bewilderment that this edict caused, not only in court circles, but throughout the Empire was enormous. Princes, officials and their families fled to the protection of the foreign concessions throughout China, whilst the masses were numbed into an incredulous silence.

One contemporary account of the incident was published some years later in the *North China Standard*, *(Peking)* November 29th 1922.

> "*The house-boy*" recounted *Ku Hung-ming,* "*brought in an Evening Express sold in the streets containing the news that the decree of abdication had been issued. . . . . The whole company simultaneously rose to their feet and turning their faces towards the north fell to their knees with weeping and sobbing knocked their heads on the floor. . . . . . . .When, after this, late in the night, before parting, I said, 'the catastrophy has come. What is there more for us to do?' He grasped me by both my hands and, with tears flowing from his eyes, said to me in a voice I shall never forget, Shih shou kuo en ssu sheng i chih . . . .*"(for generations we have received benefits from the Imperial House; dead or alive I shall remain faithful to it.)

This was almost entirely the attitude of the official class and the majority of the people. Enthusiasm seemed wholly lacking throughout the length and breadth of the Empire, for this new government; few had only the slightest conception of what a *Republic* was, and did not manifest any desire to learn.

> "*Whether the Chinese people, as distinct from a few foreign-educated reformers, do, as a matter of fact, honestly believe that a republican government is adapted to the needs of the country, is a very difficult question. It certainly has not been proved that, 'the whole nation is now inclined towards a republic', in spite of the admssion to the effect contained in the Imperial edict of abdication. Perhaps it would be nearer the truth to say that the overwhelming majority of the people of China have not the slightest idea what a republic means, and how their lives and fortunes will be affected by its establishment, and therefore hold no strong opinions concerning the advantages or disadvantages.*" [1]

If a definition of the word *republic* were insisted upon, and that definition not too narrow or rigid, it could well be argued China was far more a *republic* under the monarchy then it ever became after it.

Sun Yat-sen had reluctantly resigned his provisional presidency of the Republic in *Nanking* in favour of *Yüan Shih-k'ai* who was *prevented* from journeying south by a *mutiny* in *Peking*. He was thus confirmed as President *in absentia* on the 10th March, and empowered to govern under a provisional constitution until a parliament could be elected and a full constitutional government be established. *Yüan* was to *betray* the revolutionists who had elected him just as he had *betrayed* the *Ch'ing* court that had made him Prime Minister, yet at the time, he seemed the only man of stature capable of holding the confused situation together. *Yüan's* achievements, though based wholly on distorted self-interest, were not inconsiderable; he had ousted the Manchus, beguiled the revolutionaries, courted and received foreign recognition and maintained at least some semblance of administration through a time of great uncertainty. Thus when China's immemorial monarchy was abolished, his emergence as *president* partly cushioned the shock. But, he was not 'the Son of Heaven' nor was he able to fill the vacuum left by the abdication in any of the traditional ideological ceremonies; he was but a man.

The rank and file Chinese who had shouted the anti-Manchu slogans invented by the *overseas* revolutionaries had little concept of what they amounted to, sadly *mob-mentality* is common to all mankind and the Chinese were, and are, no exception. Daniel Defoe said that in his time there were a hundred thousand stout fellows in England ready to fight to the death against *Popery*, without any notion of whether *Popery* was a man or a horse! So it was in China, mass-suggestion took over where common sense left off. There is an apt saying in Chinese: *Ch'iang tao chung jen t'ui*, (everyone in willing to give a push to a falling wall), and there were to be many *falling walls* to be pushed over in China for the next forty-five years.

To *politically* redress the balance, the revolutionists ascribed all manner of *imaginary* virtues to the native *Ming* Dynasty that had preceeded that of the foreign *Ch'ing*. They even formed close links with the Traid society, whose founding aim long ago, had been to revive the Chinese ruling house but, whose present priorities in a changing world had also changed into an *Oriental*

Mafia, and with the open encouragement of the *republicans*, their dangerous tentacles spread, not only throughout the Middle Kingdom, but far beyond, to the rich overseas Chinese settlements from whence so many of their republican sympathizers came.

> *"The Ming dynasty was at the outset distinguished by the cruelty and bloodshed that must accompany the establishment of an absolute monarchy. On the slightest suspicion whole families were slaughtered. Executions frequently ran into tens of thousands. The people had flocked to the standard of the Ming because they were sweeping away the hated foreign dyansty,* (the *Yüan*, Mongol dyansty), *but it was soon realized that the oppression of absolutism had became immeasurably worse."* [2]

There is little doubt that the *Da Ch'ing* Dynasty had fallen on evil days, and that the wide spread cancer of corruption had severely weakened the body politic and serious doubts were justified concerning its recovery, yet the *foreign* belief (fostered by the foreign-educated Chinese student revolutionaries) that the whole Chinese population was violently anti-Manchu was very far from the truth.

> *"It is only with the decay of the ruling house, the growth of power of the revolt in the south, and the desire to find a scapegoat on which to hang the blame for all the ills of China, that a quasi-racial hatred was worked up against the Manchus, which is now being perpetuated in text books and political doctrines."* [3]

Sir Robert Hart, during the seige of the Legations by the Boxers in 1900 wrote:

> *"This alien government, the Manchu dyansty has been part and parcel of the nation for three hundred years, and the Emperor is no more hated by the Chinese that Queen Victoria by the British."* [4]

Dr H A Giles whose works on China and the Chinese language formed the backbone of sino-British scholarship in the nineteenth century and who among other things was Her Majesty's Consul at *Ningpo* and resident in China for many years wrote:

> *"Everyone who has lived in China and has kept his eyes open, must have noticed what a large measure of personal freedom is enjoyed by even the meanest subject of the Son of Heaven."* [5]

Even *Sun Yat-sen*, with all his fierce anti-Manchu protestations was forced to admit that his countrymen, rather than suffering from too little freedom under the *Ch'ing*, in fact suffered from too much, this was uttered after he had first persuaded them that they were 'slaves of alien despots'; writing after the 'revolution' he said:

> *"The Chinese people never suffered directly any of the evils of despotism, (under the Ch'ing) . . . . The Chinese, because their liberty has always been so complete, have never noticed it, just as because there is so much air in a room we do not consider its importance . . . . Why are the Chinese merely sand? What makes us like sand is the fact that our liberty is excessive . . . . China at present is the slave of ten masters, so the nation is entirely without freedom."* [6]

In the same work *Sun Yat-sen* said:

> *"To speak plainly, our object was exactly opposite to that of European, (revolutions) . . . . We revolted because our freedom was excessive, we had no cohesive quality, no power of resistance, we were just sand."* [7]

It seems hardly believable that he could make such an utterance and justify his fanatical anti-monarchial policy at the same time, yet he did and if the whole of the puerile concepts are considered in his *San-min-chu-i* it becomes sadly obvious that he was as inept at formulating political theory as he was in trying to put it into practice. If poor indecisive Prince *Ch'un* was, 'the wrong man in the wrong place at the wrong time' what then was *Sun Yat-sen*?

The *organization* that *Sun Yat-sen* bequeathed to his fellow countrymen, the *Kuo-min tang*, made sure that the evil of *excessive freedom* could no longer be complained against. The Chinese people have always possessed an abundance of vitality and common sense but at this stage in their long history it was to be still many years before the shadow of chaos had passed from the landscape. That *Sun* was hailed as the 'father' of the still-born republican movement by naive *nationalists*, is perhaps a fitting, if not flattering epitaph. It was to be another forty-five years before a worthier figure was to emerge to occupy the shrine of patron-saint of China and lead that country on its 'long march' into the twentieth century.

'Articles of Favourable Treatment' of the Manchu Imperial House.

If this compromise of allowing the deposed Emperor of the *Ch'ing* to become the near neighbour of the President of the *Republic* in *Peking* its amazing enough, to realize that though the 'Son of Heaven' was stripped of his political powers he still retained his full Imperial status and title and continued to 'hold Court' in the *Forbidden City* until 1924, thirteen years after the so-called revolution, is to   occidental   reasoning almost unbelievable. Yet, that is precisely what happened. Few Western writers seem to have paid even the slightest attention to the 'Articles of Favourable Treatment' under which the Emperor and his court transferred administrative responsibility to the new regime but, these documents are of the utmost importance, for not only do they express the *Chineseness* of the attitude towards the Dynasty, but they demonstrate the hazy policy of the new leaders. Historians both Chinese and Western have argued that these *articles* have no direct bearing on subsequent political developments, and the *Nationalists*, realizing how much they had to hide, consigned them to oblivion in their day.

The pathetic document of abdication issued in the name of the six year old Emperor by the *Lung-yu* Empress Dowager can not be regarded as standing alone, for these eight *articles* are an integral part of the same ill-thought-out compromise. The former edict set out the Emperor's contribution, whilst the latter sets out that of the republican's which were embodied under the formal title:

"Articles providing for the Favourable Treatment of the Da Ch'ing Emperor after his abdication."

1   After the abdication of the Da Ch'ing Emperor, his title of dignity is to be retained and will not be abolished; and he will be treated by the Republic of China with the courtesy which it is customary to accord to foreign monarchs.

2   After the abdication of the Da Ch'ing Emperor, he will receive from the Republic of China an annual subsidy of 4,000,000 taels. After the reform of the currency this will be altered to 4,000,000 dollars (maximum).

3   After the abdication of the Da Ch'ing Emperor, he may as a temporary measure continue to reside in the Palace, (Forbidden City), but afterwards he will remove to the Yi-ho Park, (the Summer Palace). He may retain his body-guard.

4   After the abdication of the Da Ch'ing Emperor, the temples and mausolea of the Imperial Family with their appropriate sacrificial rites shall be maintained in perpetuity. The Republic of China will be responsible for the provision of the military guards for their adequate protection.

5   As the Ch'ung mausoleum of the late Emperor Te Tsung, (the temple name of the Kuang-hsü Emperor), has not yet been completed, the work will be carried out according to the proper regulations, (relating to Imperial tombs). The last ceremonies of the sepulchre will also be observed in accordance with the ancient rites. The actual expense will be borne by the Republic of China.

6   The services of all the persons of various grades hitherto employed in the Palace may be retained; but in future

no eunuchs are to be added to the staff.

7   After the abdication of the Da Ch'ing Emperor, his private property will be safeguarded and protected by the Republic of China.

8   The Imperial guard corps as constituted at the time of the abdication will be placed under the military control of the War office of the Republic of China. It will be maintained at its original strength and will receive the same emoluments as heretofore.

The preceding 'articles' constituted only part, albeit an important part, but not all of the revolutionary compromise, there were two further documents of a similar nature. The first defined the treatment to be accorded to members of the Imperial clan; it guaranteed that Manchu Princes and nobles should retain their titles of honour, including hereditary titles. Their rights, both public and private were to be identical with other citizens of the republic, except that they were to be excused military service. They were to retain their private property which would be protected.

The second document set out the treatment of a similar nature to be accorded to Manchus, Mongols, Mohammedans and Tibetans. This document assumed their acceptance of the new form of government and in consideration under which they were to receive equal treatment with the Chinese; their rights of private property would be respected; the titles of honour of both Princes and nobles would be recognized; it even stated that help would be given to those members who might be in economic distress; that allowances hitherto granted to members of the 'Eight Banners' (members of the Manchu military system) would continue to be issued, pending reorganization, that all the old limitations and restrictions formally imposed regarding livelihood and domicile on the persons of the races concerned be abolished; that the rights of religious liberty be guaranteed.

There were other related documents which were issued at later dates; one published 19th August in the first year of the Republic,

(1912) set out the treatment relating to the people of Mongolia, in nine clauses. Mongolia was no longer to be regarded as a dependency but as an integral part of Republican China and all barriers between the two races were abolished along with the confirmation of existing titles and privileges of Mongol Princes and lamas.

The last of this series of documents appeared in December 16th 1914 and sought to clarify the original eight articles of Favourable Treatment as, apparently during the three preceding years some anomalies had occured. This document had very little new to say except that the authority of the *Nei Wu Fu* was emphasised (the Imperial Household Department) which was now a department of the Republican government. At first sight, all these documents would appear to be most generous and concessionary indeed, that is precisely how they were interpreted in the West where discarded monarchies were treated very differently, viz., France, Russia and a string of middle European kingdoms whose monarchs had been murderously dispatched with little or no ceremony.

The articles already enumerated were doubtless concessionary, but from who's point of view is debatable. This has really never been clarified. The facts are these: The Imperialists had not been defeated. They had already retaken much lost ground in central China, nearly all north China as well as north-western China and Manchuria were in their hands. They had the good will of both the Mongols and Tibetans. Many of the ablest generals and viceroys were still loyal, they commanded by far the best trained and equiped army in China and could still control the financial and diplomatic machinery of the state. Therefore, at this stage it was by no means a foregone conclusion that they could have been overthrown, certainly not without a civil war which might have raged for as long as the Taiping Rebellion.

For an answer to this most Chinese of puzzles, one name comes floating to the surface; *Yüan Shih-k'ai*, had he consolidated his early victories against the poorly organized revolutionaries and remained faithful to the throne he would certainly have succeeded. The view of the West, based largely on fragmentary evidence was, because of the decay of the Dynasty the revolution was bound to succeed. Possible, but by no means probable. If the dissolution of the Dynasty had not occured in 1911 it would have have crumbled a few years later, was the popular assumption. On the other hand, the change over from absolute monarchy to constitutional monarchy might, under skillful guidance have saved not only the day, but the Empire.

The question is still open, why did the court give way and agree to the sweeping compromise that included the abdication of the Emperor? Was it because Prince *Ch'un* and the *Lung-yu* Dowager Empress could not bear to be responsible for a protracted and bloody civil war or did they realize that any further resistance on their part was hopeless? No, none of these fits the facts; for the real explanation we need only examine the motives of one man, *Yüan Shih-k'ai*!

Yüan had, for the moment, become master of the situation. Why had he become so half-hearted about the monarchy? Was it perhaps that he could neither forgive nor forget his dismissal from office in 1908 by the Regent? He had had more than enough time to brood over the *wrongs* done him during his three years of enforced retirement, but were these *wrongs* enough to make him abandon the dynasty? True, *Yüan* had always been an ambitious man and his loyality had always needed some form of stimulation, something, that after his recall Prince *Ch'un* could not supply. But, to abandon the Dynasty? Surely that was over-reacting to an unnecessarily theatrical degree! As he had brooded during those three 'leg nursing' years, his bitterness against Prince *Ch'un*, whom he hated and despised, grew like a malignant cancer inside him, blotting out everything else, his anger grew, while his loyality remained dormant.

To what excesses his consuming ambition led him is well known, although the exact extent can only be guessed at, but as he pressed his wishes and 'advice' on the Imperial family in the closing days of 1911 it is clear that he was not negotiating for the rebels and their still-born republic, nor for the 'Son of Heaven' and the Dynasty, but for *Yüan Shih-k'ai* and his own imagined greater glory.

The articles of Favourable Treatment have only to be examined cursorily before the same conclusion is drawn, for, embodied in this extraordinary document are clauses neither favourable to Emperor nor to the Republic. Yet, *Yüan* was no fool, and his skill as a draftsman shines through, he had created a stand-off situation which left the real power in his own hands. In playing the two sides against each other his argument to each must have proved a very tricky tight-rope to walk. His arguments to the revolutionaries could be perhaps para-phrased thus:

> *"This agreement provides for the abdication of the Emperor and will give you what you want. . . . . . a republic. In return, you are asked to let him keep a purely honorary and empty title, and to pay him an annual subsidy which though seemingly large will be only a trifle compared with the cost of a civil war. The permission granted him to remain in the Forbidden City is only temporary, and when you desire him to move to the Yi-ho Park, (the Summer Palace) he will be obliged to obey. The other privileges reserved to him and his family are of no practical importance and will be in no way detrimental to the prestige and dignity of the republic. All these privileges may be regarded as a kind of insurance against his taking part in any anti-republican or reactionary activities, and will simplify the task of keeping him under observation. Taking the agreement as a whole, it gives face to the Emperor without causing any loss of face to you. You secure the substance; he is left with the shadow. Foreign countries will extol your magnanimity, and the new republic will start its career amid general applause and in a blaze of glory. For you, there will be a clear sky and brilliant sun-shine; for the Da Ch'ing Emperor, only a slowly darkening twilight."*[8]

Then, changing both costume and format he hurried to the *Forbidden City* to brow-beat an ignorant and confused woman, an equally confused and witless Regent and a child Emperor of six years old. His arguments must have followed lines similar to these:

> *"This agreement saves the throne, and the Emperor remains Emperor. All he sacrifices is cheng ch'uan, (the right of ruling).*

45

That is really no sacrifice at all; for his Majesty is only a child, and could not personally assume the Imperial responsibilities for many years to come. By giving up the right to rule, the Imperial family will save themselves a great deal of trouble and anxiety. By the time he is grown up, the revolutionary madness will have spent itself, and the Emperor will resume the powers he has temporarily delegated to a crazy organization that calls itself a republic. It will prove itself unable to govern or to keep order, and the people will grow weary of it. Then they will remember that their Emperor still lives, that his throne has never been vacant, and that he is ready to respond to the call of his suffering people. The arrangement guarantees the maintenance of the ancestral rites and the protection of the Imperial mausolea, and large revenues will be provided for maintenance of his Majesty's Imperial state. The household department will continue to function and the traditional court ceremonies will be kept up as heretofore. 'You secure the substance; the revolutionaries are left with the shadow.' Foreign countries will extol you for your magnanimity in having laid down your arms because you could not bear to see your people enduring the horrors of civil war. The throne will regain its lost prestige, and in a few years time the whole world will rejoice to see the Son of Heaven step forth to rule once more over a happy and prosperous China." [9]

Here another element emerges, for whilst *Yüan* stood firmly between both republicans and Imperialists, dazzled by the prospects of his own future, the vested interests of the *Nei Wu Fu*, (The Imperial Household Department) had made themselves felt. This largely incompentent and corrupt organization from whose funds enormous amounts were misappropriated annually and whose *influence* was felt in every corner of the *Purple Forbidden City* had to survive and doubtless *Yüan*, for a not so small fee, arranged this. Therefore the *Articles* were favourable to, republicans, Imperialists, the Household Department, but, most of all to *Yüan Shih-k'ai*, but not to the six year old Emperor. It must have been obvious to anyone that the newly formed republican government could not long afford the luxury of keeping an Emperor

The inauguration of Yüan Shih-k'ai as the first
President of Republic of China. October 10th 1913.

in the heart of *Peking* who might at any time, although he himself possessed no political power, become the axis of a monarchist revival, even as an unwilling figure-head. No one, not even his Regent father seems to have considered what effects this 'unnatural' life might have on the morals and character of the infant Emperor surrounded, as he was, by flatterers and servile eunuchs who assured him that he was semi-divine and above all men. The poor lonely boy must manage as best he could, deprived not only of the *divine right* to rule, the only justification of a King, but *imprisoned* within the decaying *Forbidden City*, susceptible to all the falseness and deceit that enveloped it. If the Imperial family had been *tricked* out of the throne, as some Western writers have stated, it was not by the republicans, who had themselves been *duped* but by the slippery *Yüan Shih-k'ai*.

Many years later the ex-Emperor was to recall memories of his confined childhood in the *Forbidden City*:

> *"Whenever I think of my childhood my head fills with yellow mist. The glazed tiles were yellow, my sedan-chair was yellow, my chair cushions were yellow, the linings of my hats and robes were yellow, the dishes and bowls from which I ate were yellow, the material in which my books were wrapped was yellow, the window curtains, the bridle of my horse.......... everything was yellow. This colour, so-called 'brilliant yellow' (ming-huang) was used exclusively by the Imperial household and made me feel even from my earliest years that I was unique and had a heavenly nature, different from that of everybody else."*

"When I was ten years old my grandmother and mother started to come and visit me on the orders of the High Consorts, (Dowager consorts of the first degree, widows of the Emperor T'ung-chih and Kuang-hsü) and they brought my brother P'u-chieh and my first sister to play with me for a few days. Their first visit started off very drearily; they just stood gazing at me with a fixed stare like attendants at an audience. It occured to me then to take them to the part of the palace in which I lived, I asked my brother; 'What games do you play at home?'

'We play hide and seek' said my brother very respectfully.

I was very excited, 'that is a very good game' I said.

I had often played this with the eunuchs but never with children of my own age. So, we started to play and very soon my brother and sister forgot their inhibitions. We let down the blinds to make the room darker. My sister, who was two years younger than me was in a ecstasy of delight and terror as my brother and I kept giving her frights by popping out from unexpected places, we laughed and shouted so much we were soon exhausted and sat down to get our breath back. I asked them to think of another game, my brother looked throughtful for a while and then looked at me with a silly smile on his face.

'What are you grinning at?'

He went on grinning even more than before.

'Tell me! Tell me!' I urged him impatiently for I was sure that he had thought of a splendid new game. At last he said, 'I . . . . . .I thought that your Majesty would be different from ordinary people. The Emperors I have seen on the stage all have long beards . . .'stroking an imaginary beard as he spoke. That gesture was his undoing for as he raised his hand I noticed that the lining of his sleve was of a very familiar colour.

'P'u-chieh! Are you allowed to wear that colour?'

'But . . . . . but . . . . . .it isn't . . . . . its apricot, isn't it?'

'Nonsense! It is Imperial brilliant yellow!'

'Yes sire . . . . . . yes sire . . . . . .' he mumbled and stood away from me his arms hanging respectfully by his sides. My sister also quickly rose and joined him, both were frightened to the point of tears.

'It is brilliant Imperial yellow. You have no business to be wearing it!'

'Yes sire'

With these two words he reverted from being my brother to being my subject. [10]

Whatever the aspects of the young Emperor's daily life may have been, they were to him, only what he had grown up to accept; row upon row of officials either in Manchu or Western dress bowing and performing the decreed *kow tow*, all the traditional pomp of the court seemed quite normal to him, he had memory of little else.

"Every time I went to my schoolroom to study, or visited the high Consorts to pay my respects, or went for a stroll in the garden I was always followed by a large retinue. Every trip I made to the Summer Palace must have cost a great deal; the New Republic's police had to be asked to line the roads and I was always accompanied by a large motorcade consisting of dozens of vehicles. Whenver I went for a stroll in the garden a procession had to be specially organized. In front went a eunuch from the administrative bureaus whose function was roughly the same as a motor horn, he walked twenty or thirty yards ahead of the rest of the party intoning the sound, 'Chir. . . . chir . . . .' as a warning to all who might be in the vicinity to withdraw at once. Next came two eunuchs advancing in a crabwise fashion on either side of the path; ten paces behind them came the centre of the procession, myself. If I was being carried in a chair there would be two junior eunuchs walking beside me to attend to my wants, if I was walking they would support me. Following came a eunuch with a large silk canopy followed in turn by a large group of eunuchs of whom some were empty handed and others carrying all sorts of things; a seat in case I wanted to rest, changes of clothing, umbrellas and parasols. After these eunuchs of the Imperial presence came eunuchs of the Imperial tea bureau with boxes of various kinds of cakes and delicacies and, of course jugs of hot water and a tea service; they were followed by eunuchs of the Imperial dispensary carrying cases of medicine and first aid equipment suspended from carrying poles. These medicines included potions prepared from lampwick sedge, chrysanthemums, roots of reeds, bamboo leaves and skins, in summer there was always essence of betony pills for rectifying the vapour, six harmony pills for stabilizing the centre, gold coated heat-dispersing cinnabar, fragrant herb pills, omnipurpose bars, colic medicine and anti-plague powder; and throughout all four seasons there would be the three immortals beverage to aid the digestion, as well as many other preparations. At the end of the procession came the eunuchs who carried the commodes and chamber-pots. If I was walking a sedan-chair either open or covered according to season, would come last. This long procession would proceed in order and silence, which I would often throw into confusion, by running about, as all young children love to do when in high spirits. At first they would all scuttle along after me puffing and panting with their orderly procession reduced to chaos. When I grew a little older and more considerate I would tell them to stand and wait for me; then apart from the junior eunuchs of the Imperial presence they would all stand there with their heavy loads and wait for me in silence. Later, when I had learnt to ride a bicycle I ordered that all the wooden upright thresholds in the palace be removed so that I could ride around without obstruction, the procession was then no longer able to keep up with me and for a time had to be abandoned." [11]

Records also exist to the unbridled appetite of the Imperial household and it was recorded that during the second year of *P'u-yi's* reign, (1910) the following supplies were consumed within the *Forbidden City* during the course of one month: 3,960 catties of meat, (over two tons), 388 chickens and ducks, 14,642 catties of pork, (at a cost of 2,342.72 taels of silver) plus extra portions of meat, 31,844 catties; pork, 814 catties, 4,786 extra chickens and ducks, not including fish, shrimps and eggs or rice or noddles.

Also from that same month a list has survived which lists the clothing made for the Emperor; it is dated the sixth day of the tenth month to the fifth day of the eleventh month; eleven fur jackets, six fur inner and outer gowns, two fur waistcoats, thirty padded waistcoats and pairs of trousers, the bill for just the edgings, pockets, buttons and thread came to 2,137.6335 silver dollars and this list does not include any of the ceremonial costume and other accessories. The Emperor recalled:

"I do not know exactly what was made, but everything I wore was always new. . . . . My changes of clothing were laid down in regulations and were the responsibility of the eunuchs of the clothing storerooms. Even my everyday gowns came in twenty-different styles, from the one in black and white inlaid fur that I started wearing on the nineteenth of the first lunar month to the sable one I changed into on the first day of the eleventh month. Needless to say, my clothes were far more complicated on festivals and ceremonial occassions." [12]

To manage the Emperor's affaris was the prerogative of the *Nei Wu Fu*, (Imperial Household Department) it had under its control seven bureaus and forty-eight other separate offices. The seven bureaus were; Storage, Guard, Protocol, Counting House, Stock-raising, Disciplinary and Constitution and attached to each were the requisite number of storerooms, workshops etc.,. For example the storage bureau was responsible for the safe keeping of silver, fur, porcelain, satin silk, clothes and tea. According to the official lists of 1909 the staff of this corrupt department numbered 1,023 which excluded the Palace Guard, eunuchs and *sulas* or servants. This figure was gradually reduced under the Republic to 600 and by the time the Imperial family was *evicted* in 1924 there were still over three hundred employees.

One of the forty-eight dependant offices of the *Nei Wu Fu* was the *Ju Yi Kuan*, The 'As You Wish Lodge', whose sole function was to paint pictures and calligraphy in outline so that the Dowager Empress or High Consorts could 'fill-in' the outlines with colour and write a title and sign their names, a practice that has tricked many an expert thereafter into assuming that this or that scroll was in fact the wholly original work of the signed artist!

The sustaining maxim of the *Nei Wu Fu* was 'taking the grass as a standard' a phrase introduced by the great *Ch'ien-lung* Emperor; he is said to have ordered that nothing in the palace, not even a blade of grass must be lost! To put his theory into practice he put some blades of grass on a table and gave strict instructions that every day they were to be counted to make sure that not one single piece was missing. Even in the time of *P'u-yi* there were the same thirty-six withered blades of grass preserved in a cloisonné canister in the Mind Nurture Palace.

Right:
The Empress Dowager Lung-yu.

Below:
P'u-yi with the Empress Dowager
Lung-yu in 1911.

When the three year old *P'u-yi* first entered the *Forbidden City* as the adopted son of both the *T'ung-chih* and *Kuang-hsü* Emperors all their surviving wives and consorts became in essence his mothers although the new Empress Dowager *Lung-yu* immediately assumed that she was the *foremost Mother* and insisted on the other *mothers* standing while she was seated. *P'u-yi* was obliged to call them all 'August Mother' whilst his real mother remained in the *Ch'un* family mansion in the Old Tartar City.

"Although I had so many mothers, I never knew any motherly love." *P'u-yi* later recalled. "As far as I can remember today the greatest concern they ever showed for me was to send me food at every meal and wait for the report from the eunuch that I had consumed it with relish." This may sound rather distant and unreasonable but the 'Son of Heaven' was forced to endure much more, when this poor lonely boy got impatient or perhaps lost his temper, the chief eunuch would offer the following diagnosis and prescription: "The Lord of Ten Thousand Years has fire in his heart; let him sing for a while to disperse it." The boy would then be locked in the small room that contained his commode in the schoolroom palace where he could rage and curse and howl, kick the door and demand to be let out; no one paid any attention and, when finally exhausted and finished "singing" and the "fire dispersed" he would be let out. This was by no means a 'cure' invented by the eunuchs of the *Forbidden City* or even *P'u-yi's* August Mother the Empress Dowager *Lung-yu*, for the very same treatment was administered to his brothers and sisters in the *Ch'un* family mansion.

CHAPTER THREE

Emperor and President

For the first thirteen years of the new Chinese Republic, that is to say, from the spring of 1912 to the winter of 1924, there dwelt in the very heart of *Peking*, (Nothern Capital), both an Emperor and a President. For the *Da Ch'ing* Dyansty this period has fittingly been referred to as the "Twilight", a somewhat extended twilight that lasted for thirteen years during which time the Emperor, deprived by the *Articles* of his most important function, the privilege of being of service to his people, continued in both title and dignity to observe the ritual ceremonies that court protocol demanded of him. The republic on the other hand faced a cold grey dawn, whose clouds, when the sun eventually broke through, were streaked with red, which even then whispered of yet another great upheaval that was to come.

This transition period, if confusing to the Chinese, was doubly so to Westerners, even those resident in China seemed to have forgotten the *Articles*, if indeed they had ever read them in the first place, and assumed that the encumbant of the Dragon Throne was the 'ex-Emperor', in conformity with European practice. Although he still had the title and dignity *P'u-yi* was really neither Emperor nor ex-Emperor, and as a compromise, he became known in foreign circles as "the boy Emperor". The confusion about the Emperor's title and status came from an ignorance of the exact meaning of these titles, the titles of all monarchs,whom Europeans quite wrongly described as 'Emperor of China' was purely Dynastic, not territorial.

The actual name of a dynasty had no connection with the area over which it ruled, thus, if the *Da Ming* Dynasty had continued to rule somewhere outside the limits of China itself, Tongking or

Burma, there would have been no reason in theory to omit the honorific *Da*, (great) whilst the new dynasty in China itself would have adopted a new Dynastic title. In fact the *Da Ming* Dynasty was completely overthrown and after a few years had no authority anywhere, it merely ceased to exist. Many Westerners have still only the vaguest knowledge of Chinese history, many assuming that the *Ming* was ousted by the *Ch'ing* but, it was not that simple. True, the Manchu onslaughts had shaken the Chinese Dynasty to its foundations but it was not the Manchu who were responsible for the suicide of the last *Ming* Emperor on the hill that overlooks the *Forbidden City*.

That tragic event was brought about by the capture of *Peking* by an army of Chinese marauders under the leadership of a brigand named *Li Tzu-ch'eng*. In the prelude to chaos, he had devastated, and made himself master of, a large portion of *Ming* China, and on successfully capturing the Northern Capital he did what many brigands had done before him, he declared himself Emperor of a new Dynasty, the *Da Shun*, and for his own reign title he had chosen *Yung-ch'ang*, the first year of his reign was 1644! Had he succeeded, his name may well have gone down in Chinese history as the first in a glorious line of *Da Shun* Emperors but, as it was, he failed, and his name is no longer remembered, in most cases he has even vanished completely from history.

The same dynastic ambitions were to bring about the eventual downfall of *Yüan Shih-k'ai* in 1916, both brigands were only 'Emperor for a Day' in company with others who, although they did not perhaps aspire to become Emperor, tried to hold the power of life and death over their fellow countrymen.

Da Ch'ing Da Huang Ti, (Great Emperor of the Great Ch'ing Dynasty) was the title of the ten *Ch'ing* Emperors, not 'Emperor of China', as popularly supposed in the West; the clause in the "Articles of Favourable Treatment" which deals with this matter clearly states, "The title of dignity is to be retained and will not be abolished". Thus the title *Da Ch'ing Huang Ti* is stated in five out of the eight Articles, as well as in the preamble. As no new dynasty was established after the abdication in 1912 the question of devising a new dynastic title naturally did not arise, and the new regime merely called itself *Chung Hua Min Kuo*, The Republic of China. If the *Min* in *Chung Hua Min Kuo* had been changed to *Ti* this would have been enough to change the meaning from Republic of China to, The Chinese Empire. One last example of the readiness of the Chinese people to accept the ancient theory that the name of the state was different from the name of the dyansty is exemplified by the Cantonese who, to this day refer to themselves as *T'ong-yan*, (men of *T'ang*), for it was under this dynasty that their southern provinces, (*Kwangtung* and *Kwangsi*) were first absorbed into the Empire; whilst northern Chinese refer to themselves as *Han-jên*, (*Han* people), which was a much earlier dynasty than the *T'ang*.

The seeming anomaly at the beginning of this chapter, in the light of the foregoing, demonstrates that, although a personage styled the *Da Ch'ing* Emperor residing in *Peking*, did not in any way undermine the authority or prestige of the new Republic. These finer points of usage may appear at first sight to be somewhat irrelevant but on reflection they will be seen to shed necessary light of the events of 1916 and the Chinese attitude towards them.

Yüan Shih-k'ai had betrayed the *Kuang-hsü* Emperor in 1898, the *Hsüan-t'ung* Emperor in 1911, and the Republic itself in 1916. The exploits of this unscrupulous selfstyled stateman who became the first president of the Republic and for whom *Sun Yat-sen* was forced to stand aside, were instrumental in the downfall not only of the dynasty, but of the Chinese people themselves.

At this time *Yüan's* military position in northern China was unassailable. Having taken the oath as President on 10th March 1912 he had no intention of attending the 'new Parliament' in *Nanking* when pressed to do so, for he was far too astute to fall into the power of this revolutionary clique, who he well knew hated and mistrusted him just as much as he did them. He therefore excused himself from journeying south on the pretext that the political conditions prevailing in the north were far too unstable, and needed his strong hand to control them. The revolutionary leaders were more than sceptical of *Yüan's* reasons for not attending the *Nanking* conference and said so. *Yüan* therefore staged the "Peking Mutiny" to satify his suspicious colleagues, that this enginered 'mutiny' cost the lives of many people and caused considerable devastation to property was a matter of total indifference to him; his point had been made, he was needed in *Peking* and there he was going to stay.

A year later, 20th March 1913 *Sung Chiao-jen* an aggressive southern leader was assassinated almost certainly at *Yüan's* instigation and, by July a new revolutionary movement was launched aimed directly at *Yüan's* overthrow. The new 'rebels', who included *Sun Yat-sen*, were defeated by *Yüan* within a month and this 'second revolution', as it has subsequently been known, failed completely, *Sun* himself was forced into exile in Japan where for a time Japanese sympathizers sustained both him and his cause but, in view of subsequent events, even the staunchist became disillusioned with both the revolution and *Sun Yat-sen*, its reputed 'father'! By the 6th October of the same year *Yüan* was formally elected President for a term of five years amid much pomp and ceremony, the 10th October marking the second anniversary of the 'new Republic'. Soon after this he managed by intrigue and financial manipulation to get himself confirmed as President for life with the power to nominate his own successor. Immediately he dissolved *Sun Yat-sen's Kuo-min tang* party, (People's Party) and this in turn led to the dissolution of parliament itself. *Yüan* was now the unrivalled strong-man of 'the New China'.

At this time he maintained an attitude of outward 'correctness' towards the Emperor and his depleted court whilst, at the same time on various flimsy pretexts, helping himself to funds and treasure belonging to the Imperial House. On the other hand the sums promised for the upkeep of the Imperial family and the court under the "Articles of Favourable Treatment" were at no time paid in full, and by the end of 1924 the 'Articles' had become a mere scrap of paper and the Emperor was owed many millions of dollars by the Republic.

Early in 1913 *Yüan* caused panic and dismay in court circles by suggesting that it was now time to comply with the third of the articles, and move the court from the *Forbidden City* to the *Yüan Ming Yüan*, (the Summer Palace)[1]. This especially struck terror into the hearts of the Imperial Household Department which saw this change of residence as the first step towards its own dissolution. In the absence of any better protest the *Nei Wu Fu*, through the willing intercession of the *Lung-yu* Dowager Empress pointed out to the President that to accede to his request would put the lives of the Imperial Family severely in jeopardy, any evil-doer could easily scale the low walls of the Summer Palace, something that was impossible within the safety of the *Forbidden City*. To satisfy this objection *Yüan* issued orders that the entire wall in question, some three miles of it, should be raised by several feet, the money for this huge task was to be supplied by the Imperial Household Department not the Republic, in other words it was to be paid for from the privy purse which the Republic had been more than forgetful in replenishing. The astute officials of the Household Department succeeded in turning even this apparent obstacle into a source of profit for themselves; the heightening of this wall proved to be an immensely costly undertaking which was carried out with such staggering inefficiency that no sooner had one section been raised to the requisite height, than another section collapsed, which in turn brought down portions of the original structure! The whole enterprise was to prove an unnecessary extravagance which merely lined the already bulging purses of the Household officials for *Yüan* relectantly agreed to an indefinite postponement of the proposed move. The reason for his apparent change of heart is not generally known; it was because he was afraid of antagonising the still powerful and influential Imperialist general and ex-viceroy *Chang Hsun*, who was in control of the *Tientsin-Nanking* railway from his headquarters at *Hsuchou* and who was therefore in a position to dominate all eastern China north of the *Yangtse*. That *Chang Hsun*, was one of *Yüan's* 'men' was well known, and that his power was the means whereby *Yüan* had kept the southern revolutionary army from marching north but, what was not known was that *Chang's* acceptance of *Yüan's* leadership was conditional on *Yüan's* scrupulous observance of the *articles* between the throne and the Republic. *Chang's* attitude was that of equal loyalties to both Emperor and Republic, as represented in the person of *Yüan Shih-k'ai*, the former was absolute whilst the latter was merely conditional.

That *Chang Hsun* was motivated by pure loyalty to the Emperor is patently clear, but unknown to him and his Imperial patrons, the Household Department, fearful of its corrupt and extravagant administration, which would have been severely curtailed by the proposed removal to the *Yüan Ming Yüan*, had dispatched emissaries to *Hsuchou* to implore his intervention on the alleged ground that the honour and personal safety of His Imperial Majesty were at stake. The *Nei Wu Fu* professed the same lofty motives as *Chang Hsun* but, in reality, as always, their interests were not the Emperor's but their own. *Chang Hsun* was convinced that by persuading *Yüan* to abandon his plan to remove the Imperial Court from the *Forbidden City* to the Summer Palace he was fulfilling the duty of a loyal subject, whereas he was merely perpetuating the evils of the corrupt and unscrupulous Household Department, this body perhaps more than anyother was largely responsible for the decay and eventual fall of the *Ch'ing* Dynasty.

Yüan relented in the face of such sustained and powerful opposition, but no doubt he had in mind that soon he would enter the *Purple Forbidden City* amid great pomp and glory as the first Emperor of a new Imperial Dyansty, then the Manchu clan would have to go, not just from the 'Great Within' but from China itself. For the moment *Yüan*, as President of the Republic of China had to content himself with that portion of the Imperial Palace that had been given over to him in his official capacity, this was the *Hsin-hua* Palace with its fine lakes and pavilions which adjoined the west side of the *Forbidden City*, which if regarded impartially was in no way inferior to the quarters occupied by the Imperial family.

For nearly two years from this date *Yüan* allowed his schemes for personal aggrandizement to mature, two years from the date of his election as 'President for life' he walked with caution seemingly content with his new position which conferred the rights of 'king' upon him in all but name. It was also a widely known 'secret' at this time that he had exercised his right in appointing his favourite son *Yüan K'o-ting* as his own successor.

Chang Hsun

He created the *Ch'ou An Hui*, (Society for the planning of Peace) through which he proceeded to manipulate the 'Will of the People' in the August of 1915. Although it was his creation, it was nominally headed by a politician *Yang Tu*, and *Yüan* took no outward part in its organization. The propaganda that poured from this organ was all aimed at the *Kuo t'e*, or form of government, a matter that must be decided by 'the People', who thus influenced by his thinly veiled policy must choose in accordance with his own secret wishes.

Yüan found himself at this time at the very centre of power and influence; there gathered around him an ever swelling throng of flatterers and like-minded opportunists, and it was a source of considerable embarrassment that this clique included some members of the Manchu clan who unashamedly sought to ingratiate themselves with this arch-enemy of their own dynasty. Prince *P'u-lun*, who was of the same generation as the Emperor and whose claims to the throne had been strenuously advocated by *Yüan Shih-k'ai*, now took the opportunity of demonstrating his gratitude to his one time advocate and outwardly supported *Yüan's* Imperial ambitions. The Prince further outraged Imperial etiquette by actually performing the *kowtow* before *Yüan* and describing himself as *ch'en*, (the term by which servants of an Emperor refer to themselves when addressing the throne). Publicly, as a member of the republican senate he posed as the representative of the Imperial family in supporting *Yüan's* proposal that he should ascend to the Dragon Throne. *Yüan* returned the compliment and entrusted Prince *P'u-lun* with the delicate mission of persuading the Imperial family to surrender the *yu-hsi*, (Imperial seals) which were always kept under lock and key in the *Chiao-T'ai Tien*, (Hall of the Blending of Great Creative forces) within the *Forbidden City*. He was unsuccessful for on the very day he had made the arrangements, with the connivance of certain officials of the *Nei Wu Fu* to carry off the Imperial seals, *Yüan's* dreams of self-glorification came crashing to the ground, and the Imperial seals remained within the *Forbidden City* in the rightful custody of the Emperor until November 1924. The Imperial seals to which such greatest importance was attached in China, much more than in any other country, had, unaccountably remained in the Emperor's keeping, yet again demonstrating the indecisive attitude of the Republic and its drafting of the 'Articles'; could it have been that they were by no means convinced that the abdication of 1912 was of a permanent nature and that the Emperor might again ascend the Dragon Throne?

Yüan's Imperial ambitions boded ill for the "boy Emperor", for although an Emperor and a President might co-exist without apparent friction in one city, it was plain to all that the same compromise would not apply to two Emperors. The stage was now set for the final act of *Yüan Shih-k'ai's* drama of Imperial dreams; thousands of telegrams, letters and petitions poured in from all over China imploring *Yüan* to give in to the popular demand for the revival of the monarchy, *Yüan's* agents had of course seen to it that this mass of adulation came from every corner of the Empire. This was followed on December 15th by the summoning of 'a great assembly of popular deputies' which voted almost to a man for a return to constitutional monarchy. The next step was for *Yüan* to issue a carefully worded mandate, announcing, that although conscious of his own unworthiness he knew it was his duty to bow to the "Will of the People" and if they wished, he, *Yüan Shih-k'ai* would become the first Emperor of a new Chinese Dynasty under the reign title of *Hung-hsien*! The climax to this "humble acceptance" of Imperial elevation came just a few days later; it was the winter solstice and *Yüan* took the opportunity of reviving the most imposing of all Chinese religious ceremonies, the sacrifice to the Altar of Heaven. This sacred ceremony could only be undertaken by an Emperor and *Yüan* , by officiating, effectively proclaimed to the whole Empire that he had already assumed the Imperial prerogatives and was imminently to ascend the Dragon Throne.

Unfortunately *Yüan's* own lack of confidence in "the will of the people", which he had so publicly proclaimed, resulted in this impressive ceremony being shorn of most of its pomp as he thought it necessary to proceed to the Altar of Heaven secure within an armoured car for reasons of personal safety. In the chill hours of dawn on that winter morning it seemed the gods were not deceived by this splendidly robed figure, perhaps they had looked deep into his heart and spurned his usurping sacrifices, knowing he was not the 'Son of Heaven', just a scheming impostor. What was in his mind as he returned, secure within his armoured car after his shameful ceremony will never be known, the stars had looked down on him as he beseeched their divine aid, but they had not given it, for if he could have read the portents of these 'heavenly spheres', they told only of his ruin and destruction. When he as last returned to his palace he received news of which the stars had given him no warning and for which he was totally unprepared: One of his generals *Ts'ai Ao* had quietly left *Peking* leaving no hint of his intentions until he had reached the confines of *Yünnan* province, there in the neighbouring province of *Kueichou* he and his fellow general *T'ang Chi-yao* raised the standard of revolt calling on all true supporters of the revolution to join with them in crushing the tyrant *Yüan* who had not only trampled on the 'will of the People' but was a traitor to both the Republic and the Dragon Throne. This 'Third Revolution' erupted in the last week of December 1915. The response to the 'call to arms' was so immediate and emphatic that *Yüan* must have realized that his dreams of monarchy were now in ruins. By the end of February the following year he was forced to issue a proclamation to the effect that his enthronement, (for which vast and costly preparations were well advanced and which had been largely paid for by 'loans' wrenched unwillingly from the Manchu ruling house), was to be indefinitely postponed. A month later he was forced to retreat still further by announcing that the *Hung-hsien* monarchy was definitely cancelled.

Even with this staggering 'loss of face' *Yüan* continued to protest, explain and extricate himself from the dangerous *cul-de-sac* into which his 'Imperial dreams' had lead him. He blamed the disastrous fiasco on everyone else, they had mislead him, the whole of China must believe that in his heart of hearts he had always been a true and sincere Republican! He had been deceived into believing that it was "the will of the People" that he should ascend the Dragon Throne and now that he knew it was not, he felt only joy and relief that he could now devote the rest of his life to serving the Republic. Luckily for the Republic, that was not to be for long for *Yüan Shih-k'ai* died less than three months after the cancellation of his enthronement, on 6th June 1916, much to the relief of both Imperialists and Republicans. His death was of course accompanied by the usual rumours of murder or suicide but there is no evidence to suspect either; the medical opinion ascribed his death to: *"Physical derangements produced by prolonged and intense anxiety and emotional disturbance"*.

That *Yüan's* monarchical movement even succeeded at all is remarkable enough but that it was voted for by elected representatives goes far to explain the then current attitude in China, which was neither anti-Manchu nor anti-monarchic, this attitude was widely held by many prominent people, China had always been monarchic, this preference was precisely what *Yüan* had played on. The 'attitude' may be best demonstrated by an article which appeared in the *Hsin Ch'ing Nien*, (New Youth) in May 1917 by an ultra-radical professor of Peking University *Ch'en Tu-hsiu*, which was published a year after the death of *Yüan Shih-k'ai*.

"I do not share the prevalent optimism about the immediate future of our republic . . . . .I am not at all sure that there will be no future attempts to change the form of government . . . . I was by no means surprised when the Ch'ou-An Society suddenly began to advocate the re-establishment of the Monarchic system. Now that Yüan Shih-k'ai has come to grief and died, it is generally supposed that the Republic is firmly established. But I have serious doubts. . . . . . Although there seems to be no general opposition to the Republican idea, the people's minds are still obsessed with the old monarchic notions. They have not the slightest idea of what the civilized democratic societies of Europe and America really are . . . . It was no idle dream of Yüan Shih-k'ai to make himself Emperor. He knew very well that the great majority of the people in China still believed in monarchy and had no faith in a Republic. Even of those who opposed the recent attempt to revive the monarchy, more than half were not generally and fundamentally opposed to the monarchic principal but merely to Yüan Shih-k'ai's becoming Emperor . . . Although Yüan is dead, the popular hankering after a monarchy, of which he tried to make use for his own

advantage, is still in existance. It seems to me that it would be easier to climb up to heaven than to establish the Republic so securely that no monarchic revivals could ever take place again. If we want to stabilize our Republic, there is only one thing to be done, we must clear out of the people's minds every trace of the antiquated monarchic ideas that still obsess them."

This, then was the mood prevalent throughout China at this time of change and transition, quite at variance with the Western interpretation of the situation.

Almost all that remained of *Yüan's* 'Dynasty' were numbers of prematurely minted coins which he had confidently allowed into circulation which bore such inscriptions as, *Hung-Hsien chi-yuan*, (The Hung-hsien reign period) and *Chung-hua Ti Kuo*, (the Chinese Empire) all carried *Yüan's* effigy in company with silver dollars minted before this in his role as president. Another contemporary judgement on *Yüan* was penned by a learned and patriotic Chinese , Dr V K Ting, who had spent several years as a student in England and Germany.

"He (Yüan) began his public career as China's political agent in Korea and was more than anyone else responsible for the Sino-Japanese War of 1894. By betraying the Kuang-hsü Emperor, who was endeavouring to reform the political system in 1898, he became the favourite of the infamous Empress-Dowager, and was entrusted with the formation of China's new army, from which have been drawn almost all the present military governors who are by common consent China's greatest curse. During the republican revolution of 1911 he betrayed the Manchu Dynasty, to which he was premier, to become president of the republic, which position he retained by first bribing then dissolving parliament. There are at least two murders of his political opponents proved against him, and finally he worked his own ruin by trying to create a monarchy by fraud. He died a miserable failure and unblessed." [2]

During *Yüan's* dance of death his near neighbour in the *Purple Forbidden City* was not unaware of his presence, nor the existence of the world beyond the high walls; sounds wafted in of the cries of street pedlars, the rumbling of wooden wheels and the sounds of singing, the palace eunuchs referred to this cacophony as the "city of sounds". The most distinguishable noise was of military bands which eminated from the palace of the president of the republic. "*Yüan Shih-k'ai* has been eating" *Chang Chieh-ho* the chief eunuch would whisper to the Emperor, "he has music at mealtimes, which is even grander than your Majesty". Saying this he would screw up his face, which was a clear indication that it made him very indignant, and there was sadness in his squeaking voice. The Emperor, though then only a boy of eight understood and listened to the "city of sounds" trying to peer into the future, his future.

At the age of five *P'u-yi* began his formal studies, a tutor was appointed by the *Lung-yu* Dowager Empress and the astrologers consulted to determine an auspicious day to commence, this day was 10th September 1911. His first schoolroom was on an island in one of the palace lakes but soon this was abandoned in favour of the *Yu Ching* Palace, (The Palace of Cultivation of Happiness), a small building within the *Forbidden City*. It contained two studies furnished in a more simple manner than were most other rooms; under the southern window was a long table on which stood hat-stands and vases of flowers, by the west wall was a *kang*, (a covered heated seat); there were two more tables by the north wall with books and stationery on them, the walls were hung with scrolls written by the first Prince *Ch'un*, (*P'u-yi's* grandfather), for his son the *Kuang-hsü* Emperor. The focal point of the study was a hugh clock measuring more than two metres in diameter whose hands were longer than the young Emperor's arms. The mechanism of this gigantic time-piece was located on the other side of the wall and to wind it required an implement like a large motorcar starting handle which could only be accomplished from the adjoining room. His principal texts were; The thirteen classics, (a standard work containing the maxims and histories of the *Ch'ing* Dynasty from its foundation). An excerpt from his diary dated 1920 when he was fourteen discloses his daily routine.

"27th. Fine. Rose at four, wrote out eighteen sheets of the character for prosperity in a large hand. Classics at eight. Read Analects, Chou ritual, Record of Ritual and T'ang poetry with P'u-chien and Yu-chung. Listened to tutor Chen lecturing on the 'General Chronological History with comments by the Ch'ien-lung Emperor'. Finished eating at nine-thirty, read Tso Commentary, Ku Liang Commentary, heard tutor Chu on the 'Explanation of the Great Learning', wrote couplets. Lessons finished at eleven, went to pay my respects to four high Consorts. Johnston did not come today as he had mild flu, so returned to the Mind Nurture Palace and wrote out thirty more sheets of characters. Read papers, ate at four, bed at six. Read 'Anthology of Ancient Literature' in bed; very interesting." [3]

Very few Chinese, after the death of *Yüan Shih-k'ai*, dared to say openly, what they frequently said in private, that republicanism was a failure. More than ninety percent of the population was illiterate and of the ten percent who were not, less than two percent at the very most took any active interest in politics. It therefore followed that any parliamentary system introduced into China must inevitably pass into the hands of professional politicans only a fraction of whom could be relied on to have the best interests of the country and its people at heart. "The Will of the People", at this stage was only a hollow phrase that *Yüan* had trampled in the mud. Another almost insurmountable obstacle to republicanism was the Confucian family system which was, so organized that the individual found it practically impossible to extricate himself from the social obligations which compelled him to put the interests of his family before those of the state. The monarchy on the other hand was quite a different matter, loyalty to the Sovereign was the corner-stone of Confucian teaching. Republicanism was wholly incompatible with the Confucian soul of China which would, if not eradicated, always lead to a restoration of the monarchy. These were the republican's great problems and they were never to be resolved.

"I am no lover of the Manchus and no monarchist, but I often wonder whether it would not have been safer and

easier for China to move smoothly towards the ideals of democratic government if it had been possible to retain the Manchu Emperor as a figure-head, and establish a constitutional monarchy instead of a republic." [4]

The understanding of the forms of government, even among the literate were lamentably limited; *"If we Chinese can not enjoy the privileges of American or French people, we may at least hope for conditions similar to those under which the British, Germans and Japanese now live."* These words written by a Chinese journalist in *Peking* demonstrates the widely held yet naive assumption that because the United States and France were republics and the other named states monarchies, there must of necessity be more freedom under the former than under the latter.

An American author writing in the same month of the same year said:

"We Americans hold that the government by the people means liberty and justice. This is not necessarily true. Democracy gives us ten thousand bosses, each one more costly than a single average monarch of Europe. England is nominally a monarchy; yet in London the American can find more home rule and common law justice than in New York and Chicago." [5]

Yüan Shih-k'ai's death, however welcome, left a vacuum that could not adequately be filled. The occupant of the vic-presidential chair *Li Yüan-hung*, who had unwillingly taken the leadership of the revolutionary forces at *Wu-ch'ang* in 1911 was now, on *Yüan's* death, automatically president. It was a task far beyond his mediocre powers. The political and military factions intrigued against him and each other, descending into an ever deepening sea of chaos. The whole situation was slipping out of focus as the inevitable "twilight" loomed over the whole nation.

To the north there was still a ray of light visible in the descending gloom; *Hsuchou* on the *Tientsin-Pukow* railway, where general *Chang-hsun* with his large army held a position of such strategic importance that no Chinese military or civil offical could ignore him. *Yüan's* death freed *Chang-hsun* from one of his two loyalties which now gave power to the other, for he had made no secret of his loyalty to the Manchu Dynasty, hence his nick-name, 'the pig-tailed general', he had never, as so many others had, cut off his queue, nor had he permitted any member of his army to do so, thus his forces were known as 'the pig-tailed army', and there is no reason to suppose that his outward symbol of loyalty to the *Ch'ing* was anything other than a 'badge of honour'.

Throughout 1916 and 1917 *Chang-hsun* organized a number of 'secret' political conferences at *Hsuchou*, these were willingly attended by not only his own friends and sympathizers but many prominent semi-independant leaders. This council within a council gave solemn pledges of support for *Chang-hsun's* plans for the restoration of the Manchu Monarchy. *Li Yüan-hung* was by no means ignorant of the path that 'the pig-tailed general' was travelling, although he had no certain knowledge. It was at this time that he invited *Chang-hsun* to visit *Peking* to mediate between the rival political factions; these included a southern party formed by *Sun Yat-sen* as a rival government at *Canton*. At this time, as well as the almost total domestic chaos that confronted President *Li*, these was the difficult question of whether China should or should not join forces with the allies and declare war on Germany. *Sun Yat-sen* was strongly opposed to an involvement on China's part in 'the foreign war', but characteristically changed his opinion when he saw the advantages that such participation would enabled China to claim as one of the "victorious allies". *Li* had reassembled the parliament that *Yüan* had dissolved, but its members seemed to have learnt little from the experience, judging from the disgraceful scenes that took place in *Peking*. It was at this time, in desperation that *Li* sought the aid of 'the pig-tailed gereral'.

It was at this decisive stage that *Chang-hsun* made a far-reaching error of judgement for, in complying with *Li's* request to mediate at *Peking*, he placed far too much reliance on both his own prestige and the promises of support he had been pledged from others and proceeded to the capital leaving the major part of his army in *Hsuchou*, travelling with only a small and badly equipped force that would not afford him real mastery of the confused situation. He entered *Peking* in June and in his initial attempts at 'mediation' ordered the dissolution of the shambles which called itself parliament, President *Li*, powerless and irresolute agreed. Already loyalists secretly summoned by *Chang* were arriving at the capital, and the subdued excitement culminated in an event that had long been foreseen; the restoration of the *Hsüan-t'ung* Emperor although, restoration is somewhat inaccurate, he had never ceased to be Emperor and had under the 'articles' surrendered only *cheng-ch'uan*, (the right to rule), not his Imperial status and dignity.

16th June, 1917;

> "Your Majesty will have no lessons today. A high official is coming for an audience with your Majesty and a eunuch will be here to announce him very shortly". The Grand Guardian Chen P'ao-shen announced.
> "Who is he?"
> "Chang-hsun, the viceroy of Kiangsi, Kiangsu and Anhwei and governor of Kiangsu."
> "Chang-hsun? The Chang-hsun who would not cut his queue off?"
> "Yes, that is the man" he said nodding with approval, "Your Majesty's memory is very good", he always flattered.

According to the protocol of the *Ch'ing* house no one was permitted to be present when a high official was received in audience by the Emperor.

> "I had tried to form a picture of what Chang-hsun looked like from the picture magazines that the eunuch had brought me, but I had not yet succeeded when I emerged from my sedan chair. A little while after I had reached the Mind nuture Palace Chang arrived. As I sat on the throne he knelt before me and performed the kowtow.
> "Your subject Chang-hsun kneels and pays his respects. . . . ."
> "I motioned to him to sit on a chair, as by this time the court had abolished the practice of having officials report from a kneeling position. He kowtowed again, thanked me and then sat down. I dutifully asked him about the military situation . . . . . . I was a little disappointed at the appearance

of this 'loyal' subject of mine; he was dressed in a thin silk jacket and gown, his face was ruddy and set with very bushy eye-brows and he was rather fat . . . . I looked carefully to see if he indeed had a queue, and he did. He spoke in very respectful terms. I remember that the audience was not over-long, lasting only some five or six minutes.

Next day my tutors were wreathed with smiles as they told me how Chang-hsun had praised my modesty and intelligence, this made me very pleased although it did not occur to me to ask why he had come for audience or why my tutors were so visibly excited, or why the household department had given him such lavish presents, or why the High Consorts had held a banquet in his honour.

About two weeks later, on 1st July, my tutors came to my school-room with very grave faces. . . . .

"Chang-hsun is here. . . . ."

"Has he come to pay his respects again?"

"No, he has not just come for that. All preparations have been made and all is now settled. He has come to bring your Majesty back to power and to restore the Great Ch'ing Dynasty" seeing that I was greatly startled, he continued. "Your Majesty must allow Chang-hsun to do this. He is asking for a mandate on behalf of the people; heaven has complied with the wishes of the people."

I was stunned by this news.

"There is no need to say very much to Chang-hsun. All you have to do is to accept but, it would not be seemly for you to accept at once; you must refuse at first and then only finally say, 'If all is as you say I must with reluctance accept'."

I then returned to the Mind Nuture Palace and received Chang-hsun in audience again. After the formal greetings Gerneral Chang said:

"The Lung-yu Empress Dowager was not prepared to inflict a disaster on the people for the sake of one family's illustrious position, so she issued a decree ordering that a republic be organized. But who would have thought that it would have been run so badly and that the people now have no way of making their living. . . . . .a republic does not suit our country . . . . . .Only your Majesty's restoration will save the people."

74

P'u-yi seated on the Dragon Throne in the Palace of Cloudless Heaven. (Taken by Johnston in 1922).

"I fear I am too young and have neither the virtue or talent to undertake so great an office" Upon this statement, Chang lavished praises upon me, then I asked,

"What of their president? Will we give him 'favourable' treatment?"

"President Li has already memorialized asking that he be allowed to resign. All that is now necessary is for your Majesty to grant his request."

After Chang-hsun's departure the audience hall was suddenly filled with many people paying me their respects and thanking me. Then a eunuch brought in nine Imperial edicts which were already written out, the first of which proclaimed my return to the throne whilst another created a board of seven regents, including Chang." [6]

Chang-hsun issued a long manifesto, part of which was translated and published in the anti-monarchist English newspaper in *Peking, The Peking Gazette*, whose editor at the time, was a native of the British colony of Trinidad, of Chinese decent, and unable to speak, read or write his ancestoral language, known to foreigners as Eugene *Chen, (Ch'en Yu-jen)*, who was later to become a high official in the Nationalist government.

3rd July 1917.

"Ever since the uprising at Wu-chang and the establishment of the republic, peace and order have been cast to the winds and good reliable people have been nowhere to be seen. Anarchists have been holding sway while unscrupulous people have been monopolizing the power. Robber chiefs are called heroes and dead convicts are worshipped as martyrs. Parliament relied on rebels for support while Cabinet Ministers used biased parties as their protection. Unscrupulous borrowing of foreign money is called finance; and bleeding the people is termed revenue-raising. Oppression of innocent people is considered self-government; and defaming old scholars is considered civilization. Some spread rumours under the pretext that they are public opinion while others secretly finance foreigners and call it diplomacy. All these are

treason practised under the fine name of statesmanship, and corruption under the mask of legislation. They even advocate the abolition of Confucianism and thus call down the wrath of the gods . . . . In name we are a republic but nothing is known of the citizens. People are called citizens but they know nothing about their country. Now the people are poor and financial resources exhausted, the very foundations of the country begin to shake. All this is the result of a bad form of government . . . . look at the root of the matter, we find that republicanism is the source of all the evil . . . . . . compare this with the continuous reign of a monarchy, wherefrom the people may enjoy peace for tens or hundreds of years, the difference is at once seen to be as great as the distance between heaven and earth . . . . . . Carefully weighing present conditions and the tendency of the people it is preferable to expel party politics and establish a firm monarchy then to invite ruin by adopting the empty name of a republic . . . . Our Emperor, who is in his boyhood, has devoted himself to study and learning to be calm in obedience to the demand of the day. The country has passed many great upheavals but in the palace there has always reigned peace and calm. Recently His Majesty has made marked progress in his sacred studies and his virtuous reputation has spread far and wide. It can thus be seen that heaven has smiled on the Ch'ing Dynasty by conferring His Majesty with unusual wisdom so that he might be able to rise at the proper moment to stop disorder and revert to right . . . . . (Chang) Hsun and others have been accumulating their energy with their weapons near at hand for the last six years . . . . On this day we have jointly memorialised His Imperial Majesty to again ascend the throne in order to establish the foundation of the country and to consolidate the minds of the people.''

The enthusiasm which greeted this proclamation in northern China and in *Peking* itself was everywhere to be witnessed. *Peking* had, for centuries lived side by side with an Imperial household and consequently had never ceased in its monarchist sympathies, this was true of the greater part of northern China also. On the very

77

day of the public proclamation the whole city was in high excitement and the Imperial dragon flag fluttered from every available space in almost every household. Some were the real article whilst others were hastely improvised with paste and paper. *Ch'ing* robes and realia, which had not been seen for a number of years suddenly made their appearance in every street. The newspapers brought out special 'restoration' issues at a higher than usual price, the whole city was ablaze with an outward acclamation for the return of the Imperial Dynasty. The shops did a booming trade, those by the *Chien Men* gate sold dragon flags as fast as they could make them; tailors and second-hand clothes shops were inundated by eager officials trying desperately to acquire the necessary court dress; even theatrical costumers were ransacked by crowds begging for this or that item, and false queues for those who now realized that they had been over hasty in dispensing with the Manchu 'pig-tail'. The scene had changed in an instant from 'revolutionary madness' to 'Imperial euphoria', which was so infectious that hardly a corner escaped. Even the *Forbidden City* was ablaze with restored colour and activity, officials paraded attired in complete court costume though perhaps on closer inspection, some items were old and a little shabby, whilst others were cleverly improvised, the sea of bobbing peacock feathers flooded every forecourt and assembly point. The Manchu dragon flag fluttered from every building but one, the republican president's palace;

"Li Yüan-hung has actually refused your Imperial Majesty's order to resign; will Your Majesty please instruct him to commit suicide at once!" demanded Chen Pao-shen the Emperor's senior tutor. The boy Emperor stared at him, taken aback for a moment by the vehemence of this usually stable and sensible man.
"Surely that would not do at all Chen Pao-shen," replied his Majesty, "How could I ask Li Yüan-hung to kill himself so soon after my return to the throne, that would not appear 'favourable treatment' at all."
"Li Yüan-hung is not only refusing to resign, he is even refusing to leave the presidential palace, he is nothing more than a rebellious traitor and a brigand. How could you mention

him in the same breath as yourself your Majesty?" continued the tutor, carried away with the heat of the moment. [7]

The old tutor was shamedfaced at his young Emperor's refusal to take his advice, it was the first time that *P'u-yi* had ever rebuffed him. Sensing the old man's embarrassment he promised to send an official to the presidential palace in an attempt to persuade the obstinate president. Unbeknown to both Emperor or tutor, *Li* had already fled to the safety of the Japanese Legation taking his seals of office with him.

To state that the situation was confused would be a misleading understatement. This was due, in part, to the Imperial Edicts issued in the Boy Emperor's name, there were nineteen of them in all and if the excited *Peking* populace had bothered to study all of them the ensuing confusion would have been even greater. One carried the lines, "Whether our subjects cut their hair or not is to be left entirely to each man's conscience . . . ." had this been known it would have prevented the 'heady' problem of acquiring a false queue, often at ruinous expense, for after the failure of the restoration it has been said that these symbols of "Manchu oppression" were so thick on the ground in places that it was like walking on the finest *Peking* carpet.

Chang-hsun had been appointed, regent, Minister in charge of the northern armies and governor-general of the metropolitan district, (*Peking*) but his 'pig-tailed army' were so badly behaved that the already fearful citizens whispered that these 'pig-tailed ones' were almost worse than the Boxers and things were getting almost as bad as 1900, during their 'rebellion'. True, they strutted about *Peking* as if they owned it, and for a time they did; shopkeepers who were 'disloyal' enough to ask payment for the goods the soldiers took provided proof positive that they must be republicans and were duly knocked on the head. Theatres had to keep in reserve any number of seats for these 'defenders of the restoration' who, if not satisfied with the performance were capable of breaking it up and the building along with it.

Peking railway station was in a state of seige as wealthy *Pekinese* made a determined effort to quit the city while there was still time, old ladies screamed and shouted at the harassed railway officials to assist them in forcing pieces of their favourite furniture into the already crowded compartments and flatly refused to allow their prize possessions to be loaded into the guards van, which they felt was decidedly unsafe. It was a sight that was sadly to become all too familiar in China during the next thirty years as the whole country slipped into the abyss of war-lord-nationalism.

On 4th July, *Tuan Ch'i-jui* the newly installed republican Commander-in-chief of 'The Army for the Suppression of Treason' issued a telegraphic appeal to the nation; "Although our system of government is not very good, it is not very bad either, and now that it has been definitely established, these frequent attempts to change it will do great harm. The Manchu Dynasty appreciated the trend of events and by a sincere abdication from power earned the esteem of the people. In return the 'Articles of Favourable Treatment' enabled the Imperial House to avoid the recriminations of politics, while retaining the dignity of its name. We have had throughout our history more than twenty dynasties, but none of them had so fortunate an end as the Manchus. The Emperor is merely a boy and incapable of contriving such a plot. As for the Grand Guardian his one desire is to abstain from all adventures of this sort. When the traitor Chang-hsun and his ruffians broke into the palace in the dead of night, the Grand Guardian begged them to desist, and kowtowed with such energy that you could not see his nose for the blood that streamed from his forehead. The Lustrous Concubine too could not have wept and lamented more if she was losing life itself. Our sympathy must go out to the boy Emperor, threatened as he is by such criminals." This roughly worded document may well have afforded the Imperial family some comfort if they had ever had an opportunity of reading it but they were by this time effectively sealed-off within the *Forbidden City* by *Chang's* forces, and he now had other priorities more pressing than paying his respects to his Emperor. The only source of information within the palace were the latest editions of the *Peking* newspapers which were stealthily obtained by eunuchs posted at the Gate of Heavenly Peace which, on examination contained only depressing news.

'The pig-tailed general' meanwhile was determined to wreck the railway lines a few miles from the capital at *Fêng-t'ai*, thus halting the advancing republicans, but the foreign diplomatic corps insisted that the lines must be kept open and dispatched a train load of their troops to ensure that the treaty rights were thoroughly respected for ever since the Boxer uprising the foreign legations had a horror of being cut off from the sea. It seemed that nothing could prevent the war from engulfing *Peking* itself and on 7th July whether by chance or design a republican plane flew over the confused capital and dropped three small bombs on the *Forbidden City* itself. One fell in a lake, the second failed to explode whilst the third did only minimal damage; this was China's first experience of aerial bombardment and the occupants of the *Forbidden City* were severely shaken:

"On the day of the air-attack I was sitting in my school-room talking to my tutors when I heard the unfamiliar drone of an aeroplane followed shortly after by a loud explosion. I was so terrified that I shook all over and the colour drained from my tutor's faces. Everything was in chaos, eunuchs hustled me over to the Mind Nurture Palace as if my bedroom was the only safe place. The High Consorts were in an even worse state, some of them lying in the corners of their bedrooms whilst others hid under tables. The air was filled with shouting voices and the whole city was in great confusion. Everyone was told to lay down in their bedrooms and all the bamboo blinds were let down, these were the only measures the eunuchs and palace guard could think of. Fortunately the pilot was apparently as terrified as we all were and the incident gave us nothing more than a bad fright. One of the bombs fell outside the Gate of Honouring the Ancestors (Lung T'sung Men) wounding one of the sedan-chair carriers; one fell into a pond in the Imperial Garden, damaging only the corner of it, whilst the third fell on the roof of one of the gate-ways in the western avenue of the palace striking sheer terror into the hearts of the eunuchs there, who were gambling at the time, but caused no damage as it failed to explode." [8]

Early the next morning republican troops were outside the city, *Chang* and his 'pig-tailed army' made preparations to fight to the death and to guard the three most sacred places in *Peking*, The *Forbidden City*, The Temple of heaven and not unnaturally their commander's house wherein *Chang's* wife and family were housed; Madam *Chang* seems from all accounts to have been an extremely forceful lady and had harangued the old general so much that he was always hesitant about returning home after one of his 'coarse carousing' nights out in the red light district of the old Chinese city. Meanwhile the republican spearhead had penetrated into the city and made contact with the foreign diplomats in the legation quarter, from whom *Chang* learnt that the republican leader *Tuan Ch'i-jui* was willing to guarantee *Chang's* personal safety and to confirm the continuation of the 'Articles of Favourable Treatment' extended to the Dynasty in 1912 on but two conditions; that the newly restored Imperial rule be abolished and that *Chang's* 'pig-tailed army' be disbanded. The Dutch Minister conveyed all this to *Chang* and offered him asylum as a political refugee. But to disband his beloved 'pig-tailed army' was too bitter a pill for the old general and he insisted to the very last that he be allowed to withdraw all his forces intact and return to his headquarters at *Hsuchou*. Before his enforced retreat *Chang* tendered his resignation from all his offices, assumed only a few days previously, and humbly bid farewell to 'the Boy Emperor'. In a last gesture of defiance he issued a telegram proclaiming to the world what had led to this unhappy end to the restoration; the republican generals who were now against him had to a man all agreed after the death of *Yüan Shih-k'ai* that a restoration of the Manchu Dynasty was imperative if China was to escape civil war and utter chaos, now they had betrayed him.

For the next few days the dynasty and the republic maintained a nervous truce, each adhering to their own accepted calendars; from 1912 the revolutionaries had used the Western calendar thus 10th July 1917 was known everywhere within China, except *Peking*, as the 10th day of the 7th month of the 6th year of the republic; but within the walls of the *Forbidden City* time was calculated on the old lunar calendar even also by newspapers and other publications as 22nd day of the 5th moon of the 9th year of *Hsüan-t'ung*.

During the following night, (11th July) the republicans succeeded in forcing entry at three of the city gates and at dawn the next morning confronted some three thousand of the 'pig-tailed army' who were guarding the Temple of Heaven. There was only token resistance, most hoisted republican flags signifying their surrender whilst others escaped towards *Chang's* mansion in the old Tartar City, which by this time had been set ablaze by some unaccountably accurate republican gunnery. They arrived just in time to see *Chang* bundled into a motor car by two foreigners and driven at speed to the Dutch legation. Now deserted by their general their thoughts turned to their own safety and, to insure this, weeping and cursing, they cut off their pig-tails, and tried to merge into the *Peking* crowds.

Chang-hsun remained safely within the Dutch legation until the following year when an amnesty was declared which freed him from his enforced confinement. He purchased a large fine house in the British Concession at *Tientsin*, for although he had lost his army he still had a hugh fortune which he had been careful to preserve. He died in 1923 in his *Tientsin* 'palace' and the Emperor conferred on him the posthumous title, 'Loyal and Brave'. His funeral procession was said to have streatched for four miles and have cost 100,000 dollars and some newspapers also reported that he had left a large endowment for the encouragement and cultivation of the pig-tail.

The Manchu restoration had lasted just twelve days;

> "My father, (Prince Ch'un) and Chen Pao-shen came to me with dejection written all over their faces. They handed me the abdication edict to read that they had just drafted; I was both frightened and saddened and I wept aloud." [9]

The decree ran thus:

> "On the twentieth day of the fifth month of the ninth year of Hsüan-t'ung the cabinet received this Imperial edict:
> Formerly We followed the memorials of Chang-hsun and others who, saying that the nation was in a state of

fundamental disorder and that the people longed for the old way, advised Us to resume the government. As our years are tender and We live deep in the Forbidden City We have heard nothing about the people's livelihood and the affairs of the nation. Remembering with reverence the great benevolence and the instructions of the late August Empress Hsiao-ching (The Lung-yu Empress Dowager) who yielded the government out of pity for the people, We had not the least intention of treating the world as Our private property; it was only because We were asked to save the nation and people that We forced ourselves to accede to the requests made of Us and assumed power.

Now, yesterday Chang-hsun reported armed risings in every province, which may lead to military insurgencies in a struggle for power. Our people have been suffering hardships for years, and their state is as desperate as if they were being burned or drowned. How could We then compound their miseries with war? Thinking upon this We were much disturbed and unable to rest. We therefore resolved that We would not keep this political power for Ourselves and thus besmirch the living soul of the August Empress Hsiao T'ing-ching by turing our backs on her abundant virute.

Let Wang Shih-chen and Hsu Shih-chang inform Tuan C'hi-jui at once, that the transfer of power may be arranged and the present troubles brought to an end, so calming the people's hearts and avoiding the calamity of war.

By command of the Emperor.

This edict, *P'u-yi's* second abdication, was never issued; in its place the Republic published the following document which included a statement by the Imperial Household Department.

By order of the President of the Republic:

> "The Home Ministry reports that it has received the following communication from the Household Department of the Ch'ing House:
> This day the Household Department received an edict; Formerly on the twenty-fifth day of the twelfth month of

the third year of Hsüan-t'ung a decree was issued by the August Empress Dowager Lung-yu in which, recognizing that the whole people were inclined towards a republic, she and the Emperor returned sovereign power to the whole country. She ordained that there should be a republic and settled that the Articles of Favourable Treatment for the Ch'ing House should be adhered to forever; for the past six years the Ch'ing House has been very well treated and has never had any intention of using political power for its own ends; what cause could it have had for going back on its word?

But contrary to expectation Chang-hsun led his army to occupy the Imperial Palace on 1st July. He fraudulently issued edicts and decrees and altered the state structure, thus disobeying the instructions of the Empress Dowager of the former Dynasty. I, a child, living deep in the Forbidden City, had no choice in the matter; in these circumstances I should have allowances made for me by the whole world. The Household Department has been instructed to request the government of the Republic to make this widely known both in the country and abroad.

When the ministers received this document they thought it right to report this matter.

As it is common knowledge that Chang-hsun the traitor and usurper was the originator of the disturbances, let the details of this document be speedily proclaimed.

For general information.

Issued by the Prime Minister Tuan C'hi-jui.

July 17th, sixth year of the Republic of China.

Thus a veil was subtly drawn over the attempted restoration and public attention diverted from the *Forbidden City* to the 'traitors' outside. The actual suppression of the instrument of abdication and its change into a more 'acceptable' document was almost entirely the work of the Grand Tutor, *Hsü Shih-ch'ang* whose reinterpretation was readily accepted by both the Republican President and Prime Minister.

The Imperial Dragon Flags that had fluttered so proudly for less than twelve days were now carefully folded away in readiness for the 'inevitable' return of 'the Son of Heaven'. The restoration attempt had been no more than an escapade and its ultimate failure was not due to the strength of the republic but the selfishness of the monarchist supporters who, jealous of each other, were even then on the brink of war-lordism, an evil that in thirty years wreaked more havoc and suffering on the Chinese people than the Ch'ing had in three hundred years.

A leading article published in the *North China Standard*, (Peking in Chinese) on September 18th 1923 puts forward a more accurate and serious view, the following is a translated extract:

> *"When he,* (Chang-hsun) *inaugurated his monarchical restoration movement he had the definite assurance of many prominent leaders that they would assist him in his scheme. But when the fateful day arrived he stood practically alone and although he resorted to the ultima ratio of war he was defeated. When we let the history of China for the last twelve years pass before our mental eyes we find the same everywhere. Whenever there is a man willing and capable of doing something he is ignominiously deserted by his so-called friends. Apparently nobody wants to commit himself definitely, nobody has the courage of his convictions. As long as this state of affairs exists there is no help for China. Even the strongest man can not do everything himself, but must rely on the support and co-operation of others. But if there are no others willing to give support and co-operation achievement is impossible."*

The immediate outcome of the 'twelve day restoration', as far as the Emperor and his Imperial Household were concerned was minimal; no advantage was taken of the 'incident' to humiliate the encumbant of the Dragon Throne nor were any of the 'articles' varied or changed, everything went on just as before. Even general *Fêng Kuo-chang*, who succeeded *Li* as republican president showed not the slightest inclination to 'punish' the residents of the *Forbidden City*. The only voices raised in discord came predictably from the southern radicals who called for the cancellation of the 'Articles of the Favourable Treatment' and the dissolution of the

the Emperor's status to that of an ordinary citizen. That these *Sunite* protests were ignored is hardly surprising, for they also repudiated the authority of the northern government in *Peking*. *Sun Yat-sen's Kuo-min tang* were the most vociferous of the southern voices raised against the Imperial Clan and they, in company with other southern left-wing revolutionaries kept up this barrage of abuse, hoping, no doubt, that it would finally serve some useful purpose. Finally in 1924 when action was taken against the Emperor and his household by a small group of irresponsible left-wing soldiers and politicians, they regurgitated their 'reasons' trying vainly to justify their ill-advised actions. Some modern historians have accorded *Sun Yat-sen* the wholly unearned title of "father of the republic", the truth is quite different, he can now be seen as the singularly unsuccessful 'professional revolutionary', he was.

The young Emperor's attitude to the failed restoration was published in a collection of Chinese anecdotes which were widely quoted at *Peking* dinner tables, and although far from true, gives an amusing contemporary view of the meeting between *Chang-husn* and *P'u-yi*:

"A few days before the restoration, Chang-hsun had a secret audience with the Hsüan-t'ung Emperor in the Forbidden City. Chang knelt and informed the boy Emperor what he proposed to do. Hsüan-t'ung shook his head and refused to agree to the restoration.
'May I invite your Sacred Majesty to tell your old servant your reasons for refusal?'
'My tutor Chen Pao-shen' replied the Emperor, 'keeps telling me all day long about how the classic of poetry says this and Confucius says that, there is never an end to it. How can I possibly find time to attend to anything more than my endless lessons?'
'If Your Sacred Majesty,' said Chang 'will only ascend the throne again, you will have important affairs of state to attend to and you need not spend any more time at lessons.'
Hsüan-t'ung immediately brightened up.
'Do you really mean' he said 'if only I become Emperor

again I may give up all my lessons?'

'History tells us,' replied Chang 'that the Son of Heaven has always been a good horseman. No one ever heard of a Tu-shu T'ien Tzu . . . . a book-reading Son of Heaven!'

'In that case,' exclaimed Hsüan-t'ung joyfully, 'let it be as you wish. I will do whatever you want me to,' "

This light-hearted anecdote concealed more truth than the gossiping Pekinese knew. If those in informed official and semi-official positions were becoming confused with the situation, then the people at large were hopelessly at sea amid a never-ending tide of rumour and counter-rumour. From the beginning to the end of the 'twelve day' restoration less than one hundred lives had been lost but, more importantly for those that remained, many an official career was in ruins, the whole country was sinking deeper into total chaos. The period that followed the abortive restoration lasted for over seven years, 'the war-lord' era which is succinctly summed up by a French Lawyer who was resident in China for much of this lawless time;

> "There was a central government in Peking. Real power was in the hands of military governors of the provinces, who made war and alliances between themselves and betrayed one another to their heart's content. Every now and then, one of them would get the better of the rest and set up in Peking a government devoted to his interests. The foreign powers would back such and such a general regarded at the moment as the strong man likely to succeed. Over and above the struggles of the militarists there were party intrigues and the intermittent proceedings of a caricature of a parliament." [10]

Under the war-lords the people were much worse off than they had ever been, they were taxed many years in advance, provincial banks were taken over and forced to print literally tons of valueless paper money. These provincial war-lords with hardly one exception, had no sense of feudal responsibility towards the people they mis-governed, let alone any vestige of patriotism, as one local tyrant replaced another in a never-ending struggle the desperate plight of the people grew more and more serious. The war in Europe had provided some impetus to industry that was

A youthful Chiang K'ai-shek standing beside Sun
Yat-sen on the warship Yung Feng.

based within the various treaty-ports but this had scarcely any effect on the country as a whole. If the war-lords were indifferent to the plight of their own people, they were far from being indifferent to the foreigners. They accepted massive loans from the West, in return granted, on their own authority, economic privileges of almost every kind. For example, the International Banking Consortium in 1913 agreed to lend *Yüan Shih-k'ai* the staggering sum of 125,000,000 dollars, even in spite of the protests of the then government, who realized that *Yüan* would use this money against them in suppressing what few democratic institutions existed. This precedent was eagerly emulated by all the subsequent war-lords including *Shan-kai-shac*, who pocketed the foreign loans and increased their own military muscle, thus the number of soldiers continued to grow; 457,000 in 1914; 900,000 in 1920 and by 1925 there were no less than 1,470,000. This undisciplined hoard of mercenaries marched and counter-marched across the face of China bringing ruin and destruction wherever they went. It made the 'bad' old days of Manchu rule seem more like a 'golden age'.

The unhappy ghost of *Yüan Shih-k'ai* lingered on to the plague his fellow countrymen: in 1914 he had finally agreed to the notorious 'Twenty-one articles' demanded by Japan, who was allied to Great Britain and at war against Germany; *Yüan* agreed to their demand, of what was virtually economic control of Manchuria as well as extensive privileges formerly enjoyed by their 'new' enemies, the Germans. In 1917 the *Peking* government declared war on Germany, although the only active part she was to take in the conflict was to supply labour corps for service in France. The real reason behind this alignment was the hope of enlisting allied support against Japan during the peace treaty negotiations. As these negotiations began at Versailles, it soon became clear that this relied upon international support was not to be forthcoming, the British and French had already, by secret agreement, confirmed Japan's right to all the former German concessions in China. The disappointment caused by this double-dealing erupted into the 'Fourth of May Movement', for on that day in 1919 a 'nationalist' demonstration was organized by students and teachers of Peking University and spread like a forest-fire throughout the whole country.

CHAPTER FOUR

"The Great Within"

The Purple Forbidden City, often referred to as 'the Great Within' was and is, a city within a city, as the attendant maps will clearly demonstrate. To fully comprehend the narrative, it is essential that the reader be made aware of the traditions and customs of this high-walled Imperial dwelling. During the period in question, 1908-1924, little had changed since the eighteenth and nineteenth centuries; the Household Department was the most powerful internal administrative body and was served almost wholly by eunuchs, as indeed were all other bureaus within the Imperial Court. Amid all the anomalies of Chinese political life at this time, as republican cabinets rose and fell, as political and military opportunists were forced to fly for safety to one or other of the foreign legations, as one clique replaced another; even amid the then familiar scenes of turmoil, banditry, disruption and civil war, there endured within the heart of *Peking*, one fragment of Chinese soil which at least preserved an outward appearance of stability and dignity; a seeming fortress against the chaotic excesses of 'republican government', where a vanishing past was lovingly preserved in an unchanging daily routine. The *Da Nei* . . . ."The Great Within".

With the abdication of 1912, certain parts of this Imperial city had been taken over by the republicans; the southern portion, though not the guardianship of the eastern and western gates, were now under republican administration. Two of the largest palaces, the *Wu-ying Tien* and the *Wen-hua Tien* had been turned into museums which housed a portion of the Imperial collection, which had formerly adorned the palaces of *Jehol* and *Mukden* and which were lossely understood to be "on loan" from the Emperor, until such time as the republicans could collect enough funds to purchase them outright. That was the official explanation, though no one was in any doubt that the real and unofficial attitude was quite different, "if you desire the luscious fruit and it will not fall, shake the tree, if it still will not fall, then cut the tree down, for then you may have all."

Three of the Imperial throne-halls had also lamentably passed into republican hands; the *T'ai Ho Tien*, (Hall of Supreme Harmony), the *Chung Ho Tien* and the *Pao Ho Tien* together with a number of subordinate buildings. However, the whole of the northern portion from east to west together with large sections on either side of the aforementioned throne-halls still remained the exclusive prerogative of the Emperor and his court, admittance was indeed *Forbidden* to all except the very few who had the entreé. Also included were all the palaces which constituted the living quarters of both the Emperor and his Imperial Family; the 'Imperial Garden', (*Yu Hua Yuan*); the *Wen Yuan Ko*, a large pavilion containing the most valuable portion of the Imperial library, the offices of the *Nei Wu Fu*, (the Imperial Household Department); the *Chun Chi Ch'u* which had been used as the office of the Grand Council of State, which, after the revolution became a waiting room for those seeking audience; the *Chien Fu Kung*, (palace of Established Happiness) which was mysteriously destroyed by fire in 1923 with the "supposed" loss of many priceless art treasures, which will be examined later in the chapter. Added to this were a number of outer buildings and pavilions which, after the revolution, ceased to serve any practical purpose. Mention should also be made of the *Feng Hsien Tien*, (Chapel of Serving the Ancestors), which was used on the first and fifteenth of each month for memorial rites generally presided over by the Emperor or another member of the Imperial Clan, the *Feng Hsien Tien* should not be confused with the *T'ai Miao*, (Supreme Temple), situated in a southern annex of the *Forbidden City* where the 'spirit tablets' of the Imperial Ancestors were preserved.

The most important of the great throne-halls was still in the possession of the Emperor, this was the *Ch'ien-Ch'ing Kung*, (Palace of Heavenly Purity), built in 1655, rebuilt in 1669 and again after a fire in 1797. It was in this Palace that the Emperor

YELLOW TEMPLE

GREAT BELL TEMPLE

FROM SUMMER PALACE

MAUSOLEUM IMPERIAL PRINCES

ALTAR OF EARTH

FIVE PAGODA TEMPLE

ZOOLOGICAL GARDENS

STATION

TE-SHENG MEN

AN-TING MEN

CONFUCIAN TEMPLE

LAMA TEMPLE

RUSSIAN ECCLESIASTICAL MISSION

HSI-CHIH MEN

PALACE OF PRINCE CHUN

HALL OF CLASSICS

BELL TOWER

DRUM TOWER

TUNG-CHIH MEN

PALACE OF PRINCE CH'ING

PALACE OF PRINCE TING

IMPERIAL GRANARY

MAUSOLEUM OF PRINCE SU

TARTAR CITY

FROM TIENTSIN AND PEKOTAI

PALACE OF PRINCE CHUANG

WALL

HOU MEN

WALL

IMPERIAL STORES

STREET

PING-TSE MEN

PAI-TA SSU

TI WANG MIAO

IMPERIAL CITY

PEKING UNIVERSITY

COAL HILL

TUNG YO MIAO

TU TUNG-CHOU

FROM WESTERN HILLS

PEI TAI PAGODA

PEH-HAI

TAZAO MEI-SHAN TIEN

PAI-TA

PALACE OF PRINCE SHUN CHIEN

DEPT OF AGRICULTURE

PETANG CATHEDRAL

HSIAN MEY

OLD R C GATE

MARBLE BRIDGE

FORBIDDEN

PALACE CITY

TUNG AN MEN

DEPT HOME AFFAIRS

ALTAR OF THE MOON

PRESIDENT'S RESIDENCE

HATA MEN STREET

ALTAR OF THE SUN

PALACE OF PRINCE CH'ING

MARBLE BROWN MOSQUE

WU MEN

WAI-CHIAO-PU TSUNG-LI YAMEN

KETTLER MEMORIAL

SITE OF OLD EXAMINATION HALL

TIEN AN MEN

CHINESE GENERAL P O

OBSERVATORY

DEPT OF EDUCATION

CHANG AN STREET

FOREIGN LEGATIONS

HATA MEN

FROM HANKOW

HSI PIEN MEN

PARLIAMENT

SHUN CHIH MEN

DEPT OF JUSTICE

TA-TSING LEGATION STREET

HSIEN MEN

WATER GATE

TUNG PIEN MEN

TO TUNG-CHOU

PAOTINGFU

PEKING HANKOW RY

GOVT RAILWAYS OF NORTH CHINA

CHIEF METEOROL OFFICE

CHANG I MEN

CHINESE CITY

SHA KOU MEN

TEMPLES

GOLD FISH PONDS

RAILWAY FROM TIENTSIN

TEMPLE OF AGRICULTURE

PING MEN STREET

TEMPLE OF HEAVEN

NAN HSI MEN (YU AN MEN)

YUNG TING MEN

CHIANG TSA MEN

(TSO AN MEN)

still held court on great occasions and anniversaries, the most important of which was the Chinese New Year, (according to the old lunar calendar) and the Emperor's own birthday, (*Wan-shou*), which fell on the thirteenth day of the first moon. In front of the Palace of Heavenly Purity was a large quadrangle in which members of the court and Imperial family would assemble to do homage to their sovereign; on the east, west and south sides of this quadrangle were various small buildings of historic interest because of their associations with former Emperors of the Manchu Dyansty: The *Shang Shu-fang*, which had most recently been used by Prince *Ch'un* as his office during his brief regency, (1909 to 1912), and had formerly been used as a schoolroom for Imperial Princes; the Hall of Industrious Energy, (*Mou-ch'un-tien*) used by the great *Sheng Tsu* Emperor (*K'ang-hsi*, 1662-1722), as a study, latterly used by those members of the *Hanlin* Academy, who had duties at court; together with the Southern Study, (*Nan-shu-fang*). At the back of the throne-hall was the *Chiao-t'ai Tien*, (The Hall of the Blending of the Great Creative Forces) of which it was said, "the divine and earthly powers of the Universe intermingled and interacted in perfect harmony". It was in this hall that the collection of twenty-five Imperial seals was preserved, for which *Yüan Shih-k'ai* had lusted; there also was to be found *Ch'ien-lung's* water clock or clepsydra; also the *Ts'e Pao* of all the Empresses of the Dyansty engraved on gold plaques and attested by golden seals (these *ts'e pao* were the equivalent of marriage lines). Immediately to the north of the *Chiao-t'ai Tien* was the *K'un-ning Kung*, (Palace of Tranquil Earth), which has been mistakenly sited by a number of writers as 'special to the Empress', this was true under the *Ming* but not so during the Manchu Dynasty, when part was used as an Imperial nuptial-chamber, but occupied only for a short time; the central portion was reserved for religious or rather quasi-religious ceremonies such as *chi t'ien*, (the worship of Heaven), and *t'iao shen*, an invocation of spirits by means of the mystic rites and dances of the *shaman* or *wu*, a cult that the Manchus imported from their homeland and kept very much in the background, this section of the palace was strickly forbidden, even to those within the *Forbidden City.*

THE PURPLE FORBIDDEN CITY

The Emperor's own palace, the *Yang-hsin Tien*, (the Mind Nurture Palace) was rebuilt in 1802 and had been the residence of several former sovereigns, including the unhappy *Te Tsung* Emperor, (*Kuang-hsü*) before he was imprisoned by the Empress Dowager *Tz'u-hsi*. The name of this royal residence containes an illusion to a passage in *Mencius*, [a Chinese philosopher *Meng-tzu* of the late *Chou* period better known under his romanized name *Mencius*, (372 to 289 BC) and an important disciple of Confucius]. *Yang hsin mo shan yu kua yu*, meaning: 'in the nurture of the mind it is of the first importance to refrain from self-indulgence'.

Before the abdication, the main Imperial entrance to the 'Great Within' was the magnificent southern gateway known as the *Wu-men*, immediately in front of the 'supreme Harmony' throne-hall. (*Wu-men*, means 'noon-gate'). This was an allusion to the supreme glory of the Emperor whose brilliance was equal to the strength of the sun at the height of noon. This was the gate used by the Emperor himself when he passed either in or out of the *Forbidden City*. After the revolutionary settlement, this gate and part of the surrounding area passed under the control of the republican authorities, and the *Shen-wu Men*, the northern gateway, became the main entrance to that part of the city which, in the strictist sense still remained *Forbidden*. This gate was tri-sectional, in common with the former and the central section was used only by the Emperor and his immediate entourage; the western section was opened daily for those who had premission to enter the Imperial precincts such as Princes, nobles and officials, all of whom were obliged to enter the *City* on foot, unless they had been granted the privilege of entering on horseback or carried in sedan-chairs. One of the greatest honours was to be granted the right to ride through this Imperial portal and on into the sacred precincts. The right to enter carried in a sedan-chair was still a high distinction and carried with it the privilege of the former. This Imperial concession was sometimes bestowed temporarily, but those who received the honour on a permanent basis, had the right to include it among their list of Imperial honours, traditionally inscribed on wooden tablets displayed at the entrance of their private residences. This privilege allowed it recipients to ride or be carried as far as the inner-gates that led directly to the throne-hall; the

eastern gate, *Ching-yun Men* and on the west the *Lung-tsung Men*.
These gates led directly to that part of the *Forbidden City* which
was occupied by 'the Son of Heaven', from that point all were
required to proceed on foot. Only one person at this time had the
privilege of being carried a little further than the rest, the Emperor's
father, and former regent, Prince *Ch'un*, who might proceed as far
as the *Yang-hsin Men* gate which lead to the courtyard of the
Emperor's own quarters.

The *Shen-wu Men*, (Gate of the Divine Warrior or Spiritual
Valour), was at the north side of the *Forbidden City*. During the
Ming and up to 1795 in the Manchu Dyansty this gate was known
as the *Yuan Wu Men*, (Dark Warrior) which was an allusion to old
astrological ideas of the attributes and qualities of various
constellations and indicates the north. The name *Yuan*, was
changed to *Shan* during the reign of the *Chia-ch'ing* Emperor,
(1796-1820), because, being part of the name given to his father,
the *Ch'ien-lung* Emperor, it became an Imperial taboo.

Outside the Gate of Spiritual Valour was an enormous open space
which, most times, presented a deserted and forlorn appeerence,
but on official occasions, was wholly occupied by Princes, nobles
and their retainers and transport, gathered in attendance upon the
Emperor. The northern side of this great square was bounded by
the walled enclosure of the hill, *Mei Shan*, known to foreigners
and Chinese alike as Coal Hill, although its more correct name was
Ching Shan or Prospect Hill. This last name is the most accurate
description, for from its summit a fine view of the gleaming tiled
roofs of the *Forbidden City* is afforded, and its slopes were
literally crowded with exquisite pavilions, roofed with bright
yellow and blue tiles.

This hill has always been the subject of legends and rumours; one
theory was that it was indeed landscaped on a vast mound of
coal which would provide the residents of the *Forbidden City*
with fuel in the event of a prolonged seige, but that has been
proved to be quite erroneous. Nonetheless the hill is an artificial
structure, according to information, it was raised from the
dredging of the Three Lakes, which were enlarged and excavated

from the marsh-lands that originally existed. Its location to the north of the *Forbidden City* requires some little explanation; according to the rules of Chinese geometry, the north is the direction from whence come the evil influences, and the function of the hill was to prevent them penetrating the dwelling place of the 'Son of Heaven'. Exactly the same rule applied, in that the Emperor's throne always faced the south with its back to the unpropitious north, the same was true in the location of temple gods and ancestor tablets.

This charming little hill appears in official topographical records as, *Da Nei chih chen shan*, 'The Protecting Hill of the Great Within' ,and was also known as *Wan-sui Shan*, 'The Hill of a Myriad years'; the usage of *Wan-sui* being the equivalent of the English, "God Save the King". Even after the revolution this Imperial hill remained under the control of the Imperial Household Department, for within its walled enclosure it contained the *Shou Huang Tien*, a sacred ceremonial hall where the bodies of deceased Emperors were laid in state before being taken to the Imperial Mausolea. Here too, were kept the *Lieh Sheng Yu Jung*, a series of portraits of the Manchu Emperors.

The Forbidden City as it stands today is often said to be mainly the work of the *Ming* Emperor *Ch'eng-tzu*, (*Yung-lo*, 1403-1424), the first of that dynasty to choose *Peking* for his capital but, on examination this is not so; for apart from the outer walls and some portions of the older palaces it is doubtful if much of the building from this period remains. A large portion of the *City* was burned and looted by *Li Tzu-ch'eng* in 1644 before being engulfed by the advancing Manchu, and there have, since that time, been many fires and much rebuilding.

Adjacent to the 'Three Lakes' were the palaces which had formerly belonged to the Imperial family but which, as already stated, were now the official residence of the President of the Republic. There as neighbours resided the president, who was the the real ruler of China, and beside him, the Emperor, who ruled, not one inch beyond his enclosed citadel.That this anomaly existed at all is unexplainable, but that it continued for more than thirteen years is incredible; incredible, that is, to Western understanding, but it was not so in China, where the whole bizarre situation was merely taken for granted.

No description of the "Great Within" could be complete without a mention of that most Chinese of institutions, the eunuch. The eunuch system is said to have been introduced into China during the *Chou* Dynasty, (1122-221 BC). At this time there were five major methods of punishing criminals; tattooing the forehead; chopping off the toes; slicing off the nose; castration and finally decapitation. The most chronicled case of castration as a punishment was inflicted on *Ssu Ma-chien* the compiler of the ancient historical records, *Shi Ki* during the *Han* Dynasty, (206-220 BC). The tale goes that a celebrated general *Li Ling* had valiantly lead his troops against the invading Mongols and had won a series of great victories during the early part of his campaign, this so pleased the Emperor *Wu*, that he proclaimed *Li* the hero of the hour and celebrated his victories with an elaborate feast. However, when *Li* returned to the battlefield he was far less successful, and his forces were routed and he himself taken prisoner by the enemy. The Emperor was so enraged that he immediately ordered the death of *Li's* entire family. *Ssu Ma-Chien*, shocked by this unnecessarily harsh punishment, interceded with the furious Emperor on *Li's* behalf, which only made matters worse, for not only would the Emperor not reverse his decision, he ordered *Ssu's* castration and imprisonment for life. Thus deprived of his liberty, and worse, he languished in prison but through the good offices of a friend he was given writing materials and he resignedly commenced the now famous *Lung Men* History and completed the *Shi Ki*, which is now regarded as one of the great masterpieces of Chinese literature. The mental anguish he suffered during his confinement is poignantly revealed in a letter to his old friend *Yin An-kung*, which itself is now included as part of this ancient classic. A free translation will serve as an indication of *Ssu's* state of mind at this time:

"General Li is only an acquaintance with whom I have neither dined nor conversed, but I know him to be a respectful son, a loyal friend and a brave soldier. He has often been known to

say; 'One should never hesitate to give ones life for ones country'. When he again led his five thousand troops north- ward in battle he advanced far into the enemy's territory but because of their greater numbers and better weapons he and his force were routed and did not enjoy their earlier successes. With most of his brave force lost, and he himself seriously wounded he had no other choice than to be taken prisoner. This, as you know, caused great consternation in our capital and I interceded on Li's behalf with the angry Emperor. For every good instance of Li's loyalty and bravery I raised the Emperor grew more and more enraged, he accused me of giving countenance to this ignominy and extenuating General Li's cowardice. I was subsequently thrown into prison and subjected to the punishment of castration. This is the most terrible and despicable of punishments. It is worse than death. I am physically impaired and my reputation is gone. I am publicly ridiculed and despised by the peope. As we must all die sometime, I have thought on death which, can be as light as a feather or as heavy as a mountain. Why do I want to live on in such disgrace? Famous men of the past, who have produced the most outstanding literary achievements have suffered tragedies, and as an outlet for their mental strain, they have written masterpieces. My work in compiling the 130 books of history, [chüan, (book) really means chapter in Chinese although it is translated here as book for the sake of clarity] *is far from complete. My only wish is to finish this task, so that it may be handed down to posterity. This may perhaps vindicate my sorrow and disgrace. I am now the subject of jeers and laughter; what dignity or honour have I left? What can now cleanse me from the present ignominy? My spirit flutters and reels; my senses are numb and I know not the difference between east and west. Wherever I walk I lose my way, for I no longer have any sense of purpose or direction. Why is this so? It is because my poor heart is so heavy with shame and agony that, each day when I but think on it, cold sweat soaks my clothing. All that is now left for me, is to hide myself away in some remote cave and live only from one day to the next.''*

The public attitude which is clearly expressed in *Ssu's* letter, was one of contempt and scorn for those who had been so mutilated, engendered, no doubt, by fear and a determined effort not to identify with the despised victim.

Confucius displayed a somewhat like attitude when he offered his services to the Emperor of the *Wei* court, (560 BC) and was forced to take his place in an ox cart with a eunuch whilst the Emperor rode in a chariot. History states that this worthy sage thought he was deserving of much better treatment and that he should have been invited to take his place along with the Emperor rather than to ride with a detestable eunuch! He immediately left the kingdom of *Wei* determined to offer his services to another ruler who would appreciate both his learning and dignity. The summary castration of men and boys who were engaged in menial labour within Imperial palaces was thought necessary, especially for those who worked within the secluded 'inner palaces' which housed the Imperial Concubine-Consorts and secondary wives of the Emperor which was in itself a 'city' of women. Because the Chinese throne was hereditary through the male line, every precaution had to be taken to guard against possible falsification of descent. This pre-requisite of exact paternity was more than any other the 'sharp blade' that separated literally hundreds of thousands of young Chinese from their natural future during China's long history.

Eunuchs were also employed by male as well as female members of the Imperial family, thus almost from the very beginning of the system they became trusted confidents and grew in power and influence. It is a little known fact that one of the responsibilities of the chief eunuch was to keep a connubial register in which was recorded the name, date and very hour of each concubine who passed the night in her Emperor's bed. The selection was made from a set of ivory tablets or *hu* [1] upon which was engraved the name of each consort; the Emperor would choose the one appropriate to his mood and hand it to the chief eunuch who then summoned the lady in question and recorded the necessary information into his register. Therein lay the opportunity for intrigue for, if the chosen lady could, within the fullness of time present the Emperor with a son her own position would be greatly elevated to *Imperial Mother*.

103

Because of the unlimited possibilities open to the ambitious eunuch, strict laws were enacted to keep the eunuchs in order;they were administered by the Minister of the Imperial Household; not allowed to hold official or noble rank (which was to be eroded dramatically during later dynasties), not to participate in politics or leave the capital without special authorization. However stringently these measures were administered they did not prevent a great many *crows* (as the eunuchs were somewhat unkindly called) from rising to positions of rank and power and in a number of instances even became the power behind the Dragon Throne.

Not that eunuchs were peculiar to the Middle Kingdom; they are mentioned in Matthew 19-12 and adorned the Papal choir until the accession of Pope Leo 13th and even in recent time the practise has continued in the Moslem world.

It was during the *Han* Dynasty that this *castrate clique* had its first real taste of power, (206 BC - 220 AD) which was mainly the result of the laxity shown by succeeding Emperors and it is recorded that during the reign of the Emperor *Ling* their pernicious influence permeated every corner of the state. Those foolhardy enough to speak against them were quickly eliminated. The chief eunuch at this time was one *Chang Yang* whom the Emperor elevated and gave him the more than inappropriate title of *Imperial Father* and even addressed him as such. *Chang Yang*, the *Imperial Father*, confirmed in his power fully exploited his Imperial relations; he intercepted all personally unfavourable memorials to the Emperor and had the senders murdered; he sold rank and official positions on a wholesale basis and intercepted and rechannelled the states taxes into his own purse. All the while the Emperor was blissfully ignorant and believed his reign and state to be 'perfect before heaven'; it was far from so and crumbling daily and was soon to die in one of the most dramatic and bloody episodes in Chinese history. Yet succeeding dynasties seem to have fallen into the same eunuch error, strict at the beginning but soon allowing the eunuchs to creep back into power. The *Ming* is a classical example, for when China was restored to the Chinese with the ousting of the *Yüan* in 1368 there was popular rejoicing and a national confidence that this

Chinese dynasty would revive the glories of the *Han* and *T'ang* past. There is at least one notable exception in the history of 'wicked eunuchs'; this was *Cheng Ho* who was by all accounts a loyal and upright man and faithful servant of the *Ming* Emperor *Yung Lo* who breaking all the rules sent his chief eunuch *Cheng Ho* as emissary to the South Seas in 1405. *Cheng Ho* was of *Yünnanese* origin and known as the *San Po* eunuch. On the appointed auspicious day he set sail with sixty-two vessels which carried seven thousand Imperial troops and officers and cargoes of porcelain, silks, gold and jade as gifts of Imperial favour for the leaders of those vassal states who acknowledged allegiance and paid tribute to China. This colourful flotilla called at Indo-China, Malacca, Sumatra and finally reached Java, anchoring at the port of Semarang. *Cheng Ho* is said to be the first Chinese to set foot in Java, but this is open to doubt; however he was received with much honour and all due ceremony as befitted a representative of the Great Emperor of China. *Cheng* was a devout Buddhist and well known for his supposed powers of divination and not unnaturally he was approached by his hosts to forecast their furtures, this he did by predicting that the year ahead would bring both drought and famine, which much alarmed his naive hosts. Seeing their despair he tried to console them by adding that this tragedy could be averted if they sacrificed to the evil spirits, chanted prayers to wash away their sins, worked harder and fasted for thirty days; thus the evil spirits would be appeased and leave them in peace.

As *Cheng Ho* was regarded by the superstitious as something of a demi-god himself they avowed to follow his instruction to the letter and the very next day began their fast. By the time three days had elapsed they were dizzy from the pangs of hunger which had been greatly heightened by their hard work and constant praying, but they dared not break their fast for fear of the terrible consequences. A number of the shrewd native elders resolved to visit *Cheng Ho* and enquire what effect the three day fast had had on him; they were amazed to behold that the eunuch displayed none but looked serene and happy. They retired puzzled and confused and decided to investigate further; spies were posted around *Cheng's* residence, slowly they edged closer and at last were able to peer through the windows, what they saw filled them with rage and consternation. There was this *demi-god* seated before a table literally groaning with delicious food which he consumed in a most enthusiastic way. The elders were informed of this fast-breaking and immediately resolved to face *Cheng* with his wickedness; what explanation did he have? "Why, none", replied the elegant eunuch as he rose slowly from his banquet, "I asked you to fast for thirty days, but I did not ask you to forgo food after sunset. Go, eat all you will after night has fallen, for surely you know that the evil spirits cannot see in the dark". The famished natives thanked him, and rushed home to their cooking pots eager only to satisfy their hunger and not dwelling upon the shaky logic upon which *Cheng* had based it.

The following year *Cheng's* remedy to the bad omen was seen everywhere throughout the length and breadth of Java to have indeed worked, it was a most prosperous year with abundant crops. In gratitude the Javanese set one month aside each year during which food was only taken after sunset and the tradition of this *starving month*, as it became known, is still observed in Java to this present time. The port of Semarang where *Cheng* had first landed was renamed *San Po Lung* after him and in the nearby town a temple was erected in his honour which contained a deep well which was said to have its source in China. *Cheng* made some seven trips in all to Java and eventually died there and is said to have been ceremoniously entombed within this temple.

During China's turbulent history much blame has attached to this army of *semi-men*, and nowhere were they more in evidence than during the *Ming* and *Ch'ing* Dynasties. Despite the strict measures enacted to prevent them from attaining high office many succeeded in holding noble rank and excercising great influence. The fourteenth ruler of the *Ming*, the Emperor *Wan-li* ascended to the throne in 1573, by all accounts he was irresponsible and much given to the pursuit of pleasure rather than the responsibility of government, a fact that was quickly taken advantage of by the intriguing eunuchs. This mis-rule continued for the following twenty years of his reign and the state became like an apple diseased from within. When his son succeeded to the throne in

1620 the eunuch cancer had spread to every branch of the court and far beyond, and he found himself powerless to check it, for there seemed to be no official that this corruption had not touched. But, he was determined to rid the dynasty of these voracious leeches and in a bold attempt he dismissed all the highest eunuch officials. For a short time they feigned genuine humility and acquiescence but, harboured in their hearts a deep and bitter hatred of their Imperial Master. The *Tai-chang* Emperor met his death less than two months after he had ascended the throne, dying in great agony of a mysterious poison. The eunuchs had had their revenge. From this moment their power flourished like a veritable sea of noxious weeds fatally and irrevocably entwined around the slowly dying dynasty. The following years brought drought, flood and famine that devastated many provinces; the people starved dying in their thousands and the little aid that issued from the administration was snatched away by the avaricious eunuchs for their own use, only a trickle reaching those who were so severely in need. The dark clouds of impending civil war began to envelope the corrupt and unjust *Ming* Empire. The *Chung-cheng* Emperor in a desperate attempt to rout the impending danger dismissed all the eunuchs from office. This merely had the effect of throwing the eunuch-manipulated administration into almost total chaos, the treasury was empty and what loyal ministers and generals remained could in no part stem the tide of impending rebellion. *Chung-cheng*, like a drowning man clutched at the only straw that might save him, he reinstated the eunuchs to their former offices in the vain and desperate hope that they, who had so much to lose, might at last quell the unrest.

The first flames of the rebellion had been kindled in *Shensi* and quickly spread north-eastward with ferocious speed, at its head was *Li Tse-sheng*. Soon *Tai-yuan* fell and *Peking* itself was encircled by the cleansing flame. Inside the beseiged city pandemonium now reigned supreme, the Emperor had been deserted by almost all his followers and the people were panic-stricken at the sounds of battering-rams pounding on the great southern gates, parts of the city were already ablaze and as the smoke and flames leapt heaven-ward so too rose the temperature of their terror.

Within the *Forbidden City* the pall of smoke from beyond its massive walls snow-flaked ashes over the gilded pavilions, the Emperor could not fail to recognize their portent, all was now lost. He ordered his own remaining eunuch-attendant to summon the Empress and her two daughters now, completely alone the Emperor determinedly composed himself for the farewell to his family, the usually clear pale-blue sky that canopied Imperial *Peking* was shot with crimson and the sounds of explosions washed the horizon with thrusts of black and grey smoke. Turning from the window, his wife and children stood before him and as he opened wide his arms they swiftly sought refuge within them. The situation was desperate, they must not fall into the hands of the advancing enemy, motioning to his last faithful eunuch, he made his farewells, the eunuch stepped forward, in his outstratched hands was a cushion upon which were three jewelled daggers. The Empress and her two children died by their own hand, facing south entoning the Emperor's name. *Chung-cheng* stood transfixed for a moment, tears glistening on his cheeks, then, turning to the eunuch, whose eyes were also filled with tears, he hurried from the palace, across the deserted courtyards towards the northern part of the city. Soon 'Prospect Hill' came into view and he and his attendant climbed the scenic paths to the summit. . . . . . there the magnitude of the disaster could be clearly seen, most of the southern part of the city was in flames, unable now to control himself his whole body convulsived with anguish, he shouted to heaven and cursed himself for his failure in life, then, regaining some composure he asked for paper and quickly wrote just twelve characters in a shaking hand and pinned the note to his gown, it read; 'I know you will mutilate my body, but do not hurt any of my subjects'.

The pale sunshine had almost vanished from the sky and dark crimson now afforded an unearthly twilight; turning to his eunuch he thanked him for his loyalty, then, taking the girdle from his own gown he looped it over a stout branch of an acacia tree and hanged himself. The eunuch fell to his knees weeping and calling his masters name, then, emulating his master he also hanged himself from a nearby tree.

108

At this same time the loyal *Ming* general *Wu San-kuei*, who was garrisoned at the Great Wall sought the assistance of the powerful Manchu Bannermen in stemming the revolution. This was the moment the Manchu Princes had been waiting for and they flooded over the border easily taking over all the strategic positions and with the population war-torn and leaderless they took the Dragon Throne as well.

In occupying the Chinese Dragon Throne the Manchu had learned one important lesson; to avoid the curse of the Chinese eunuch system, it had brought down the *Ming* Dynasty, it would not be allowed to led to the same fate for the *Ch'ing*! Almost immediately on assuming power, laws were promulgated to eliminate the influence of the eunuchs; none could hold a higher rank than the fourth degree civil, none were allowed to participate in any official administration, all were forbidden from, 'gaining the ear of the sovereign or influencing him in any way'. These Imperial Restrictions were engraved on a bronze plaque which still stands in the *Chung Ho Tien* within the *Forbidden City*.

For two centuries after this the eunuchs were kept in strict submission. In 1861 when the eighth Manchu Emperor *T'ung-chih* was in his minority, two regents were appointed, the young widow of the lately deceased *Hsien-fêng* Emperor, *Tz'u-an*, who was senior to *Tz'u-hsi* who had been an Imperial concubine and was now known as the Western Empress, not only because she occupied a western part of the palace but because she was the mother of the young Emperor and although *Tz'u-an* might be senior in theory, having been the legal wife of the deceased Emperor, *Tz'u-hsi* was determined to be far more omnipotent in practice. It was this constant feuding between the two Empress-regents that gave the long-dormant eunuchs their chance. Quickly they aligned themselves with which-ever of the Empresses they thought would eventually win. At this time a young, intelligent and uncommonly handsome eunuch, *An Teh-hai* used every means within his power to ingratiate himself with *Tz'u-hsi* whom he felt sure would be successful. He was young and dashing, possessed of likeable manners and a smiling countenance and soon found favour with the young lonely Empress; she made him, within a short while, chief of all the eunuchs and her confident. At this time there were above three thousand eunuchs within the *Forbidden City* so *An's* power, not only with his royal mistress but throughout the whole *City* was not inconsiderable. There was however, one flaw in *An's* character which was eventually to led to his downfall and death, he lacked stability, which in turn lead him to assume attitudes above his station. His restless spirit longed for travel and now that he found himself the powerful Western Empress's favourite his yearnings turned to other things. In his desire to break from the confines of the *Great Within* he ventured to express the wish that he might be allowed to visit *Shangtung; Tz'u-hsi*, overconfident of her newly acquired power agreed to his request, although this was a serious violation of all the Dynastic rules. Both servant and mistress had allowed their vanity to conquer their prudence. The pretext upon which *An's* excursion was based was also an error in judgement, he was to collect tribute in her name.

An Teh-hai set off for *Shangtung* at the head of a fleet of dragon-barges on the Imperial canal and naturally he assumed all the attendant prerogatives. On arrival he was shown all due respect by the somewhat startled local officials but, this was not enough to satisfy *An's* now greatly enlarged ego; his demands became more and more outrageous, was he not the appointed envoy of her Imperial Majesty? Was he not deserving of more pomp and a great deal more largesse than he was at present receiving? They must satisfy his every wish or on his return to the capital he would report their discourteous and neglectful behaviour to his Imperial Mistress, then what would happen to these provincial dullards?

The governor of *Shangtung* grew so alarmed at *An's* 'Imperial' behaviour that he secretly sent an urgent message to Prince *Kung* in *Peking*. The Prince had every reason to hate *An*, for just a few months before he had sought urgent audience with the Western Empress only to be rebuffed with the answer, that she was in delightful conversation with *An Teh-hai* and could not be disturbed for a mere Prince. Now Prince *Kung* went straight to the Empress *Tz'u-an* and induced her to sign a decree ordering the immediate arrest and decapitation of *An Teh-hai*, convincing her that not only would her rival regent be put firmly in her place, it would also put a stop to the eunuchs getting above themselves. Some ten days later when *Tz'u-hsi* received the staggering news that her favourite had been executed, she flatly refused to believe it, it was inconceivable that anyone would dare to challenge her power or to harm her representative. *An's* death however was soon confirmed, and his Imperial Mistress turned upon her conniving co-regent and her counsellor Prince *Kung*; this time they had outmanoeuvred her and she was forced to let the matter drop, she had been proved to be in the wrong; although she would neither forgive nor forget *An's* death. His place was soon taken by an equally intelligent eunuch, *Li Lien-ying*, who, learning from his predecessors fate quickly acquired the virtue of stability. *Li* was as ugly as *An* had been handsome, none the less he became a power to be reckoned with for over forty years until *Tz'u-hsi's* death in 1908.

Castrations were performed just outside the walls of the *Forbidden City*, the cost being usually about six taels, an extremely low sum. However, this was vastly augmented by the resale of the severed genitalia, for this operation was not just castration but the removal of the entire organ; whilst the unconscious victim lay strapped to the operating plank his genitalia were placed into a labled container which had to be shown at the annual inspection which was carried out in the *Forbidden City* by the chief eunuch, without this proof he could neither retain his place or according to Confucian ideology gain spiritual perfection after death. All Chinese wished to be buried whole and this was especially true of the eunuchs. Apart from the obvious loss, a man who had offered himself for emasculation forfeited his right to be buried with his family. . . . . . a severe penalty for the ancestor-worshipping Chinese. Eunuchs were therefore buried in their own grave-yard just outside *Peking* and worshipped at their own temple.

The surgeons who specialized in the gruesome operation usually came from *Chili* province, as indeed did most of their patients. Applicants for this emasculation would ideally be boys who had not attained puberty, for operations after this time on either men or boys could be extremely dangerous. The technique varied, but in many cases followed the traditional formula: the boy was given a bowl of 'nerve stunning' herbal tea, his body was then firmly bandaged around the abdomen and groin and then strapped to a sloping wooden plank; attendants were close by to steady the body and legs; a cloth was then placed over the boy's face and the genitals are carefully bathed several times in a hot lotion containing herbs and pepper. This accomplished the 'surgeon' took a four-inch scimitar-shaped knife, with one sudden stroke he swiftly and deftly severed the entire organ. Immediately a three inch silver pipe was inserted into the urethra, followed by liberal appliactions of herbal powder to arrest the bleeding. Pads of absorbant paper, soaked in water were then used to cover the wound. These were then secured in place by bandages and the boy was unstrapped, then, supported under the arms was walked around the room for at least three hours; he was not allowed any liquid for three days nor might he urinate. A week later the silver plug was removed and more healing powder applied as the bandages were removed. It took upwards of one hundred days for the wound to heal if there were no complications, but the ill-effects could linger for months or years.

The fatality rate, contrary to commonly held views, was remarkably low, three or four per cent at most but the bodily changes were severe, the voice became a rasping falsetto, hence their nick-name of *crows*; both facial and body hair disappeared; premature aging in almost all cases resulted and a eunuch of forty looked more like a man of sixty. There was a common crude saying; ". . . . . .he stinks like a eunuch, you get wind of him at five hundred yards". They were universally despised and any mention of a tea-pot without a spout or a tail-less dog offended them deeply. The mental repercusions of this unnatural operation were sometimes more severe; an eminent psychologist recorded; *"In most cases, castration against the subjects will may produce many very disturbing mental effects, anti-social tendencies and criminality."* [2]

The most powerful of the eunuchs, as far as the nineteenth century was concerned was *Li Lien-ying*, he was allowed undreamed of liberties by his Imperial Mistress *Tz'u-hsi*, to whom he talked-back and bullied, all-be-it in a playful manner. There was hardly a high official or Prince who did not try to gain his approval, knowing he had the ear of the Western Empress and for this service he extracted huge amounts in 'red-packet money', (the traditional way of offering money as a gift in China, which is still used), and amassed a huge fortune estimated at millions of dollars. This was the eunuch dominated court that *P'u-yi* entered as a child and his own diaries have many references to them.

> "They waited on me when I dined, dressed and slept, accompanied me on walks and at my lessons; they told me stories and played with me. They never left my presence and were the main companions of my childhood, they were both my slaves and my earliest teachers."

Their duties, according to the 'Palace Regulations' were indeed very extensive; transmitting Imperial Edicts, leading officials to audience, receiving memorials, dealing with various documents of the Household Department, receiving money and grain sent from provincial treasuries, keeping a constant fire watch, looking after the libraries, antiques, paintings, robes, weapons and Imperial paraphernalia. Being responsible for all fresh and dried fruit, obtaining all building and repair materials used within the *City*, attending to the incense burners within the various temples and before the Imperial Ancestor portraits and gods, monitoring the comings and goings of officials of all other departments, keeping the registers of attendance of both the Hanlin Academicians and the officers of the Imperial Guard, the safe keeping of the Imperial seals, recording all the actions of the Emperor, the flogging of all offending eunuchs and servant women, feeding the various live creatures within the *Forbidden City*, the cleaning of all palace buildings and gardens, regulating and winding of all the clocks, preparing all the medicines, singing in opera and acting in the Imperial Theatre, reciting the classics and officiating in the Imperial Taoist temple, and, many hundreds of subordinate duties, in fact, whatever their royal masters and mistresses required.

It is little wonder that over the years they became indespensable, and in consequence, extremely powerful. Although it had been firmly stated in the regulation that no eunuch could rise higher than the fourth degree the aforementioned *Li Lien-ying* was promoted to the second by his doting Mistress the Empress

Dowager *Tz'u-hsi*, the same honour was accorded to *Chang Chieh-ho* the chief eunuch of the 'Boy-Emperor' *P'u-yi*. The eunuch system was subject to strict grading: Chief eunuch; those in attendance upon either the Empress, Empress-dowager or Emperor. Head eunuch; those subordinate to the chief eunuch and, those who were head of the households of consorts and other minor Imperial families who were denied by law the attendance of a chief eunuch. Then, came all the others who were in every was subservient to the chief and head eunuchs. Most were officially graded between the fourth and ninth and the lowest were ungraded.

Their 'official' salaries were rather low, the highest was eight taels of silver, eight catties of rice plus three hundred copper 'cash' per month but with all the extras, legal and illegal, their actual incomes were much higher, particularly the seniors. As an example, *Juan Chin-shou*, who was deputy chief eunuch to *P'u-yi* was reported to be so rich that he wore a different fur gown every day of the winter, one that was famous made of sea-otter, which he only wore on New Year's day, was so costly, that it represented a lifetime's expenditure for a minor official. Many lived in high style within their own apartments with their own servants, cooks and attendants. The humbler eunuchs on the other hand lived a spartan existence, poor food and accommodation and if they were expelled for any reason, which they often were, they faced a life of begging and starvation outside the protective walls of the *Great Within*.

> "Chang Chien-ho was my first tutor and travelling companion. He used to play at racing me, though of course he always let me win. I also remember that one New Year when the high consort Ching-yi invited me to her apartments to play dice Chiang was banker; every number I staked my money on always won and soon I had cleared out the bank; he did not seem to mind, why should he? All the money I had won was the High Consorts!" [3]

Just like any other child, *P'u-yi* was very fond of being told stories, and the eunuchs enthusiastically entered into his world of make-believe, the stories could perhaps be divided into two categories, ghost stories, about the palace, and tales of the benevolent spirits whose sworn duty it was to assist the 'Son of Heaven'. According to these stories the eunuchs told the wide eyed 'Boy Emperor' related, that literally everything in the palaces, bronze cranes, golden jars, trees, wells, rocks had all at one time or another manifested themselves in spirit form and demonstrated their magic powers. All tried to gain the Emperor's favour, which only led to the logical conclusion, logical that is to a small boy, that he was a being of supreme importance. One of the eunuchs stories concerned the large bronze crane that stood in one of the throne ante-rooms, it had a large dent in one of its legs, this, they explained was caused by the fact that it had turned itself into a crane-spirit to protect the *Ch'ien-lung* Emperor who was on a hunting trip and the bird had interposed itself between the Emperor and the arrow of a would-be assassin and was wounded in the leg, they even pointed to the rusty dent in its leg as proof of their invention. *P'u-yi*, like any small boy loved all their stories, especially the one concerning the great pearl that had adorned the hat of the *Ch'ien-lung* Emperor, (a pearl, being the Imperial prerogative of rank); they told that one day when the Emperor was strolling beside a stream in the *Yüan Ming Yüan*, (Summer Palace), he noticed something gleaming beneath the water, he took his bow and arrow from an attendant and shot at it but the glistening object immediately vanished, unable to restrain his curiosity he ordered the stream dragged but all that was found was a huge clam, which when finally prised open revealed a large and magnificent pearl, the Emperor was delighted and ordered this gem to be attached to his official hat; but their story did not end here, for the pearl had a life of its own and longed to be reunited with its mother within the safety of its watery home and would fly away out the windows of the palace and had to be retrieved many times. The Emperor grew more and more displeased, until finally he ordered his court jeweller to bore a hole through this restless gem and affix it to his hat by a secure gold mount, then the clam shell was sent on a long sea voyage and dropped into the deepest part of the China Sea, the pearl at last remained in its new Imperial home and the Emperor was finally satisfied.

The following incident is translated from *P'u-yi's* own words:

"Once, when I was ill, at about the age of seven or eight Chang Cheng-ho, (the chief eunuch) brought me a purple pill to take. When I asked him what sort of medicine it was, he said, 'your slave has just had a wondrous dream; an old man with a white beard held out this pill in his hand and told me it was the pill of immortaility and that he had especially brought it as a humble present for 'the Lord of Ten Thousand Years'.I was so pleased and excited to hear this that I forgot all about my own illness and, recalling the story about the "twenty-four filial sons", I took the pill at once to the palace of the four high Consorts in order to share it with them. Chang Cheng-ho must have made some sign to them as they all looked overjoyed and highly praised my filial piety. Some months later when I happened to go to the Imperial dispensary I noticed some pills that looked just like the 'pills of imortality' and I was much puzzled, so I commanded the eunuch in charge to put the appropriate label on the container and that they were to be strictly reserved for Imperial use, for I remembered the tale of the old man and although I was dissappointed to learn that they were in fact 'ordinary' pills, still I was determined to retain some belief in Chang's ingenious tale."

The ghost stories on the other hand had the effect of making an already nervous boy quite terrified for, according to the eunuchs' stories the ghosts and spirits dwelt in every corner of the *Forbidden City*. The lane behind the *Lasting Peace Palace* was supposed to be the place where ghosts grabbed people by the neck; the well outside the *Ching Ho* Gate was the home of a swarm of she-devils, and had it not been for the heavy iron cover over the gate they would have roamed abroad every evening; it was also said that every three years a ghost would appear and drag a passer-by off the bridge and down into the murky depths of the lake. The more *P'u-yi* heard such stories the more frightened he became, the greater his fear, the keener his appetite became for these spine-chilling tales. Even from the age of four he became an avid reader of such stories of the supernatural, Taoist literature is brimming with them and the eunuchs supplied all the books he could read. His tension must have been heightened by the eery ritual that occured every evening at dusk as the *Great Within* was prepared for night; all the days visitors, on whatever business, were ushered from the *City*; from the *Chien Ching* Palace, (Palace of Cloudless Heaven) issued a blood-chilling shreak: "Clear the City! Draw the bolts! Lock up! Take care of all lanterns!" As the last high-pitched wailing died away on the twilight air a chorus of ghostly responses issued from all corners of the city, rising and falling in eery counterpoint. This practice had been instigated by the *k'ang-hsi* Emperor to keep the eunuchs alert and the practice continued as long as there were eunuchs within the *Purple City*. This had the effect of making the 'Boy Emperor' even more fearful, he refused to be alone after sunset for a moment and would never venture out at night for many years. There is little doubt that the eunuchs were themselves very superstitious and believed the stories they told the young Emperor, *Chang Chien-ho* was said always, when faced with a problem or difficult decision to consult 'The Record of the Jade Box', and all were diligent in their offerings to the 'palace gods', which were the especial protectors of the eunuchs.

The 'Palace gods', according to the eunuchs had been elevated to immortals of the second degree by a former Emperor; the eating of beef was taboo and any eunuch who transgressed stood in peril of his life, it was said that their gods would inflict a horrible punishment for this sin. Whenever the eunuchs went into an empty hall or apartment they would always shout in a loud voice, "Opening the Palace!" before they dared open the door thus they might avoid being punished for coming face to face with one or more of their vengeful protectors. Offerings were made to these 'Palace gods' on the first and fifteenth of each month consisting of the customary incense together with eggs, dried bean-curd, wine and cakes. At New Year and other important festivals the offering would consist of whole pigs and sheep, mountains of fruit which, for the eunuchs of the lowest rank meant great hardship, but they gladly contributed in the most-times vain hope, that it would protect them from the constant beatings they received.

117

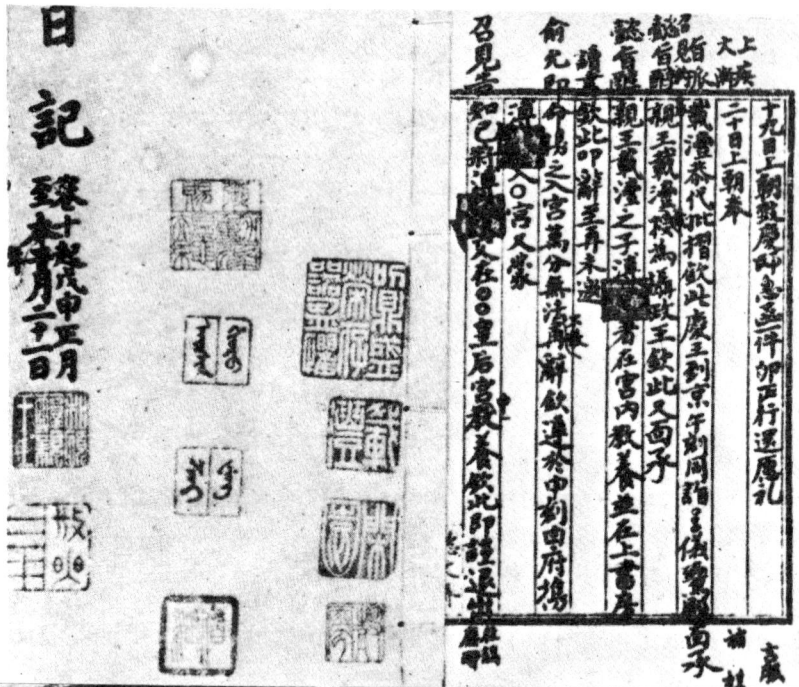

Top: A page from Prince Ch'un's diary.
Bottom: The gate of Spiritual Valour. C. 1920.

The oft chronicled talent of the eunuchs for extracting large bribes from all and sundry to supplement their meagre official salaries is well illustrated by the story of wedding preparations for the *T'ung-chih* Emperor: It seemed that the Household Department had overlooked one section of the palace when distributing the *red-packet* money customary on such occasions and, on the day of the wedding, the ignored eunuch sent for an official of the offending department and pointed out that a pane of glass in the palace was cracked; now, an official of the Household Department was not allowed to mount the terrace, unless he had been imperially summoned, he had to view the crack in question from a distance. He was terrified at what he saw, or rather what he thought he saw, if this got back to his Imperial Masters he would be in severe trouble, for it was an ill-omen of the worst kind to see a broken window on a wedding day, and an Imperial wedding day at that! The eunuchs tried to calm the panic-striken official by assuring him that there was no need to fetch workmen and thus risk discovery, they themselves would attend to the inauspicious pane, the official realized he had no choice and agreed and handed over a sum three time as much as the 'red-packet' would have contained, had it not been overlooked. This accomplished they set about 'restoring' the window, it was not very difficult, the 'crack' was merely a strand of hair that had been stuck to it.

Another amusing tale that testifies to the pecuniary preoccupation of the eunuchs has survived: *Chung-lun*, one time comptroller of the Imperial Household Department was found niggardly in his distribution of bribes and on his way to an audience with the then Empress Dowager, for which he was already late, huddled in his sable jacket, for it was in the middle of the harsh *Peking* winter, he turned the corner of one of the minor palaces he was drenched with water which had mysteriously issued from an upstairs window; the offending eunuch begged his humble pardon and pleaded not to be punished, *Chung-lun* knowing that on no account could he keep the great Empress Dowager waiting, desperately begged the eunuch for assistance. The eunuch immediately produced another sable jacket, saying "Here, take this jacket your humble servants will be very grateful if we can but share a part of your good fortune; we know that you will be generous". The every resourceful eunuchs always kept a full range of official court clothing to be 'loaned' on short notice to needful officials, for the right fee of course; *Chung-lun* was no exception, he fully realized that he had been 'soaked' on purpose, hurriedly paid up and scurried away to his impending audience.

When the fateful year of 1924 arrived and the Imperial family were driven from the *Forbidden City*. the former chief eunuch to the late Empress Dowager *Lung-yu* set up house in a magnificent mansion within the British concession and lived in the exalted style of a war-lord with hosts of servants. When one of these servants fled from his mansion to take refuge in the British Police station to escape his master's cruelty, he was immediately returned, whereupon his eunuch master *Chang Yuan-fu* ordered the runaway to be beaten to death, so great was his wealth and power that none dared protest, not even the 'fair-minded' British.

CHAPTER FIVE

"The English Tutor"

With the possible exception of a number of Imperial Princes, those who took precedence over all others at court were without doubt the Imperial Tutors. This may be difficult to understand from the Western point of view but the extreme deference shown in Old China to a teacher by his student is at the very heart of Confucian philosophy.

In the *Kuo Yu*, each human being is dependant on others and should be served with equal devotion; one is the father, who gives life, the second is the teacher, who shows how life should be lived, the third is the prince who provides the social stability that allows a good life; another section of this famous work states: *"Without a father, there is no life; without physical nourishment,* (provided by the 'prince') *there is no growth; and without a teacher there is no wisdom."*

One of the standard works of Chinese classical literature, the *Li Chi* states the following:

> *"When a pupil meets his teacher on the road, he should hasten towards him and bow. If the teacher addresses him, he should give a respectful and fitting reply; if the teacher is silent, he should retire quickly....... A pupil should wait upon his teacher and serve him without regard to mere conventions. As long as his teacher should live he must serve him faithfully, and, upon his death he should pay him the honour of three years of sincere mourning. If a ruler is desirous of civilizing his people and making them well-bred, it is in the school-room that he must begin. Uncut and unpolished jade cannot be fashioned into a serviceable*

vessel; if men are uneducated they do not know how to properly conduct themselves. Thus it was that the wise rulers of old, when establishing their states on solid foundations . . . made education their first care. It is from the teacher that the ruler learns the art of government. Thus, nothing should be of greater concern than the selection of a teacher. There are two men in the realm whom the ruler cannot regard as his subjects; the man who at ritual sacrifices to the dead impersonates the royal ancestors; . . . . . the other is his teacher. . . . . when the teacher is addressing the Son of Heaven he should not face the north, that is how honour was shown to a teacher." [1]

The reference to facing north, perhaps needs clarification; it has always been the Chinese custom that the enthroned Emperor sits facing south with his back to the north, therefore those who approach him must face north, this is just one of the essential distinctions between Emperor and subject.

Thus it can be readily seen that the relationship between Emperor and teacher is quite unlike Emperor and subject; the Imperial custom was still observed in the last days of the *Forbidden City*, the tutor was seated at the east side of the school-room table facing west whilst the Emperor sat at the north side facing south. Another mark of respect was shown by the Emperor to his tutors, he would rise whenever one of them entered a room, protocol required the tutor to advance to the centre of the room, bow once and then both Emperor and tutor would sit in their appointed position. If, during the lesson the tutor had to rise for the purpose of getting a book, or for any other reason the Emperor would remain standing until the tutor resumed his seat.

This profound respect, which was rigidly observed by the Manchu was misinterpreted by the Jesuits of *K'ang-hsi's* time as respect for their 'god', they were, of course much mistaken. An account survives of a eulogium pronounced in 1726 by the *Shih Tsung* (*Yung-chêng* 1723-1735) Emperor on his deceased tutor *Ku Pa-tai*:

"*Ku Pa-tai,*" entoned the Emperor, "*who formerly held the office of first president of the Board of Rites, was a man of*

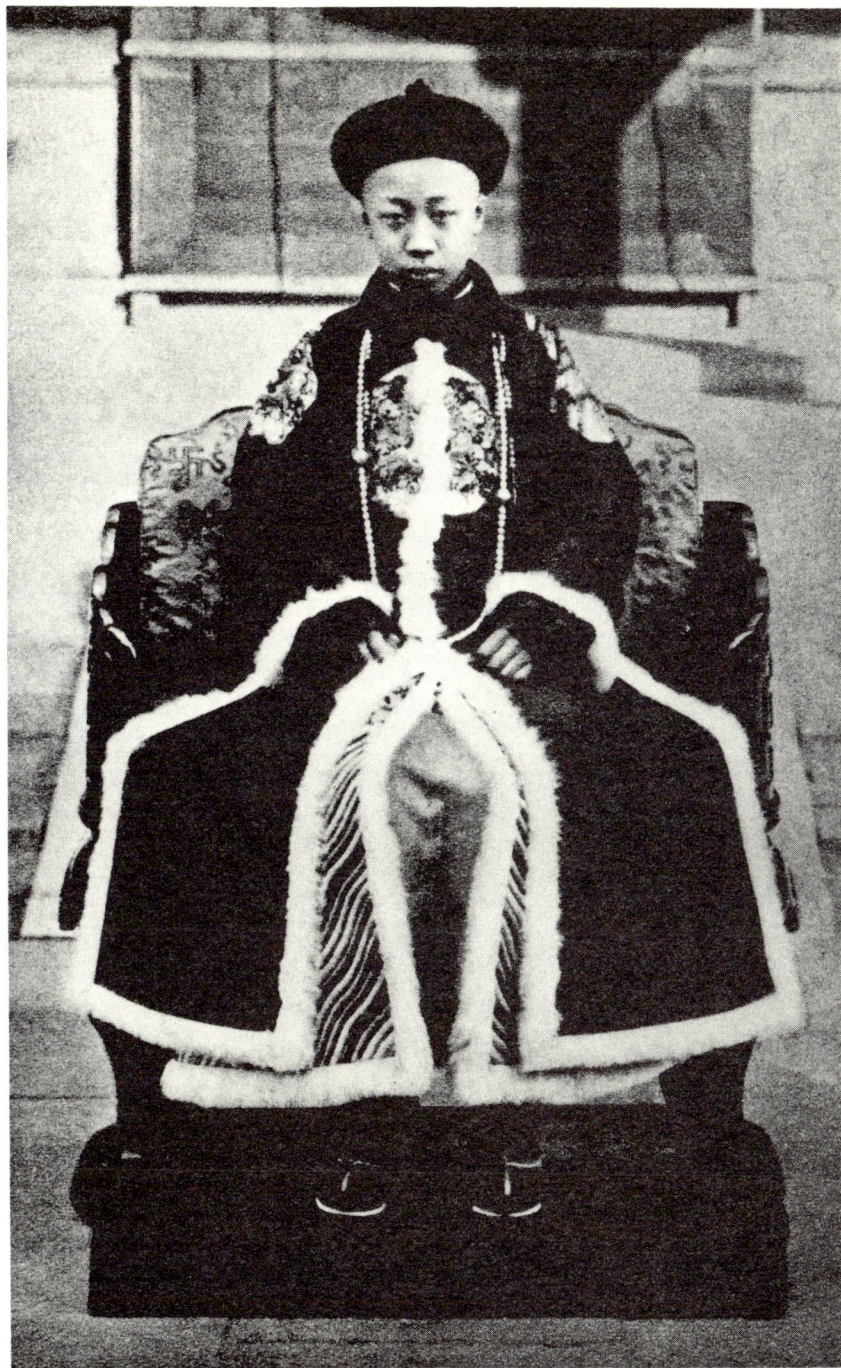

P'u-yi at the age of 11 in 1917.

*irreproachable character, moderate and well-regulated in all
his conduct and full of knowledge and virtue. My father, the
Emperor Sheng Tsu,* (temple name of the *K'ang-hsi* Emperor,
1662-1722) *who held him in high esteem, employed him in
affairs of a most difficult nature . . . . as he excelled in the
military art no less than in scholarship, he was astonishingly
successful in the enterprises assigned to him . . . . . . As he was
distinguished for his vast erudition, and his actions were such
as to make him a worthy model for our imagination, my
father selected him to be tutor to several of the Imperial
princes. I was one of those whom he taught. Filled with
indefatigable zeal, he laboured from morning to night in the
work of giving us instruction and in engraving upon our hearts
the purest and noblest maxims of fidelity and piety . . . . . .As
soon as I heard of his death, wishing to carry out the duty
that a disciple owes to his teacher, I went personally to his
house to take part in the last rites and to mourn before his
coffin. When his funeral took place I sent several of my
officials to represent me and to carry out the prescribed
ceremonies in my name . . . . .I should not forget so wise a
master, and I wish to give him a mark of my gratitude."*

The Board of Rites was instructed to deliberate upon the case of
the Manchu tutor *Ku Pa-tai* and to submit recommendations
regarding posthumous honours. In the due course of time the
departed tutor was awarded the title, *Wen Tuan*, (Scholarly and
upright), and was given a place in the National Memorial Temple
which was dedicated to honouring those who had served their
country well. [2]

The Emperor also conferred a large sum of money on *Ku Pa-tai's*
needy relations. There was nothing unusual in the honour done
the former Imperial tutor by the Emperor, it was customary and
fully accepted and expected. His position in life was much more
than that of a privileged friend for his post was in no way inferior
to that of say, a viceroy or grand councillor for, even before he set
foot in the palace he would have already passed the gruelling state-
examinations and obtained the 'ruby hat-button' of the first degree
civil and the 'mandarin-square' with the crane which, was enough

to place him above most of his new palace colleagues. Then, attendant on these other honours were bound in the normal course of events to be conferred upon him; the right to wear a sable robe, the single or even the double eye peacock feather and perhaps the right to enter the 'Great Within' carried in a sedan chair. These honours and titles would be retained to the end of his life and posthumously after his death. Automatically he had the right to sit in the Emperors presence when even a senior viceroy had to kneel and if his influence with the Emperor was strong there was no telling what other 'concessions' he might in time add to this already substantial list.

The principal *maxima debetur puero reverentia*, was used by Confucian teachers long before it ever reached a Roman ear.

In 1911 a book titled, *A Chinese Appeal to Christendom Concerning Christian Missions* was published which caused such screams of outrage from the missionary societies of Britian and the United States that little else was discussed. The author of this "wicked" work was a Mr *Lin Shao-yang*, who, when the red-faced clergy had partly calmed down and began to re-read the three hundred pages, was surely better-read that any of their number; there was not a tract, journal, pamphlet or book published during the last fifty years that he had not read! His material was so collated that he was able to rebuff by accurate argument all the hundreds of publications he cited in his long text. Chinese, they knew had a flair for languages and could master both English and French with equal dexterity, but the sheer scope of his learning baffled them. As the flames of righteous indignation subsided the hot coals of concentration continued to puzzle over this serious denunciation of their holy work among the Chinese; "was it perhaps not written by a Chinese after all?" When the truth finally surfaced, as even the best kept secret eventually must, it was even more shocking. The writer was a respected Scotsman holding an official post in the Colonial Office and administering the British territory of *Weihaiwei* in *Shangtung* province.

Reginald Fleming Johnston, the real author of this work that put the "meddling missionaries" in their place in 1911 was, later in life convinced that its publication had destroyed his chances of becoming Governor of Hong Kong, a post he had set his heart on. If that were the case, he had ample reasons for consolation for his diverted path was to take him on a journey that no European had ever made before; he was to become the first English tutor to a reigning *Ch'ing* Emperor in history.

Reginald Fleming Johnston had arrived in Hong Kong as a cadet in 1898, at the age of twenty-four, and knew, from the very first moment, that China was his spiritual home. The gloom of his youth among the methodist mists of parochial Scotland vanished. He discovered in Confucian China the spiritual values that were the true background of his life and he became determined to protect the 'Celestial Kingdom' from the destructive encroachment of Christianity. He made no secret of his pro-Chinese feelings although it won him few friends among the ex-patriots and no doubt caused many a Chinese official to puzzle why this *devil face* should have an attitude so different from his fellows.

When the question of an 'Imperial tutor' was first raised in official British circles, the first choice was an American educationalist, but when he turned the post down, to the undisguised relief of the English, who were quite rightly disturbed at the prospect of an 'American accented' English speaking Manchu Emperor, the post was fortuitously offered to Reginald Johnston, who immediately accepted it.

Some twenty years before, Johnston had met his future pupils father, Prince *Ch'un*, when the Prince had passed through Hong Kong on his way to Germany to make formal apology for the murder of the German minister at the hands of the Boxers. In 1911 during the revolution whilst Johnston was stationed at *Weihaiwei*, Lord *Li*, son of *Li Hung-chang*, took refuge in the concession, both men soon found that they had much in common and became firm friends. When *Hsu Shih-ch'ang* was elected to the presidency of the republic in 1918 he still retained his honorary guardianship of *P'u-yi*, the 'Boy Emperor' and wished to do something for his former sovereign in the field of education. 'The Son of Heaven' should learn English, but who was to teach him? Lord *Li*, who was an old friend of the newly elected president took the opportunity to bring Johnston's name forward recommending him as a fine 'British Confucianist'. The formal request was issued from the office of the President of the Republic, though the British Minister, and the British authorities soon agreed. Johnston was seconded from this official duties at *Weihaiwei* and all was ready, the stage was set for the entry of 'the English tutor' into the world of the *Imperial Purple Forbidden City*.

Inside the 'Great Within' every thing was far from being settled, the proposed appointment of a *devil face* as tutor to the 'Lord of Ten Thousand Years' caused a commotion and strenuous opposition from the conservative members of the Imperial family and the Household Department. They feared, and not without just cause, that this foreigner would influence the impressionable *Hsüan-t'ung* Emperor to adopt too modern an attitude and thus seriously undermine his respect for the traditions of the court, especially its outmoded administration. The President was adamant, and soon persuaded some of the more liberal minded princes, such as *Tsai T'ao*, to accept the idea and thus a compromise was effected. This *devil face* tutor was not to be given any rank or title, after all he was not a graduate of the state examination system, he could not expect to be accordingly honoured; he was to be engaged merely to give English lessons and must on no account aspire to the privileges of other Imperial Tutors, which gave them the right to tender advice on matters of policy. He would be regarded officially as an employee of the Imperial Household Department and would received instructions from the comptroller. The controversy was still raging when Johnston arrived at the gates of the *Forbidden City* to take up his duties, indeed, it was several months after this that he realised the extent of the 'in-fighting' that had been precipitated by his appointment. From the beginning he was treated with Oriental courtesy and consideration, and was soon on friendly terms with both members of the Imperial family, as well as the suspicious officials of the Household Department.

The first time *P'u-yi* had seen foreigners had been at an audience held by the Empress Dowager *Lung-yu* when she had received the wives of the foreign ambassadors, as her illustrious aunt-mother

Tz'u-hsi had. The Boy Emperor was fascinated by their strange clothes and frightened by the colour of their eyes and hair. At this time he had never seen a foreign man but had some idea of what they looked like from the illustrated magazines; he saw that they wore many whiskers on their upper-lip, there was a straight line down the leg of their trousers and always seemed to carry sticks. The eunuchs, who could always be relied upon to embellish a story, told the 'Son of Heaven' that the moustaches of the *devil faces* were so strong and stiff that you could hang large lanterns on the ends of them and they would not bend; their legs were completely stiff and all you had to do when fighting them was to knock them over with the aid of a bamboo pole and they would then be incapable of getting up! The sticks they always carried, the eunuchs told the wide-eyed Emperor, were called, *civilization sticks*, and were used for hitting people to make them more *civilized*. All these eunuch fantasies remained in *P'u-yi's* mind, and when he was informed that he was to have a *foreign devil* tutor he was both alarmed and apprehensive.

The first meeting between teacher and student took place on 4th March 1919 in the *Yu Ching* Palace. Prince *Ch'un* and the Emperor's Chinese tutors introduced him to Mr Reginald Fleming Johnston, the Emperor seated on the Dragon Throne, Johnston moved forward and bowed, then according to protocol when receiving foreign officials, the Boy Emperor rose and hesitantly offered his hand, Johnston took it and shook it firmly, *P'u-yi* was trembling with a mixture of fear and excitement and dared not look directly at his new tutor. Johnston bowed once more, the Emperor bowed to him, the student showing due deference to the teacher. This formal audience concluded, lessons were to begin that very morning in the Imperial class-room. The young Emperor left the throne-room and returned to the school-room carried as usual in an Imperial sedan-chair draped completely in acid-yellow silk. On entering the room he saw Johnston and his own Chinese tutors, they bowed and he returned their honourable courtesy; Johnston was the first to speak and for a moment both the Emperor and his tutors were openmouthed with amazement, Johnston spoke fluent Peking dialect, which the young Emperor later recalled was much easier to understand than either *Chen*

Pao-shen's Fuhkienese or *Chu Yi-fan's* Kiangsi dialect. As he spoke in the proscribed formal way, *P'u-yi* hesitantly looked at him for the first time, he was clean shaven, there were no stripes on his trousers, he had no *civilization stick*, he seemed older than Prince *Ch'un*, but his movements were deft and dignified. His back was so straight that *P'u-yi* was sure that he must wear an iron frame under his clothes, but what almost hypnotized him were Johnston's plae blue eyes, he had never before seen such a colour, they shone so brightly that he was sure that they could look right into his very soul, and it was to be many moons before he got over his uneasiness when every Johnston looked at him.

Johnston's first encounter with the eunuchs resulted in a victory for the canny Scot; he was approached for the customary largesse expected of all newly appointed members of the court, which would be distributed among the eunuchs and thus ensure his future credit in their eyes. It was a large amount but after some astute bargaining he agreed to pay, but only if they would issue him a formal receipt for the proposed sum. The eunuchs somewhat abashed informed him that as it was an unofficial demand, they could not furnish an official receipt, where upon Johnston withdrew his offer to pay and the eunuchs withdrew in confusion, although Johnston was proficient in both 'mandarin' and Cantonese dialects he overheard some words that he could not immediately translate.

The 'incident' with the eunuchs slowly grew into a feud, for about a month later when he was instructing his Imperial student he suddenly turned to *P'u-yi* his face flushing red with anger and pointed to the lone eunuch attendant;

> "I am being treated with great discourtesy by the Household Department." He protested, his usually perfect Chinese become heavily accented with English. "Why, when I am teaching you do I have to put up with a eunuch standing there, when your other tutors do not? I do not like it! I do not like it at all, and I am going to bring the matter up with President of the Republic himself, after all it is he who invited me here." [3]

This was of course the trump card in Johnston's hand for, although he himself was not fully aware of it, his appointment had been accepted at court mainly because the President of the Republic had proposed it and the court was more than desirous of continuing the 'Articles of Favourable Treatment', which naturally meant not upsetting the President in any way. Although Johnston did not fully realize the circumstance, he soon became aware that he had only to threaten taking the matter to the President or even go slightly red in the face for Prince *Ch'un* and the other officials to acquiesce immediately. So it was in the case of the school-room eunuch, he was withdrawn at once.

P'u-yi also realized that Johnston was used to being obeyed and attended to his lessons in a much more diligent manner than with his other tutors; he dared not talk about other things during a lesson nor would he order a holiday when he got bored, as was his custom with the Chinese tutors. When Johnston first entered the *Forbidden City* in 1919 there were four Imperial tutors already in residence, three Chinese and one Manchu. *Liang Ting-fen*, was already a very ill man at this time and Johnston never met him, as this Cantonese tutor died towards the end of that year. According to popular belief Canton and the two Kwang provinces had always been the breeding-ground of revolutionaries; this is far from the truth, for Canton had been the home of many of the staunchest conservatives and most devoted loyalist and monarchists the *Ch'ing* Dynasty had ever had. The Cantonese had acquired a politically bad name because of such rebels as *Hung Hsui-ch'üan* the pseudo-christian leader of the Tiaping uprising and later *Sun Yat-sen* who fathered the still-born republic, but these misguided men were in no way typical of the Cantonese as a whole. It was men such as *Liang Ting-fen* who were indeed typical, *Liang* had obtained his doctorate in the prescribed way by passing the Classical examinations and by 1880 had risen to be chief justice of *Hopie* province. He was an honourable, if somewhat outspoken man, and incured the displeasure of *Tz'u-hsi* for his criticism of some of the Imperial princes and court officials, and had it not been for the timely intervention of his patron and protector *Chang Chih-tung*, a powerful viceroy, *Liang* would doubtless have suffered the severest of penalties. He was suspected of being an active member of the 'Hundred Days' reform movement in 1898, but in fact he was far too conservative to approve of the new liberalising policies which he denounced. The abdication of 1912 caused him great pain and he journeyed to the 'Western Tombs', there prostrated himself before his departed Emperor's tomb, when his pleading with the new Republican officials failed to produce the *Ch'ing* restoration he sought. Subsequently, on the recommendation of *Ch'en Pao-shen*, he was appointed minister in charge of construction of the late Emperor's tomb; some time afterwards, on the death of *Lu Jun-hsiang*, (one of the three Imperial tutors appointed in 1911), *Liang* was appointed to the vacant post.

His poetry, a requisite of all true Chinese scholars, followed in the main the *T'ang* and *Sung* models and two lines written after the fall of the dynasty typify not only his own personal feelings but mirror the almost national sadness and melancholy the passing caused.

Chiang shui pu k'o hao, Wo lei pu k'o kan.

(The water in the river never runs dry, nor do these tears ever cease to flow).

During the summer of 1917 when the restoration rose and fell, an incident occured that illustrates both the courage and loyalty of this great Cantonese scholar. Fierce fighting was taking place in the immediate vicinity of the *Forbidden City* between *Chang Hsun's* troops and *Tuan Ch'i-jui's* republican forces; the appointed hour came for *Liang Ting-fen's* attendance on his Imperial pupil and master. To reach the palace gates he was obliged to travel by pony-carriage through streets thronged with undisciplined soldiers, he refused to stay at home nor to turn back when the danger was pointed out to him; at last he arrived at the gates opposite 'Coal Hill' where he found his official sedan-chair waiting for him as usual, the attendants begged him not to proceed into the palace as the opposing forces were exchanging fire across the courtyards. He seated himself in his chair and gave firm orders to proceed to the *Yu Ching* palace, the bearers obeyed with some reluctance, concerned for their own safety as well as that of the old scholar. They had progressed only a little way when rifle-bullets struck a wall close by them and a shower of plaster and brick fragments covered the chair; the attendants were terrified and again begged the old man to allow them to take shelter; from inside the sedan-chair a voice like thunder answered them: *Pu k'o wu ch'ai shih, pu k'o wu ch'ai shih!* (My duty is not to be neglected, my duty is not to be neglected!). It would have been an unbearable disgrace had the old scholar, through thinking of his own safety, failed to keep his appointment with his Imperial master and pupil. It may be assumed that when he reached the *Yu Ching* palace, little school-work was done that day, but it was not because the Imperial tutor had failed to keep his appointment. At his death the *Hsüang-t'ung* Emperor conferred upon him the posthumous *Wen Chung*, 'Learned and Loyal'.

The senior Imperial tutor was *Ch'en Pao-shen* who was at that time something of a national celebrity.[4] By 1919 he was the proud possessor of a number of honours; *T'ai Pao*, (Grand Guardian of the Heir-apparent) *T'ai Fu*, (Grand Tutor), in this year he was seventy-two years of age and a man of courtly manners, vigorous in both mind and body, a celebrated poet and calligrapher, in all a highly accomplished scholar. Born in *Fuhkien* province he retained much of his native accent throughout his long life, although he prided himself on the precision of his spoken Peking, he was none the less, misunderstood on occasion, not least by his Imperial pupil.

This Confucian scholar became a close friend of the "British Confucian" who had become his fellow Imperial tutor, and in company they visited many of the surrounding beauty spots. One of their favourite haunts was a remote valley in the Western Hills where Johnston had acquired, due to the kindness of President *Hsu*, a small retreat which he named "Cherry Glen", in true Scots fashion. *Ch'en Pao-shen* honoured his first visit to Johnston's fairy-tale retreat by writing a poem which he addressed to him, written in his own fine and gentle calligraphy which Johnston much admired, this was in the full-mooned autumn of 1920.

Chu I-fan was a native of *Kiangsi* province and younger than *Ch'en* by some ten years. Early in his career he had been a member of the Hanlin Academy, in 1904 he became literary Chancellor of

Shensi, in 1906 head of the Education Department of *Shangtung*, and in 1907 a vice-director of the Imperial Clan Court. He had been an Imperial tutor for nearly four years before Reginald Johnston arrived in the *Forbidden City*. His provincial accent was said to make his court mandarin almost unintelligible, it was not only Johnston who experienced difficulty in understanding him. He was severely conservative in outlook and quite frankly expressed a thorough dislike for everything Western, supporting even the most inept of ancient Chinese traditions, which did not endear him to the new "English tutor". His hobby, if hobby it really can be called, was Chinese medicine; although the palace staff included a number of physicians *Chu I-fan* was permitted to combine his function as tutor with those of physician to the young Emperor. Whenever the Emperor was indisposed *Chu I-fan* was always the first to be summoned, *k'an yu mo* (to take the Imperial pulse).

One of *Chu's* less practical theories was that his Imperial pupil should not be encouraged to take strenuous physical exercise; his reason were twofold, one, that it was not seemly that an Emperor's demeanour should be anything but solemn and dignified and two, it was well known that all human beings possessed but a fixed stock of "vital energy" which, once expended could not be replenished. His royal pupil had other notions, and so did Johnston.

The only Manchu among the Imperial tutor was *I K'o-t'an* whose only official task was to make sure that the young Emperor grew up not totally ignorant of his ancestoral native tongue. By all accounts he was of a sociable and genial temperament, very popular within the *City* and "notorious" outside it, especially in the *sing-song* district of *Peking*. Whether his knowledge of the Manchu language was profound or not, is open to question, the lessons seemed to be conducted in a light-hearted way and his pupil seemed to be able to speak and write a little, the depth of his interest can be gauged by the fact that, after *I K'o-t'an's* death in September 1922, lessons in Manchu were suspended in favour of English.

When Reginald Johnston passed throught the Gate of Spiritual Valour on March 3rd 1919 and entered the *Forbidden City*, he entered a world that was old before the foundations of Rome were laid. In one step he passed from the New China of the twentieth century into the Old, behind him lay a city of over a million people full with new hopes and ideals, trying to make their capitol worthy of the great new Republican democracy. In front of him, rising in splendour was the centre of the oldest throne in the world, the *Forbidden City* of the 'Lord of Ten Thousand Years'. Inside the gate, he saw palanquins bearing stately mandarins adorned in their official court robes, ruby and coral hat-buttons appended with shimmering peacock feathers, squares of embroidered silk displaying cranes and golden pheasants applied to their blue-black silk surcoats; high court officials in sable coats; young handsome nobles on horse-back, their magnificent embroidered robes covering both saddle and stirrups; eunuchs, each robed according to his rank, standing motionless; hordes of sula, (servants of the 'Great Within'), waiting in patient readiness to assist the alighting great men and lead them to the throne ante-rooms where they would be served the indispensable and inexhaustible bowls of tea; there officials of the Household would be nervously scrutinizing the lists of those who were to be admitted to Imperial audience. Then, on entering the inner hall of The Mind Nuture Palace, seated on the high Dragon Throne was a boy of thirteen slim and gentle . . . . .the last encumbant of world's oldest throne, 'The Son of Heaven', the *Hsüan-t'ung* Emperor of the Great *Ch'ing* Dynasty. The new Republic could have been a thousand miles, a thousand years away, instead of just a few hundred yards.

Outside the *Forbidden City* the year was 1919, the eighth year of the republic; inside the old lunar calendar was still observed, the year was the eleventh year of the *Hsüan-t'ung* Emperor. The famous old *Peking Gazette*, which was said to have been first issued during the *T'ang* dyansty more than a thousand years ago, continuèd, even after the revolution, to be issued in the *Forbidden City*, though in a much abbreviated form. At this time its circulation was confined to members of the Inner Court, (those who had the right of Imperial audience), and because of the very small numbers, each copy was hand written. This Gazette, which is probably the oldest newspaper in the world, (*Ching Pao* or *Kung-men Ch'ao*), contained important Imperial rescripts and edicts, lists of promotions and degradations, memorials from ministers of state and other information purely of an offficial nature. One or two translations of typical announcements will help to illustrate the nature of this important "Newspaper":

> *The master of ceremonies memorialises that at the Ch'en hour,* (between seven and nine am), *of the 20th day of the eleventh moon, work has commenced on the making of the spirit-tablet of Kung-su Huang-kuei-fei,* (the deceased dowager consort). *He also memorialises that the 24th day of the eleventh moon will be the date of the winter solstice, at which the usual sacrifice to Heaven must take place, and requests instructions. Rescript by his Imperial Majesty: Let the sacrificial ceremonies be performed on Our behalf by Tseng P'ei.*

(This refers to the most important and famous of all court ceremonies, the sacrifice to Heaven which was always carried out by the Emperor himself at the Altar of Heaven. After the revolution it was no longer conducted there, but observed within the *Forbidden City*. It will be recalled that *Yüan Shih-k'ai* usurped this Imperial privilege on the eve of his expected enthronement, albeit in a somewhat debased form).

> *Memorial from the Imperial Household Department. The master of ceremonies having requested a date to be named for the changing of winter hats for cool hats at court, an Imperial edict has been issued ordering that the change be made on the 28th day of the third moon.*
> *24th April 1922*

Even in the twilight of the *Imperial Forbidden City* the great ceremonies were conducted in strict accordance with the rites and usuages the Manchu ruling house had inherited, ritual observances that went back centuries. Apart from the Manchu official costume and the ceremonial utterance of certain words of command in the Manchu language, there was little that would offend the unhappy ghosts of former dynasties if they returned to visit the 'Great Within' of *P'u-yi's* time.

Apart for the purely religious observances, the two most important celebrations to take place within the court were the Emperor's birthday and Chinese New Year; others of a less elaborate nature were observed, on the fifth day of the fifth moon, the so called "Dragon Boat festival", which was and is a misnomer of Western origin, in name at least. The Mid autumn festival held on the fifteenth day of the eighth moon; all dates, as already stated were based on the lunar calendar within the walls of the *Forbidden City*, this 'Chinese' calendar was still adhered to by millions of Chinese throughout the whole of the Middle Kingdom, despite strenuous efforts by the Republicans to suppress this "bad old system". Only once a year did the Manchu court even acknowledge that there was another dating system, on the fall of the Western New Year Day, the Emperor would send formal greetings to the President of the Republic, the compliment would be returned on the Emperor's birthday by an official of the Republic, usually the Master of Ceremonies.

Wan-shou sheng-chieh, (the sacred birthday of the Lord of Ten Thousand Years) was the official court phrase. The main celebration of this Imperial event took place in the throne-hall and adjacent quadrangle of the *Ch'ien Ch'ing Kung*, (The Palace of Cloudless Heaven). Early in that morning the Emperor, or his duly appointed dupty, usually an Imperial Prince, would make a formal announcement of the Imperial birthday to the spirits of the august ancestors in the *Feng Hsien Tien*, (the temple for serving the ancestors). By as early as eight in the morning the court guests, which included princes, ministers, grand councillors and other officials gathered, in full court costume, in the *Mou-ch'in-tien* and various other buildings which flanked the great quadrangle in front of the Palace of Cloudless Heaven. Then the Grand Marshall and a body of court musicians would take up their place on the marble terrace in front of the throne-hall while the waiting official guests were served refreshments.

The crimson-clad musicians performed stately antique ritual music, many of the instruments dated back to the *T'ang* period and included; jade bell-chimes, gongs, drums and sonorous stones. During the fruitless embassy to the *Ch'ien-lung* Emperor in 1793 Earl Macartney described the unearthly and beautiful sounds of this official court music. With the appearance of the state-canopy the guests left their waiting-rooms and arranged themselves in order of rank; Princes of the blood went up to the high terrace; the Imperial tutors in the front of a lower terrace and the others on and back over the quadrangle, this complete, the musicians began a short chant accompanied by sonorous music, the Imperial state-canopy was held up blocking the view into the throne-hall; this was the eagerly awaited moment of *Sheng Tien*, the arrival of the Emperor and his ascent of the Dragon Throne. The Son of Heaven was held as too sacred a being to be gazed upon before he was seated on the throne and the state-canopy hid him from view even from the princes nearest the entrance doors. Immediately he was seated the music changed and the canopy removed, just visible within the dim glowing interior was the 'Lord of Ten Thousand Years' attended by his four eunuchs of the presence and the Household Chamberlain, who remained with him throughout the ceremony.

After a momentary pause, one of the princes on the upper terrace came forward and entered the throne-hall by a side door which was especially opened for him; this was the Emperor's father Prince *Ch'un*; some minutes elapsed and he emerged again, having greeted his Emperor son in the proper manner in accordance with the prescribed rites. During Prince *Ch'un's* private audience he carried the curved sceptre, which many Western writers have wrongly assumed confers some authority on the holder, not so, this is really not a sceptre in the true sense, in Chinese it is called *Ju-i* (the wade romanization, J indicates a retroflex tongued R), it is regarded as a tangible token of respectful greetings and the word *ju-i* means, 'as you wish' or in a non abbreviated sense, 'may happiness, peace and prosperity be yours in abundance'. These beautiful objects are given as formal presents on birthdays, weddings and anniversaries and may never be self-awarded for, if they are, it was believed to act in the very reverse to that intended, bringing bad luck instead of prosperity. The Emperor's father advanced to the steps of the throne dais, bowed and slowly ascended to the throne level, bowed again and with outstretched hands placed the *ju-i* into the Emperor's hands, they exchanged bows, the Emperor resumed his seat and the Prince backed away and finally withdrew without a single word being spoken on either part. Prince *Ch'un* was the only member of the court who was not required to kneel in the Emperor's presence, not because he was the Emperor's father, for technically since his nomination as heir-apparent he was no longer officially the son of Prince *Ch'un* but of the departed *Kuang-hsü* Emperor.

This completed it was now the turn of the other princes to pay their respects, the Grand Marshall gave the Manchu word of command and the princes filed into the throne-hall; then the words rang out *Hsieh En!* All then went to their knees and performed the triple *Kow-tow*, touching their heads to the floor three times three, which was repeated on the command, *Hsieh En!*

The first group of triple-kow-tow was performed in silence, and was a greeting, a reaffirmation of loyalty, whilst the second group was in gratitude for the 'Imperial Bounty' they had, and were hopeful now to receive, for it was the custom of the Emperor to bestow rich gifts on all the princes and higher grade mandarins at all official celebrations, generally these gifts had been delivered to the recipients the day before the ceremony.

So the procession moved slowly forward; next came the Imperial Tutors, the senior officers of the Household Department and then officials of the first two degrees and ranks, those graded from three to nine were confined to the quadrangle outside. Many at this time were old officials who had held office under the *Ch'ing*, and had refused to serve the new Republic, and who had journeyed from distant provinces to greet their Emperor. Their court robes were, in many cases old and a little the worse for wear but they stood proudly before their sovereign even though their rank and costume had been abolished by the 'modernising' Republic, who had, in so many instances, foolishly dispensed with the old ways, but failed to replace them with anything half so ordered or beautiful.

As J O P Bland stated in his 'China, Japan and Korea'; *"For a little while these men who call themselves republicans may be content to see earth's most beautiful song without words, the Temple of Heaven, abandoned to sordid uses of neglect; they may see fit to wear frock-coats and top hats, instead of the most dignified and decorative garments ever devised by man; but surely before long, they, or others in their place, will be compelled to restore the ancient faith, the ancient ways."*

Reginald Johnston was one of the 'frock-coated top-hated' modern men at some of the great ceremonies at this time, surrounded by a sea of dancing peacock plumes, washed with rustling silk robes. Both the young Emperor's birthday and the New Year festivities took place in the cold raw wind of *Peking* winter and those officials who had been awarded them, wore the court sable coat and fur-trimmed hat whilst, others not so lucky were known to underdress with many layers of soft Chinese cotton completed by an unofficial fur lining to their surcoat, *(p'u-fu)*. The main reason for both republicans and Westerners wearing European morning dress was politically expedient; it precluded them for performing the *kowtow* although Johnston frankly acknowledged his willingness to do so; this ceremonial bowing was in no way a humiliation despite the inflexible Western view to the contrary, the *kowtow* was merely an accepted act of obeisance. After Johnston had been awarded full Imperial tutor status and was recognized as *Ti Shih*, (Imperial tutor), he was awarded the right to enter the *Forbidden City* in a two-bearer sedan chair, which was provided for him by the palace authorities. Just a few months after this he was invested with the 'sable robe' and raised to the second degree civil, with all the attendant rights and privileges, and in 1922 he was elevated to the first grade, (ruby hat button and crane insignia 'Mandarin Square'). The eunuchs, whom the 'canny Scot' had severely ruffled on his arrival in the 'Great Within', still haboured both dislike and mistrust for the *devil face* tutor and a story was spread about that Johnston, who had been so delighted at his elevation to the mandarinate, could not wait to try on his official robes, persuaded some official of the Household Department to let him into the Imperial costume store, there, when alone he dressed up, trying on this robe and that hat until when at last the doors were flung open by two high officials, there was the 'Imperial English Tutor' dressed in the costume of *Kwan-yin*, Goddess of Mercy; the two astonished officials were in a severe state of shock and *kowtowed* their way out as quickly as possible for, what Johnston did not the realize was that the costume he wore had been a favourite of the late Grand Dowager Empress *Tz'u-hsi*, and although the present apparition had piercing blue eyes they were convinced that it was the ghost of the *Old Buddha*, returned from the spirit-world. Whether this was a true story or more likely a malicious concoction of the revengeful eunuchs, it earned him the nick-name of the *Old Foreign Buddha* among the lower orders of the palace staff.

In addition to honours, gifts were bestowed from time to time on all officials, including the Imperial tutors; these took the form of jade, books, pictures, works of art and 'red-packets', for which the formal thanks expressed at audience would be *hsieh en*. A typical report of such an incident as the arrival of gift-bearing messengers appeared in the *Peking Shih Pao*, and translated reads:

> *"It is reported that Chin Kuei-fei,* (sister of the murdered Chen-fei, 'Pearl Concubine') *of the Ch'ing House, fearing that the English Imperial Tutor Johnston may, by his labours in the Yu Ching palace lose the natural moisture of his throat, has bestowed upon him a special present of several pounds of Chinese and foreign ginseng. This is indeed a mark of exceptional favour."*

Even after Johnston had been made a mandarin and wore his official robes in the presence of his pupil-Emperor, he was restrained from performing the *kowtow*. Until the real end of the *Ch'ing* Dynasty in 1924 Johnston alone, was the only Westerner ever to be allowed to witness and attend the great Imperial ceremonies, the Household Department was completely opposed to the admission of strangers, foreign or Chinese, at any time but particularly on these important ceremonial occasions. Johnston, who had by this time, been in Asia for over twenty years had become more Chinese than the Chinese themselves; he was exceedingly well versed in all aspects of Chinese culture and was a true connoisseur of classical Chinese poetry;

Reginald Johnston dressed as a Ch'ing official
of the first degree. 1922.

> "I used to see him wagging his head as he chanted the T'ang poems, just like a true Chinese scholar, his voice rising and falling and always pausing correctly" [5]

Slowly a close and intimate relationship formed between Johnston and his Imperial pupil, *P'u-yi* began to sense Johnston's sincere love of all things Chinese and warmed to the flame of his tutors kindness. Johnston's behaviour too, was slowly becoming less formal, and it soon became apparent that they enjoyed each other's company. During the English lessons, Johnston would bring the young Emperor Western books and magazines, explain all they contained, and answer the hundreds of questions his eager pupil asked. Once he brought a tin box of fruit-flavoured Western sweets, *P'u-yi* was delighted and eagerly opened the silver inner wrapper; Johnston then told him that the flavours were produced by various chemicals and made by machine, the boy was confused, a machine that made fruit-sweet? How could that be? However his interest soon turned to his 'Imperial ants', which lived in the cypress tree just outside, he decided to see if they liked these strange chemical-machine sweets and before Johnston could protest, he had disappeared, returning much later informing his indulgent tutor that the ants seemed very pleased with the 'foreign sweets', the tin of which Johnston was still patiently holding.

> "I gradually came to realize how diligently Johnston was trying to teach me and I was very pleased and so became much more willing and obedient. He did not just teach me the English language for, in his eyes it was even more important to train me along the lines of 'the true English gentleman' he so often spoke about . . . . .When I was fourteen, I decided that I would like to dress in Western clothes like him, so, I sent some of my eunuchs out into the 'outside' city to buy me a large amount of Western clothing and waited impatiently for their return. At last they arrived and I tried on a number of garments which were all to big for me, at last I settled on one outfit and glowing with pride went along to the school-room. As I entered the room Johnston, who was reading, looked up, I shall always remember the look on his face which slowly went crimson

with anger; I must have looked a peculiar sight to him, my tie hanging outside my collar like a length of limp rope and my baggy trousers and jacket and a hat three sizes too large for me. Johnstone rose, quivering with anger and ordered me to go at once and take those 'dreadful' clothes, I obeyed him at once, even though I was the Emperor.

Next day I was rather nervous about facing him in the school-room he looked at me sternly and then said, 'It is far better to wear your Manchu robes than ill-fitting Western attire . . . . If you wear clothes from a second-hand Peking shop you will never be a true English gentleman, you'll be . . . . 'what I would be he never said as just then the tailor he had summoned from the outer city was announced and Johnston told me smiling that if I wanted to wear Western clothing so badly I might as well have the very best tailor-made garments and instructed the trembling tailor just what was required.

'If Your Majesty ever appears in London there is little doubt that you will be invited to tea very often. Tea parties are informal but important occasions and usually take place on Wednesday. At them one can meet all sorts of desirable people, peers, scholars, celebreties and just the sort of people that Your Majesty will need to meet. There is no need to be overdressed on such occasions but manners are very important. It is not done to drink tea as if it were water or to eat cakes as if they were a real meal, or make too much noise with your fork or tea-spoon. In England tea and cakes are 'refreshment', not a meal.' " [6]

P'u-yi listened attentively to all that his tutor said, he devoured mounds of magazines, making careful note of anything that should take his fancy and then dispatching the somewhat confused eunuchs to the 'outer' city to purchase them. He ordered the Household Department to buy foreign furniture and a polished wooden floor to be laid in the largest room in his private apartments; soon the whole place was a hotch-potch, neither wholly Chinese nor wholly Western and although Johnston's enthusiasm was noticeably restrained, his young Imperial pupil was in a cloud of delight. In imitation of his tutor he acquired all manner of Western trinkets to hang about himself; watches and chains, rings, tie-pins, cuff-links, boxes of silk neck-ties, the list was endless and it was no easy matter to persuade the delighted *P'u-yi* that a watch chain was not usually hung around the neck nor was it customary to almost cover a golfing cap with tie-pins.

> "I thought that everything about Johnston was 'first-class' and even went so far as to regard the smell of moth-balls that always came from his clothes as fragrant. He made me feel that Westerners were the most intelligent and civilized people in the world and I thought him the most kind and learned. I do not think that even he realized how deep an influence he was having on me. The beautiful woolen cloth of his suits made me doubt the value of all the silks and satins in China and the gold fountain-pen in his pocket actually made me ashamed of writing with brushes, his cream note-paper I thought far finer than our hand-made Chinese paper. . . . . Once he arranged for a British military band to come to the palace and play for us, I was so excited I almost cried and thereafter considered Chinese music hardly worth listening to, even the ancient and stately ceremonial music seem far less majestic. . . . . Once Johnston remarked that the English word for the Chinese queues was 'pigs tails'; I was horrified and shocked and within the hour had cut mine off!" [7]

This last remnant of Manchu 'domination', the queue had been the subject of many letters from the Home Ministry of the Republic since 1913 and the Household Department had been politely dodging the issue ever since. Now, within just a few days of Johnston mentioning 'Pigs tails', quite in passing, almost everyone else followed the Emperors example and over a thousand queues disappeared, only a few high officials on the Household Department and the old tutors retaining theirs. This in no way added to the 'English' tutors popularity at court, the eunuchs were right, he was the *Old Foreign Buddha*, and was starting to exercise almost as much power, but there was more to come.

At this time the payments formally promised to the *Ch'ing* court under the 'Articles of Favourable Treatment' were always at least a year in arrears. In order to meet the expenses in maintaining the *Forbidden City* the Household Department was obliged to either sell or pawn antiques, paintings, silver, porcelain and indeed anything else that would keep the inhabitants of the "twilight City" solvent. The Great Household Department was, even in these hard times, lining its own pockets out of the proceeds of such sales, only a fraction of the purchase price ever reached the privy purse. Johnston was well aware of the massive corruption taking place, and the Household Department was aware, that he was aware. Both watched the other, waiting for a slip that could be taken advantage of. Johnston had already intimated to the Emperor that there was something "fishy" about this wholesaling of Imperial antiques. The works of art made of gold and silver were being sold on the open market in *Peking* for just their metal value, and in many cases realized even less than this scrap metal value. Johnston was seriously concerned and remarked to *P'u-yi* that this must, stop for only a "fool" would act like this. Some days later the Emperor was approached by officials of the corrupt department for permission to sell a gold pagoda, which was some six feet tall and encrusted with precious stones, when they told the young Emperor that they intended selling it according to its weight he, remembering Johnston's words, burst into a fury:

> "Are you all fools? Have you not one ounce of sense amongst you? Never dare to ask me such a thing again!" [8]

The crafty officials were temporarily taken-aback and retired in bowing confusion but, on reflection they soon realized that it was Johnston's doing, and they determined to settle with this meddling foreigner. Having been refused by the Emperor, they decided to implicate Johnston in their plot to dispose of the gold pagoda, and with some difficulty had it secreted in his apartments, and intended to inform the Emperor that Johnston had agreed to sell it for them, in return for his 'usual' commission. Fortunately for Johnston, and most unfortunately for the Household officials, he walked in and caught them red-handed with the gold pagoda in his apartments. He glared at them, then slowly walked towards them, in a voice that was more a hiss than a whisper said, "If you do not take that away immediately I shall summon his Majesty and have you all flogged." He stood commandingly before them never taking his bright blue eyes from them for a second, there was a cold silence, then, without a word they took up their weighty burden and departed, but, there was little doubt that both parties were now openly at war.

The special relationship that existed between pupil and master in China has already been discussed and this relationship now existed between *P'u-yi* and Johnston.

> "By the last year of my study in the Yu Ching palace, Johnston had become the major part of my soul." [9]

Both were charmed by the others company, their formal lessons together soon became informal relaxed conversations, Johnston even admitted much later that during the five years of English studies, his pupil never became anything like proficient in the language. They were always in each others company, talking and laughing, even making plans for the future, for it was the cherished wish of both that the young Emperor should study in England, and that Johnston should naturally accompany him. This caused alarm and despondency in the court who knew that if "the tree fell, the monkeys would be scattered", what would they do? Where would they go? Who then would fill their rice bowls?

> "Our time together was spent more and more in extra-curricular topics . . . . .He told me about the life of the English Royal family, the politics of different countries, ... about the Great British Empire on which the sun never sets, ...the possibility of an eventual restoration and the unreliable attitudes of the war-lords . . . .
> 'One can see clearly from all the papers', he once said to me, 'that the Chinese people are thinking about the Great Ch'ing and that everybody is bored with the Republic. I do not think that there is any need for Your Majesty to worry about those military men; nor need you take much trouble in trying to assess their attitude from the papers; . . . . .Tutor Chen

is quite right in saying that the most important thing is for Your Majesty daily to renew your scholarly virtue but, this cannot be accomplished within the Forbidden City alone. You can acquire much more essential knowledge and widen your horizons in Europe, especially at Oxford University, which is in the land of His Majesty the King of England where the Prince of Wales studied . . . . ' " [10]

During this time Johnston did everything in his power to widen his pupil's horizons; he brought high British officials to meet the Emperor, admirals, generals, even the Governor of Hong Kong and *P'u-yi* was much impressed by their manners and respectfulness. He became intoxicated with the European way of life and began to copy Johnston in everything, which caused the 'canny Scot' much embarrassment on occasions, and always resulted in a 'correction' session for the submissive and outwardly repentant *P'u-yi.*

"On the subject of clothes for example, our opinions differed, even though he had a 'special' interest in me." [11]

It was during this time, when Johnston was in his second year as Imperial tutor, (1920), that he put forward the suggestion that his lone Imperial pupil should have a companion in the classroom, this was considered quite acceptable as it was already an established practice to have a *pan-tu* (reading-companion, or friend) present during lessons. What did cause a minor tremor was the boy Johnston chose, *P'u-chia* the eldest son of one of the Emperor's uncles, Prince *Tsai-tao*. Quite unknown to Johnston at this time was the enmity existing between Prince *Tsai-tao* and his brother the ex-regent and father of the Emperor, Prince *Ch'un*. However the matter was soon settled by the selection of a second *pan-tu*, *P'u-yi's* younger brother *P'u-chieh*.

Also at this time *P'u-yi* asked Johnston to select English names for himself and his brothers and sisters. Johnston was not at all sure that this was a good idea, but his affectionate pupil soon whittled away his objections. From the list of English royal names *P'u-yi* chose Henry, *P'u-chieh*, William, *P'u-chia*, Arthur and the Emperor's third sister Lily, and so on. *P'u-yi* was delighted and with some pride even imitated Johnston's way of speaking, which was a mixture of Chinese and English when addressing his class-mates:

" *'William* sharpen this *pencil* for me. . . . . . .*good*, put it on the *desk. Arthur*, tell *Lily* and the others to come around this *afternoon* to hear some foreign military music on my *gramophone.*' Just then Chen Pao-shen came in and heard this Westernized conversation and 'Screwed his face up as if he was suffering from toothache.' " [12]

This christian name of Henry has been misused by journalists and writers over the years, referring to *Henry P'u-yi*, which Johnston never intended; "There was never any intention that 'Henry' should be used along with *P'u-yi*." [13]

The whole question of English names was intended only as a classroom prank, and if Johnston was dismayed at its widespread use, then he must have been severely shocked at its subsequent reoccurance in journalistic parlance in later years.

"My relations with my pupil were friendly and harmonious from the first, and became increasingly so as time went on. The qualities that I found most attractive in him, were his general intelligence, his frankness, his eager interest in the affairs not only of China, but of the world, his impulsive generousity, his artistic gifts, the lack of any indication of vindictiveness or ill-will against those who had wronged him or had been enemies of his house, his kindness and sympathy with suffering, his courage in the face of grave physical danger, and his keen sense of humour. . . . . . .His proficiency in Chinese calligraphy, however, gave him an interest in penmanship, and he soon wrote English in a well formed hand that many an English schoolboy of his age might envy . . . . .he had an active and intelligent mind, but had a frivolous as well as serious side to his nature . . . . When he had grown out of childhood I used to discuss this matter with him very frankly. I often told him that there were within him, 'two Emperors, not one', and that he would never be able to do justice to himself and to his ancestors unless the better of the two Imperial personages succeeded in reducing the other to a permanent state of obedient vassalage .... He invariably took my criticism of his character and my admonitions very good-humouredly, even if they did not always have the desired effect. Indeed the patience and good temper with which he listened to my complaints, and the complete lack of any sign of resentment, were among the most conspicuous and charming of his characteristics. I was often told by my Chinese colleagues, however, that he was not equally submissive and receptive with them; and as it gradually came to be recognised in the palace that the Emperor would listen more patiently to his 'English Tutor' than to anyone else, I was repeatedly appealed to, not only by his Chinese tutors, but also by his father and uncles to make representations and suggestions to him which they themselves despaired of doing with any hope of success." [14]

The wise old Chinese tutor *Ch'en Pao-shen*, described the frivolous side of the young Emperor character as *fou*, which strictly means, to float, to drift; volatile; unsteady, and it was this bubbling side of *P'u-yi's* nature that Johnston tried, albeit, without success, to rechannel. It was obvious that the *fou* side of his character was a direct inheritance from his day-dreaming father Prince *Ch'un* whilst, the undoubted intellectual ability he possessed came from his mother who, was the daughter of *Jung-lu* the great Manchu Viceroy.

Once when Johnston was attempting to illustrate the difference between an absolute and constitutional monarchy, he put forward, as an example, the case of a ruler who wielded such immense power that he could indulge his whims by ordering the execution of any of his subjects he wished, or perhaps delegate this awesome power over life and death to a favoured minister;

> "Then," remarked the Emperor, "all my predecessors must have been irresponsible despots!" [15]

Johnston, not unnaturally was somewhat flustered by this telling reply, and quickly changed the subject, *P'u-yi*, exercising great

151

self-control managed, just, to hold back the waves of impish laughter that were welling up within him. However, although Johnston might have quickly forgotten the incident his Imperial pupil did not; some days later whilst Johnston was sitting reading in his cloistered garden, a servant announced that there was a palace eunuch with an important message from the Emperor which had to be delivered in person. The eunuch was duly admitted and formally handed Johnston a gleaming object which, on examination turned out to be a sword-stick.

> "This sword" intoned the eunuch, "is from *Wan-sui-yeh*, (The Lord of Ten Thousand Years), and he has ordered me to say, he confers upon you the privilege of killing anyone you like. . . . . *sui pien sha jen*." [16]

The eunuch withdrew with just the hint of a smile on his lips, and Johnston sat holding the Imperial gift slowly realizing that *P'u-yi's* impish sense of humour was paying him back for his absolute, if hardly constitutional blunder. He smiled, rose to his feet and unsheathed the blade and made a few thrusts at an imaginary victim, who now he could dispose of with complete impunity, his servant, who was just then bringing tea into the garden, saw this blood-thirsty display, shrieked, dropped the tray and fled, Johnston's laughter reverberated around the tiny garden, how he loved the Emperor, how he loved China, and as he turned from the garden into the house he was chuckling still.

Once, in the school-room, Johnston noticed his Imperial pupil turning around to tell the time from the large wall clock, rather than the small table-clock in front of him, Johnston enquired why, and received the answer that the small timepiece was just a blur. *P'u-yi* had been suffering from headaches for some time past and now Johnston realized why, he immediately brought the matter to the Household Departments attention and offered to bring in a competent Western oculist. A storm of outraged protest was the only result, "a foreign doctor meddling with the eyes of the Son of Heaven? The Lord of Ten Thousand Years wearing glasses!" This 'English Tutor' had gone too far, his *devil face* ways had been tolerated long enough, it was not his place to dictate to the Imperial court! Johnston stood his ground, the Emperor's eyes were 'ill', did they not understand? If they thought that he would neglect his duty in any way, then, they had seriously underestimated him! If they did not follow his advice, then he would have no other choice but to resign. At this, the court could hardly conceal its delight, at last they would be rid of the *Old Foreign Buddha*; but when the Emperor declared that he would never let Johnston go and that he intended to see the foreign doctor no matter what any of them said. Prince *Ch'un*, finding the water deeper than he had bargained for, withdrew and sulked for days over his lack of influence with his own son. The oculist diagnosed severe myopia and forthwith prescribed glasses. *P'u-yi* now enjoyed clear vision for the first time he could remember, and never missed an opportunity of showing-off his new spectacles to the disdainful court who feigned not to notice them.

This incident, in company with others, demonstrated the Emperor's restless, and sometimes to them, his rebellious spirit, precipitated the question of his marriage, after all he was sixteen years of age in early 1922 and it was, according to traditional law time for him to take an Empress. Not that this choice need necessarily concern him, for by Chinese law the consent of the parties was not necessary as long as the senior member of the families agreed. Johnston, when informed, was gruff and non-commital, "there is plenty of time for a lad of sixteen to think about marriage." The Emperor himself left no-one in any doubt that he was completely against any such arrangement and gave his Imperial family a severe telling-off if they even mentioned it. True it was a usual adjunct to coming of age, which meant that he could at last tell others what to do instead of being dictated to, that was quite acceptable, but take a wife, a woman he had possibly never met and share his apartments with her? He was horrified at the very idea and told Johnston as much, did he really have to participate in these, *Grand Nuptials*, as the Household Department called them?

P'u-yi and his Empress Wan-jung at the time of
their wedding in 1922.
Their Dragon-Feng-huang bridal bed.

CHAPTER SIX

The Reluctant Bridegroom

On 11th March 1922, the Peking Court Gazette contained the following breif announcement: *"Jung-yuan chih nu kuo chia shih li wei huang-hou"*; (*kuo chia*, daughter of *Jung-yuan*, is hereby created Empress). Nothing more, not even the inclusion of the customary auspicious salutations.

This has led Westerns to assume that the wedding had already taken place, not so; one curious feature of Chinese Imperial law made it necessary for the elevation of the young woman to Imperial rank before her actual marriage, this notice in the court gazette was all that was needed to achieve this. Months could elapse, (as in this case) before the 'grand nuptials' took place. What was interesting, was the behind the scenes manoeuvring that had culminated in this particular choice.

The court quarrels started as soon as the subject of the Emperor's marriage was brought forward; each of the consorts wanted her particular favourite to be the future 'Empress'; then Prince *Ch'un* and the other Imperial clansmen put forward their candidates, the resulting chaos continued for some time, rendering the 'Great Within' a bridal battleground. All this time *P'u-yi* and Johnston were occupied with their own thoughts and the usual lessons. According to Manchu Dynastic law the choice had to be a Manchu girl, although there was a great deal of chatter about the inclusion of one or two Chinese hopefuls, whose selection would do much to politically unite the two, now almost indistinguishable races. However, traditionalism prevailed and *P'u-yi* was sent photographs of the Manchu maidens who had at last been short-listed to four, and was told to mark the photograph of his intended 'Empress'. He took the whole thing rather lightly, rather like a game, none of them were beauties; "To me, the girls seemed much the same, their bodies looked as shapeless as tubes in their dresses." [1]

Their faces were small and *P'u-yi* could not discern beauty in any of them, the only difference he could make out between them were their clothes! Becoming bored with the obligatory choice he casually drew a circle around what he considered to be the prettiest face and handed the photograph to his eunuch attendant and went back to his book. The Dowagers, on receiving the Imperial decision were perturbed to say the least; how had this girl's photograph been included in the first palce? Her family was too poor to merit any real distinction and she herself, (*Wen-hsiu*), was hardly 'Empress' material, no, the Emperor must choose again. So, the whole tedious process was repeated, much to the clearly expressed annoyance of the Emperor. This time whether by good fortune or stage-management his choice fell on the Lady *Wan-jung* a mongol by descent and coming from a family of good standing, long resident in China. Then the behind the scenes wrangling started in earnest, the Emperor's first choice must be the new 'Empress' and his second a consort. *P'u-yi* was furious, he had not felt the need for one wife, now he protested that he certainly did not need two! In that same issue of the Peking Gazette that had proclaimed the appointment of an 'Empress' there was also an announcement of a 'secondary consort', (*Shu fei*) whose personal name was *E-erh-te-t'e*, the daughter of *Tuan kung*, who had held the rank under the dynasty of Expectant District Magistrate. All this time the Peking press had been indulging in a spirited 'guessing-game' which daily put forward its favourite candidate and, when the official announcement came were sorely disappointed as neither Empress nor consort were Chinese, as many Chinese loyalists had hoped.

The next spate of official announcements appertaining to the forthcoming double Imperial wedding appeared on March 14th. They related that *Jung-yuan* had been graciously granted Imperial audience to return thanks to the Emperor for the elevation of his daughter to Imperial dignity. At this time several marks of Imperial favour were bestowed on the *hou-fu*, father of the Empress. He received the ruby hat button of the first degree, became an officer of the Imperial bodyguard, was granted the right of riding on horseback in the *Forbidden City*, together with the right of access to the Imperial presence.

Some little time after he was made, *Nei Wu Fu Da-ch'en*, (a minister of the Imperial Household Department) and was finally raised to the rank of Duke. The prospect of having to share his privacy with not one, but two unknown females, (for both Manchu and Chinese custom, not to mention Court etiquette, made it impossible for him to meet either before the wedding), did little to tranquilize the Emperor's already restless spirit. He finally acquiesced to his betrothal, that, he felt was concession enough, and expressed no enthusiasm at the prosepct. But, what really threw the court into shocked confusion, especially the Imperial Dowagers, was the Emperor's vehement protest against being provided with more than one unwelcome fianceé. It was pointed out to him that according to immemorial precedent there should in fact be not just one *fei* but several, and he was already breaking this custom. Civilized monarchs in the West did not practice polygamy and he saw no reason why the Manchu Court should countenance the 'evil' practice either! It was this point that caused much tearful protest and the most tearful and most protesting of the Dowagers was undoubtedly the only surviving consort of the *T'ung-chih* Emperor, *Ching-yi T'ai Fei*.

Through most of this 'family' wrangling Johnston had kept quietly in the background, consoling his indignant pupil and trying to put the best complexion on what must be. It was he who was blamed by the sorrowing Dowagers for the Emperor's horrifying monogamic principals, and the Peking press, both foreign and Chinese, accused him of trying to turn the young Emperor into an "English Dandy", in reply he made the following repudiation: "The only opinion I expressed at court, or in conversation with the Emperor, on any aspect of the matrimonial project was that as he was only a boy of sixteen, the question of his marriage was one which might advantageously be discussed at a later date." [2]

The Emperor's betrothal accordingly took place in March and occupied little of either Johnston's or *P'u-yi* attention during the following weeks, principally because of an incident that took place in June. Johnston wrote a letter to an English-speaking ex-official on 8th June 1922 which explains the details, and is here reproduced in an edited version:

Dear . . . .

During the recent dragon-boat festival holidays, I was absent from Peking and did not return till the morning of the 3rd. On reaching home I heard of the sudden resignation and departure of president Hsu, which had taken place the day before. In the course of the morning, his Majesty, having learned by telephone of my return, sent me by confidential messenger a pencilled Chinese note asking me to go and see him in his private quarters in the palace at 3 o'clock. He also directed me to have two motor-cars waiting outside the Tung-hua Gate at the same hour, but did not state his reasons for this order. Finally, he desired me to treat his note as strictly secret, so far as the Imperial household and his other tutors were concerned.

I went to the palace in my own car at the time appointed, and ordered a second car from a public garage . . . . . . I found his Majesty awaiting me in the Yang-hsin-tien. No third person was present during the interview. It lasted over an hour, and was one of the most trying experiences of the kind I have ever gone through. The first point of importance was that his Majesty wished me to take him at once to the British Legation. He had made up his mind so definitely on this subject that he was unwilling, at first, even to discuss it with me. This explained his instructions as to the motor-cars. He and I were to go together in one car, and a few of his personal attendants were to follow in the other. His Majesty went on to say that as soon as he arrived at the Legation he intended to issue a telegram to the people of China, stating that he was ashamed to remain in the position of an idle pensioner of the State, and wished to surrendered not only the $4,000,000 a year which the Republican Government undertook to pay him as the price of abdication, but also to renounce his Imperial title and all rights pertaining thereto, including the privilege of occupying the Imperial palaces. After despatching this telegram, he proposed to make immediate arrangements to visit Europe, and would trespass upon the hospitality of the British Minister only until the necessary arrangements for the foreign tour should be completed.

I should explain that this resolve on His Majesty's part was only intensified, not caused, by recent political developments. As I have already informed you, he and I have often, during the past year or two, discussed the question of his position with regard to the republican government, and he has come to realise, more and more vividly, the anomalous and humiliating nature of his present circumstances. Even if there had been no upheaval in Peking politics, he would not have remained quiescent much longer. He is no longer a child. He has arrived at an age when he is perfectly well able to form opinions of his own, and having come to the definite belief that there is something fundamentally wrong about his present position, he will not rest until he has had it changed . . . . I pointed out that His Majesty was probably wrong in assuming that the British Legation would, on this occasion, receive him as a guest. It is quite true that when civil war broke out a short time ago and there was a possibility of serious disorders in Peking, the British Minister, on my representations, was good enough to promise that, if His Majesty were threatened by personal danger, quarters would be found for him within the British Legation. But the present circumstances were quite different. No actual danger threatened the Emperor's person, and the grounds upon which Sir Beilby Alston had agreed to grant him British protection no longer existed. It was His Majesty's frankly avowed purpose to use the British Legation as a place from which, without interference from the Imperial familya nd the palace officials, he could draft his telegram to the nation and make preparations to leave the country. Such being the case, it seemed to me practically certain that Sir Beilby Alston would find it impossible to offer His Majesty the hospitality of the British Legation. Even if he were personally willing to do so, it seemed to me highly improbable that the British Government would allow itself to be involved in action which might easily be construed, however unjustly, into an unwarrantable interference in China's internal concerns. I offered to settle the question at once by going to the Legation and laying the matter before the Minister, and pointed out that I could easily bring back his reply within an hour. This, however, proved to be unnecessary, as His Majesty very reluctantly agreed, in deference to my views, to postpone all action for the present . . . .

In the first place, let me point out that the Emperor is intelligent and thoughtful, and is an omnivorous reader of newspapers of all shades of political opinion. He knows more about the present condition of China than many well-read adults, and is under no delusions whatever about his own position. He now knows far more about political and social conditions in Western countries than his Chinese tutors, whose learning is confined to the history and literature of their own country, and he is able to make comparisons which to them are impossible. He has a thorough grasp of the history of his own dynasty and of the various causes that contributed to its fall . . . . .During all the years of his childhood he naturally accepted things as they came, and it never occurred to him to question the wisdom of those who were responsible for the sordid bargaining which took place between the prince regent or his advisers and the revolutionary leaders at the time of the establishment of the so-called republic in 1912. During the last three years, however, as I can testify from my own knowledge, His Majesty has come to feel more and more vividly the shame of taking an enormous subsidy from the State in return for no services whatever. The fact that there are at present large unpaid arrears does not affect the principle . . . .

A second reason for urgency, from the Emperor's point of view, is His Majesty's growing disgust with the corruption which he knows is rife throughout the palace. He has himself spoken to me with intense irritation of the malpractices of persons whom I prefer not to name even in a letter to you; of cases of unblushing robbery, bribery and falsification of accounts, of thefts of palace treasures and the division of the spoils among high and low. He has told me with horror of how the eunuchs attached to the palace of Chuang Ho, the Imperial consort who died last year, struggled with one another for the treasures stolen from the very chamber in which the deceased princess lay in state; with even greater indignation he has told me of how, when he wished to make and example of these ruffians, he had to stay his hand owing to the solid wall of opposition raised against him by princes, ministers and, of course, the whole fraternity of eunuchs. Is it any wonder that His Majesty's desire to renounce his title and subsidy is intensified rather than diminished by his knowledge of the fact that the renunciation would necessarily involve the collapse of this system of organised roguery? Naturally, the members of the Imperial household would not contemplate with equanimity the loss of all their lucrative opportunities, and it is by no means improbable that if they knew of the Emperor's intentions they would devise some means of forcibly preventing him from carrying them out. It is perhaps a vague knowledge of this that suggested to His Majesty the advisability of seeking a temporary home outside the Forbidden City as a preliminary to the issue of his proposed telegram of renunciation. However that may be, it need cause no surprise that His Majesty feels under no obligation to cling to his subsidy for the sake of those who now have the spending of all but the small fraction of it that suffices for his personal requirements. That he himself should be supported in return for no services, at the expense of his suffering and almost bankrupt country, is humiliating enough; but the humiliation is many times intensified by the knowledge that by far the greater part of the subsidy goes to support a huge staff of unnecessary and more or less worthless parasites.

The treaty with the republic which is still in force, and which His Majesty hopes to abrogate, provides *inter alia* for payment to the Imperial family of an annual subsidy of $4,000,000.

Obviously, this sum was vastly in excess of the amount actually needed to support in comfort and dignity the abdicated Emperor and the few remaining princesses and ladies of the Court. For that modest purpose, indeed, no subsidy from the republic was necessary at all, as the movable and landed property of the Imperial family was in itself far more than sufficient for such needs. That property has, of course, been disgracefully mismanaged and pillaged during the past dozen years; but, whatever may be its extent and value today, there is no doubt that in 1912 it could, under competent and honest management, have been made to yield a revenue which would have placed the Emperor and those properly dependent on him far above the reach of poverty. His Majesty holds the view, which is fully shared by me, that the real object of the promoters of the treaty on the royalist side was not to safeguard the welfare of the Emperor and the Imperial family, but to provide for the indefinite maintenance in idleness and luxury of the hordes of court officials, eunuchs and hangers-on of every description, who would have been appalled at the prospect of having to go out into the world and earn their own livings, and whose one desire was to save for themselves as much as they could from the wreck of the monarchy. The impression I have gained from my three years' experience in the Forbidden City is that the real welfare of the Emperor was not taken into consideration at all, and that his true interests have never been consulted from that day to this . . . . .I have now given two of the main reasons why the Emperor regards this proposed renunciation of title and subsidy as a matter of urgency . . . .

The third main reason for urgency is the possibility or likelihood of the revival in the near future of the so-called old parliament, or some similar assembly representative of the extreme republicans. In any such assembly there will probably be many who will favour a drastic revision of the terms of the treaty with the monarchy. If this parliament settles down to regular work it is more than likely that the question of the future treatment of the Imperial house will be brought up for discussion . . . . It would distress him very deeply if his voluntary act of renunciation were interpreted by the people not as the outcome of his own determination to do what was right, but as the result of a mere desire to "save face" by anticipating the coercive action of parliament.

In addition to the three principal reasons I have given for the Emperor's desire to have this matter settled quickly, I may mention a fourth, which is mine rather than his, and which might be regarded as comparatively unimportant by those who have never seen the inside of the Forbidden City and know nothing of the mode of life of its inmates. To my mind, however, this reason would of itself justify the Emperor's immediate renunciation of his useless and cumbersome privileges. I allude to the physical and moral unhealthiness of his present surroundings . . . . Chen Pao-shen, his senior Chinese tutor, tries to console him with the reflection that all the Emperors of the dyansty have had to lead lives of rigid isolation, and reminds him that they were all subjected to various limitations on their freedom of action and bound by innumerable irksome conventions. The obvious answer to this is that his Imperial predecessors did at least receive certain compensations. They were real monarchs and exercised real power, whereas their unhappy descendant of today is well aware that he has nothing but an empty title, that his only subjects are eunuchs and court officials, and that even in his own palace his most reasonable wishes are constantly thwarted by people whom he distrusts and despises . . . .

I have urged upon His Majesty another reason for delay. I have pointed out that, as China is at present without a parliament (and for the moment without even a president), there is no organ or body which would be competent to accept his renunciation of the subsidy and Imperial title. He might, as he desires to do, address his telegram to the people of China, but there would be no man or body of men competent to receive or acknowledge it - and surely it would deserve an acknowledgment. His Majesty has admitted the force of this argument, and I think it will help me to keep him from taking any rash action . . . . .Nevertheless, if there is any undue delay in the reassembly of the old parliament or in the summoning of a new one, I doubt whether His Majesty will be content to allow a matter of such grave importance to himself to be indefinitely shelved while loquacious politicians are quarrelling among themselves over the prospective spoils of office.

There is one important consideration upon which I have not yet touched. When I first reported to you and Liu Chien-chih some months ago that His Majesty had confided to me his wish to surrender his annual state subsidy, you advised me to remind him that it would be unwise to take this step until a thorough investigation had been made into the financial position of the Imperial house. It was pointed out that, owing to the gross mismanagement, peculation and other corrupt practices of the palace officials during the past twelve years, it was quite impossible, at present, to say what the assets of the Imperial house really were, and to what extent, if at all, they exceeded the liabilities. Thus it was desirable, in His Majesty's interests, to refrain from renouncing the subsidy until it had been definitely ascertained that the real and movable estate still remaining in His Majesty's possession would provide him with adequate means of support. On my advice, he agreed to appoint a special committee to make the necessary investigation, and as it was obviously hopeless to expect the present ministers of the household, if left to themselves, to conduct a scrupulously honest enquiry - which would necessarily result in painful disclosures as to past mismanagement and corruption - His Majesty wisely decided not to confine the membership of this committee to those who had had the handling of the Imperial finances in recent years. He therefore willingly accepted my suggestion that you and Liu Chien-chih should be appointed independent members of the proposed committee, and also gladly agreed to signify his trust and confidence in yourself by making you a Grand Guardian, which would, of course, give you a high status within the palace and the right to audience at any time. As you are aware, both these appointments were very strongly opposed by interested persons, and the fact that they have at last been made is solely due to the inflexible determination of His Majesty to have his own way. He told the Ministers of the household quite frankly, and directed them to inform the ex-regent, that he refused to be treated any longer as a puppet, and that in this matter he intended his will to prevail. The language which he used in addressing the Ministers on this occasion (he showed me afterwards a written draft of what he had said) will probably never be forgotten by them as long as they live.

Nevertheless, I think I ought to warn you that you must not expect His Majesty to allow this matter of the renunciation of the subsidy to remain in abeyance during the long period that may elapse before your committee has completed its investigations and drawn up its report. Personally, I am in entire sympathy with His Majesty's present point of view, which is that the renunciation of the subsidy should not be dependent on whether his private property is or is not sufficient to yield him an adequate income. After all, there would be very little courage or nobility of character shown in postponing the act of renunciation until His Majesty were fully satisfied that his private resources were sufficient to yield him ample means of support. . . . .

While I am touching on this question of enquiring into the financial position of the Imperial house, I venture to draw your attention, as you will probably be the most influential member of the investigating committee, to the urgent necessity of arriving at a definite understanding with the republican government as to what movable property may be regarded as belonging to the Emperor and at his absolute disposal. If you read the Peking Chinese press you cannot have failed to notice the paragraphs that have appeared from time to time during the past months regarding the sale of certain palace treasures. Several protests have been raised against these transactions on the ground that the articles disposed of are State property and that the Imperial family has no right to sell them. Today's *Shun-t'ien Shih-pao* contains a paragraph to the effect that recently some articles of great value have been sent from the palace to a foreign bank, "a certain foreigner" having acted as intermediary, and it is hinted that the intention of the palace authorities is to sell them, in which case these "priceless treasures will probably be lost to China".

The Emperor himself has given me to understand that the statements contained in the paragraph are accurate in the main, though, if the reference to "a certain foreigner" is meant to indicate myself, that part of the paragraph is wholly false. Anyhow, I think you will agree that this is a matter in which the honour of the Emperor and the Imperial family is deeply involved, and no time should be lost in separating what may rightly be regarded as Chinese national property from the personal property of the Imperial family.
. . . . .Sir John Jordan once made the remark to me that perhaps some day, after the Emperor had completed his education and travelled abroad, he might be elected president, That indeed is a conceivable possibility; but only if the palace system is dissolved and the republican subsidy and the Imperial title are renounced for ever. Otherwise, it is pretty certain that none but monarchists would support his candidature, and that their action would be interpreted by their political opponents as a direct challenge to republican principles. . . . .

I need hardly say that my colleagues in the Yu-ching kung [the Imperial tutors] have nothing whatever to do with palace scandals and intrigues, and are morally above all reproach. As scholars of the old school, however, they are totally out of touch with all modern political, social and literary movements in China, and have a far narrower general outlook than the Emperor himself . . . .

My relations with His Majesty have always been most cordial, otherwise, indeed, I should have resigned long ago. Externally, my relations with the ex-regent and the other Imperial princes, the Ministers of the household and my colleagues are also all that could be desired. But I feel that they hold me (not without cause) largely responsible for the fact that during the past year His Majesty has been growing more and more discontented and restive, less and less willing to order his life according to the routine and conventions of the court, and increasingly dissatisfied with his position, both in its personal and in its public aspects. If the present conditions in the palace are to be maintained, and the Emperor is to be compelled to acquiesce in those conditions, it will be quite impossible for me to continue to occupy my present post, as I shall be forced to realise that my efforts on His Majesty's behalf have failed . . . . As one who was known to have closer and more confidential relations with His Majesty than any other member of the court or household, I should not unnaturally - and probably rightly - be held mainly responsible for the disaster which had befallen all who had made a living out of the palace system. The fact that I am a foreigner would add to the bitterness of feeling with which they would regard me. This in itself might cause me small discomfort, as I should be conscious of having done no more than my duty; but I could not allow it to be assumed and believed that, while causing a multitude of others to lose their means of livelihood, I had taken good care to safeguard my own position as His Majesty's tutor or confidential adviser . . . .

Yours sincerely,

R F JOHNSTON [3]

This telling document is illuminating on a number of counts, not the least is Johnston's own unshakeable loyalty to his young Emperor-pupil and his sound 'canny' advice on political matters. Certainly, the situation was fraught with difficulties; if the Emperor resigned and repudiated the annual republican subsidy and renounced his title he was sure to become the figure-head of Monarchist propaganda, which, because of the binding effects of 'The Articles of Favourable Treatment', had hitherto not directly implicated him, but as soon as he quit the *Forbidden City* and took up a 'private' residence, he was bound to be surrounded by a monarchist clique who would naturally look to him for active leadership. It would also be unreasonable to expect a high spirited and intelligent lad of sixteen or seventeen to remain unmoved when they called upon him to become, 'the Saviour of China' and become the second illustrious founder of his Imperial house.

It was also doubtful if the Emperor's voluntary surrender of his privileges would meet with anything like the desired "grateful response", that such an act deserved. On the contrary, his motives would inevitably be misjudged by the enemies of the dynasty as merely ridding himself of his obligations under 'the Articles' so that he might intrigue with his monarchist followers against the republic. In addition, as Johnston pointed out plainly in his letter, the British Minister might well have to refuse asylum within the Legation, on the grounds that Britain could not openly be seen to be meddling in internal Chinese politics, and even if he were admitted, he might well be officially restrained from issuing any policy statements from behind the walls of the British Legation. Further, the political climate within the Middle Kingdom at this time was becoming increasingly anti-British, directly encouraged by the Soviet embassy, erupting in the anti-British outburst of 1925. The atmosphere was such, that soon anything and everything that the British government did was suspect, and there was no doubt that if the Emperor had carried through his plans at this time and taken up even temporary residence in the British Legation, the whole episode would have attached but one label, 'A British plot against the Chinese people'. Even Johnston was the subject of slander and denuncation from all sides, especially from the republican dominated Peking popular press, which no doubt received many of its juiciest titbits from the disgruntled Household Department, and those among the princes and ministers who saw their influence with the Emperor eroded by this "English Tutor".

The honest reasons for the Emperor's renunciation of his rights would have been completely ignored, he would doubtless be denounced as a mere 'puppet' in the hands of the 'British Imperialists', who had been seduced and led astray by their 'secret agent' Johnston. The situation was alive with possibilities, none of which were anything less then disastrous. Again, it was Johnston who evolved the only really workable plan; the Emperor without delay should summon the princes and officers of the Household to a palace conference; once assembled he must insist on that clause within the 'Articles' and abdication settlement, that provided for his eventual removal from the *Forbidden City* to the *Yüan Ming Yüan*, (the Summer Palace); that the proposed committee for the investigation of the finances of the Imperial house should begin at once; that the said committee should draw up a scheme for the drastic reduction of palace expenditure and the reform and reorganization of the Household Department; that the Emperor should, as soon as possible after his removal to the Summer Palace initiate friendly negotiations between himself and the republican government for the revision of the 'Articles of Favourable Treatment' and the voluntary surrender of all rights and privileges which the Emperor felt were anachronistic. When this had been achieved, to the complete satisfaction of the Imperial house, (as distinct from the Household Department), and the republican government, the Emperor would be free at last to realize at least one of his long-cherished ambitions, to travel to Europe and study at Oxford University.

Johnston had formulated this solution without taking into account one important factor, which, at this time was unknown to him; the existance within the *Forbidden City* of the vast stores of valuable works of art and other treasures that even the Emperor himself had seen only a thousandth part of, and which had been acknowledged by the republican authorities to be the private property of the Imperial family. References had appeared in the Chinese press from time to time protesting at the sale of such items which in their view rightly belonged to the State. This was not the official attitude of the republican government who raised no objections to such transactions, on the contrary, they realized that they were themselves directly responsible for the financial difficulties of the Imperial household by their failure to meet their obligation in the matter of the annual subsidy, legally payable under the terms of the abdication agreement.

In addition to the vast hordes of treasure still under the direct control of the Imperial family and the *Nei Wu Fu*, only a tiny fraction had been disposed of by sale, gift or even theft, there was also an enormous collection which, after the revolution of 1911, had been transferred to *Peking* from the Imperial palaces of *Mukden* and *Jehol*. By 1916 these treasures were deposited in the three throne-halls that had been taken over by the republic, whilst the greater portion were placed in the *Wu-ying* and *Wen-hua* palaces, (two large buildings in the eastern and western sections of the *Forbidden City*) which were opened to the public towards the end of 1916 as museums of Chinese Art. Access to this collection, which became the core of Palace Museum collection, was obtained, not through the northern gate of the *Forbidden City*, which remained strictly private, but through both the *Tung Hua* (Eastern Glory) and *Hsi Hua* (Western Glory) gates.

This 'national' museum which, as already stated housed the Imperial treasures from *Mukden* and *Jehol* was not, as universally assumed, the property of the State at all, but were on 'loan' from the Imperial family and had been the subject of lengthy negotiation between the two parties. An official document dated 11th September 1916 sets out the background to this agreement;

> In January 1914 the republican government and the Imperial household had sent a joint deputation to Mukden and Jehol to collect and bring to Peking the treasures contained in the palaces there; these treasures were acknowledged to be the private property of the Imperial family; independant experts were called into value all the articles, (which numbered over seventy thousand); some items were not to be included in this valuation because of their exceptional value and rarity; that by mutual agreement between the two parties, all items, except those specifically withdrawn by the Imperial family, were to be bought by the republican government at the figure valued; that for the time being, because of the governments inability to pay the purchase-price, the said treasures were to be regarded as 'on loan' until such time as the republic met the financial requirement; that in the meantime the Wu Ying palace, which contained most of the treasures was to be

opened to the public as an National Museum; that the collection would be entrusted to an official of the Household Department, (*Chih ko*), who would be responsible for their safety to both the Imperial family and the Republic.

The official valuation of the treasures was: *Mukden:* $1,984,315, *Jehol:* $2,081,731, Items retained: $554,571 Thus the balance due to the Imperial family by the republic was: $3,511,476 (the value of the dollar in question at this time was about 10 new pence).

Not one dollar of this sum was ever paid, the republic had in fact ignored its written undertaking and confiscated the entire private collection. It would seem that this agreement along with the articles were merely scraps of paper to the republic, and it is doubtful if they ever intended to honour them. Also, the so called 'valuation' of the Imperial treasures from *Mukden* and *Jehol* were alarmingly underestimated, obviously by design. But, if these provincial palace treasures were so desirable to the officials of the new republic, how much more desirable were those still housed within the *Forbidden City*? This huge private accumulation of precious works of art eclipsed the former in quality, quantity and value and, unknown to the principal actors in this Imperial Tragedy, all the treasures of the 'Great Within' was similarly to be confiscated without the slightest pretence of legal right or justification in the years to come. The confiscation, disbursement, theft, call it what you will, robbed China of countless thousands of its art treasures during the first fifty years of this century; there is hardly one Western museum or collection that does not contain at the very least, one piece of 'loot', and if but a small fraction was returned to its rightful home, China would need to increase its museum space many thousands of times over; one of the greatest collections of 'war-lord loot' sits arrongantly across the East China Sea facing *Fuhkien* province, and although many of the spoils of war have mysteriously disappeared over the years, the remainder is immense and the source of constant sorrow to the Chinese people to this day.

The Emperor's betrothal, or rather the announcement of the 'creation' of an Empress by Imperial decree had taken place on

11th March 1922 and between this date and the actual wedding on the 1st December, the court was a flurry of nuptial activity; there were edicts to issue, which proclaimed the successive stages according to court protocol. In the same issue of the Peking Gazette that reported to elevation of the future Empress's father, was a edict appointing four Imperial commissioners to take charge of the wedding arrangements, (*Da Hun Li Da Ch'en*); these four were Prince *Tsai-t'ao, Chu I-fan*, (an Imperial tutor), *Shao-ying* and *Ch'i-ling*, who were both ministers of the Household Department.

The next step in this ritual was to convey the future Empress to *Peking* so that she might come within the Imperial families sphere of influence and be suitably instructed in court etiquette. Accordingly on the 17th March, she was ceremoniously brought by special train from *Tientsin* to *Peking* accompanied by palace officials, eunuchs and officers of the palace guard. At the station she was met by a group of ministers of the Imperial Household Department in full court regalia, a cluster of ladies-in-waiting and a guard of honour supplied by the republican government, who emphasized their respect to the Imperial family by giving orders that the 'august Empress to be' was to be saluted by both republican troops and police on her drive from the station to her father's residence. This residence was situated in the old Tartar City of *Peking* in a quiet street named *Ma O'rh Hutung*, (Hat Lane) in the north-east quarter which lay about three quarters of a mile from the Gate of Spiritual Valour. From the very moment of her arrival her father's house was known as *Hou Ti*, (the Mansion of the Empress) and although her father continued to live there, he was obliged to yield precedence to his now Imperial daughter.

All this time *P'u-yi* grudgingly acquiesced to the prescribed rituals which inevitably surrounded his unwilling pratication in the 'Imperial Nuptials'. Very early on the morning of 6th April, the young eunuchs of the 'betrothed' Emperor dressed him in ceremonial robes for his required visit to the *Shou Huang Tien*, (a hall at the back of Prospect Hill), which contained the 'ancestor' portraits of the dynasty. There, in strict accordance with the traditions of his dynasty he solemnly announced his betrothal to the august spirits of his ancestors; the same, but greatly elaborated ritual was repeated two days before the actual wedding, when the approaching event was reported with more ceremony to the Imperial ancestors in the innermost halls (*hou tien*) of both the temples of Serving the Ancestors and the Supreme Hall of the Ancestors (*T'ai Maio*). The three most important pre-marriage ceremonies were; 'Sending of the Betrothal Presents', which occured on 21st October; 'The Marriage Contract Rites', on 12th November; and the 'Rites of the Golden Seal and Scroll', on 30th November. The date for these three ceremonies were arrived at by astrological calculation and considered to be the most 'auspicious'. There were certain similarities between the three ceremonies, though mostly of a superficial nature; each began with a state procession from the Palace of Cloudless Heaven in the *Forbidden City* to the 'Mansion' of the bride's father in 'Hat Lane', where he would greet the representatives of the 'Son of Heaven' kneeling on a crimson cushion outside the main entrance of his now 'Imperial' residence. On each occasion the procession was headed by a 'Prince of the Blood', (an Imperial Commissioner) who carried the staff of Imperial authority, the *chieh*.

On 21st October the princes, nobles and officers of the Household Department gathered in the great quadrangle of the throne-hall and when assembled in their respective places by the grand ushers and marshals, a herald appeared and proclaimed the following: "We have already issued Our Edict declaring that We have elevated *Kuo Po-lo*, daughter of *Jung-yuan*, expectant-taotai and hereditary noble of the sixth rank, to the dignity of Empress. We now command Our officers of State to take the symbol of Imperial Authority and carry out the ceremony of Sending the Betrothal Gifts." These 'gifts' were not selected at random but in strict accordance with dynastic precedent; included were, two horses with saddles and bridles, eighteen sheep, forty pieces of satin and eight rolls of other carefully selected cloth.

The *Chieh* was reverently lifted from its resting place in front of the Imperial throne and handed to the principal Imperial commissioner who then placed himself at the head of the procession and after slowly negotiating the inner paths of the *Forbidden City* issued from the Gate of Spiritual Valour into the streets of *Peking* which were crowded with curious towns people and the occasional *devil face*. Accompanying the opulent procession were not only the court musicians and the palace guard, but the way was lined with republican soldiers both mounted and on foot stretching from the *Forbidden City* to the *Yuan* mansion in Hat Lane. This curious, and apparent anachronism, was not lost on the excited crowds who interpreted the display of Imperial Pomp, guarded and honoured by the republic, as further evidence of 'auspicious' co-existence.

The *Da Cheng Li*, (Rites of the Great Proof or Marriage Contract), took place some two weeks later. Once more the Imperial Herald made a proclamation to the assembled nobles: . ."Take the symbol of Imperial Authority and carry out the rites of the great Proof."

Gifts were again at the centre of this ancient ceremony, but this time of a more significant value; those sent to the 'Empress' included; 100 oz of gold, 10,000 oz of silver, a gold tea set, two silver tea sets, two silver bowls, 100 rolls of silk-satin, and again two horses with fine saddles and bridles, On this occasion her parents also received; 40 oz of gold, 4,000 oz of silver, one gold tea set, one silver tea set, forty pieces of satin, one hundred rolls of other cloth, two horses with ornamental bridles and saddles, two complete sets of court robes, two sets of winter garments, and one belt of honour, (an Imperial symbol largely discarded by the later *Ch'ing* house but historically honoured by the Manchu who had first been recipients of the *Ming* originals before their conquest of China). To the Empress's two brothers, (one of whom was still a child of ten), eight rolls of satin, sixteen rolls of other cloth and a fine set of writing materials. Nor were the *Yuan* servants forgotten but were given the sum of four hundred dollars to be divided amongst them.

The last of the three ceremonies was by far the most imposing of the prenuptial observances, the " Rites of the Golden Seal and Scroll". This took place on 30th November, the eve of the actual wedding. On this occasion three ceremonial tables were placed in front of the dragon throne, the Imperial symbol *chieh* was placed in the centre; on the eastern table the Golden Scroll, (Imperial

Letters Patent), and on the western table the Golden Seal. Both Seal and Scroll were intended to pass into the possession of the Empress who would return them when she entered the *Forbidden City* as the Emperor's bride.

Mention should also be made of one other important ceremonial article, the great bridal sedan-chair which, at this time, for the purposes of sanctification, was housed in the Palace of Cloudless Heaven and would be carried by twenty-two bearers conveying the young Empress from her father's home to the palace of her Imperial bridegroom. This *feng-yu* derived its name from the *feng-huang*, which western writers have erroneously labelled the 'phoenix', and it is quite wrong to suppose that this Chinese *feng* has anything in common with the phoenix of Greek lore, except the fact that they are both mythical birds. This *feng-yu* bridal chair was sumptuously covered with traditional scarlet silk and by far the most prominent of the many auspicious symbols was the Chinese *feng-huang*, which is synonymous with a happy and prosperous bride, and is so to this day. The other prominent symbol was the character double happiness and although in the beginning of their dynasty the Manchu disliked red, feeling it was unlucky because it was the court colour of the *Ming*, this most Chinese of hues soon reasserted itself, and its historic connotations were conviently forgotten. As the *Lung*, (five clawed) dragon is the emblem of the Emperor then the *feng-huang* was the prerogative of the Empress.

The final and most important stage of this ceremony was completed by the Emperor himself, for when the procession was ready to proceed he appeared in his full robes of State entering the throne-hall to inspect the Golden Seal and Scroll before they departed from his keeping, then assuring himself that all was in order with his last and most important gift to his future bride, he mounted the dragon throne. This was the signal for the court musicians to commence a special composition entitled, 'The Central Harmony' which was attributed to the Emperor *Shun* who began his reign in 2255 BC. When the last sounds of the ancient music had died away the princes, nobles, court officials and Imperial commissioners marshalled themselves and performed the

three-fold kneeling and nine-fold *kowtow*, then the Imperial
Herald read aloud the third Imperial proclamation and the Seal
and Scroll were handed over to the senior Imperial commissioner
for conveyance to the home of the Imperial bride. The procession
again formed up in the great quadrangle and the Emperor slowly
descended from the throne which was the musicians cue to
commence the 'Joyful Peace' section of the previously mentioned
work. When the procession eventually arrived outside the *Yuan*
family manison the bride, for the first time, became an active
participant in the great ritual. On the arrivial of the Imperial
procession the Empress-to-be had to take formal and ceremonious
possession of the Scroll and Seal, and personally attend the
reading of Imperial Rescript appertaining thereto. During this
reading she was required to kneel and afterwards to go through an
elaborate form of salutation which consisted of standing six times,
arms by her side and head slightly forward, kneeling three times
and bowing three times. This was regarded as the female
equivalent of the male nine times *kowtow*. Early in the morning of
the same day, (30th November) the Emperor's *shu fei* or
secondary consort, entered the *Forbidden City* as a bride. This
custom, then as now, may seem odd to western observers, but
from both a Manchu and Chinese point of view was quite proper,
and it should be remembered that a *Shu fei* was by no means an
ignoble position, but in fact one of great dignity; she might, in
certain circumstances be elevated to the rank of Empress and her
son could well become Emperor. The ceremonies surrounding her
betrothal were much the same as those already described, although
observed with a lesser degree of pomp. The principal reason for
her early arrival was simple and indeed pure, (contrary to low
rumour), it would allow her to be present at the head of the court
ladies to greet the Empress on her arrival the following morning
and thus be the first to welcome her. The time fixed for the brides
arrival was at four the following morning, (1st December), for,
unlike Chinese weddings, Manchu nuptials were always nocturnal
ceremonies. At the appointed hour the moon would be bright and
the sky serene and cloudless and the 'Great Within' would be
bathed in enchantment.

The *feng-yu* sedan-chair played its own important part in the 'Imperial Nuptials' and its conveyance from the Palace of Cloudless Heaven to the bride's home was accorded due solemnity; first it was carried by bearers of the Imperial Equipage Department as far as the first courtyard, here it was handed over to eunuchs, who, on arrival, placed it in the principal reception room fronting the auspicious south-eastern quarter, (which had been ascertained by astrology and divination) being at the hour prescribed, ruled over by the god of Happiness.

The bride, in all the sumptuous splendour of her wedding robes was ready and waiting when summoned by the mistress of ceremonies, entered the silk lined confines of her *feng-yu*, which was immediately raised by the attendant eunuchs and transported through the various halls out into the courtyard where the regular Imperial bearers were waiting to carry it to the *Forbidden City*. It was not permitted that any member of her family should accompany her, only her father could venture as far as the main entrance where he watched his Empress-daughter carried out of sight, whilst he remained tearfully kneeling on a crimson cushion, whilst this almost unearthly scene was washed with pale moonlight.

The bridal procession wound its way, escorted by republican cavalry and infantry and a squadron of police, soldiers of the Imperial Palace guard, two bands both playing Chinese and Western music, sometimes simultaneously. Also in the early dawn caravan were three traditional *Peking* carts draped in yellow silk each surmounted with a silver knob and a similarly covered sedan-chair which were intended for the Empress's future use for, the *feng-yu* could, by law never be used again. As the music rose and fell sometimes a little discordantly, the moonlight procession bobbed along the narrow streets and lanes from the old Tartar city; there were some sixty bearers of large palace lanterns, over seventy attendants carried 'Dragon-Phoenix' flags and state ceremonial canopies, eunuchs carrying yellow silk 'pavilion' chests containing the Seal and Scroll and the bride's trousseau.

During this time there was an underlying tension within the midst of the Imperial Family; neither the Princes nor the Dowagers felt much confidence in *Li Yüan-hung*, (now president of the republic for the second time) who, in their eyes was not half so reliable and predictable in his attitude towards the Tartar Court as *Hsü Shih-ch'ang* had been, and it was generally feared that the new president might well interfere with the nuptial ceremony and the traditional pomp of the occasion. As it turned out, *Li* was the very soul of helpful consideration; the republic's ministry of finance wrote a letter couched in the most humble terms to the officials of the Imperial Household Department, explaining that they were experiencing severe difficulties in meeting their present expenditure, and were therefore unable to pay the full amount due under the 'Articles'; they would however, make a special payment from tax revenue of one hundred thousand dollars to help with the expenses of the 'Grand Nuptial', of which twenty thousand was to be considered as a gift from the republic. Extensive plans had been made for the disposition of literally thousands of soldiers and police to provide public ceremonial and Imperial protection for this great occasion.

From the moment the winding procession bringing the new Empress entered the confines of the *Forbidden City*, the wedding celebrations commenced and lasted five days, three of which were taken up with Imperial theatre performances and the statutory granting of new titles.

Presents poured into the palace from all over China and beyond, *Ch'ing* veterans appeared, as if from a long and tranquil sleep, converging on *Peking* in their thousands, determined to demonstrate their undying loyalty to the dyansty, and to wish their young sovereign everlasting happiness for, his ascendance would surely mean the reinstatement of theirs. "Offering of President Li Yüan-hung of the republic of China to the Hsüan-t'ung Emperor" read the note written on the red card which accompanied his wedding gifts; four large antique vessels of cloisonné, rolls of different silk and satin, (bearing the mark of the Imperial silk factory *Nanking* which the republicans had taken over for 'the good of the people'), a pair of scrolls wishing the Emperor the traditional Chinese greeting of, Longevity, prosperity and good fortune and a number of other items. From ex-president

Hsü Shih-ch'ang, came twenty thousand dollars, a fine Chinese carpet with the appropriate 'Dragon Feng-huang' motif, twenty-eight pieces of antique procelain and many other valuable gifts, (if any real evidence was needed as to *Hsü's* 'missappropriation' of both republican funds and Imperial dues this was enough, but, no one mentioned it). War-lords, politicians, officials, government officers all seemed to forget their supposed 'anti-Manchu' and 'Monarchical' prejudices, swept along by the national love of ceremony and feasting. The official representative of the republic at the wedding was *Yin Chang* chief *aide-de-camp* to the president who, in any ways typified the attitude towards the throne at this time. He formally congratulated the Emperor on his wedding, rather as he would a foreign monarch, but after bowing in a restrained manner he said, "That was my official duty on behalf of the republic, now, your slave will greet Your Manjesty as a private subject as his heart dictates", this said, he fell to his knees and performed the *kowtow* as if he were an official of the court. The *Ch'ing* veterans present were delighted at this 'courtesy' done their Emperor by one of the 'republican revolutionaries'. The whole atmosphere throughout *Peking* was festive in a way that had not been experienced for over ten years, it seemed that all strata of society were anxious to forget the misery and upheavals of recent times, smiles crept across lips that had been thin and sullen, *Peking* had come to life again, no matter what the cause, it was a time of celebration, perhaps the dragon was not vanquished after all. The Peking press, so long critical of everything Imperial, gave up their carping about the "foreign wedding" as they soon realized that their readers enthusiasm could not be dampened by any amount of criticizing the Imperial Nuptials.

When the young Empress's procesison had finally arrived she was conducted by princesses and eunuchs through a door at the back of the throne-hall to the Palace of Earthly Peace, *(K'un Ning Kung)*, which stands a short distance from the Palace of Cloudless Heaven. There, nervously waiting, was her sixteen year old bridegroom, he had never given the wedding any real thought until that moment, his Empress entered and stood before him, the silence seemed endless, then two ladies-in-waiting stepped timorously forward and removed the bride's vail, which was attached to her traditional *kai-t'ou* headress. Sixteen year old bride and groom gazed on each other's face for the very first time. *P'u-yi* was all this time turning over in his mind the question of how this lavish ceremony actually altered his life, "I have an Empress and a consort; I am married, but, how does this make things different from before!" he puzzled, "what is different, I have come of age, and were it not for the revolution I could start ruling without the regents. I must recover my ancestral heritage". All this while as the Emperor was preoccupied with his thoughts the bride and her entourage had stood motionless, waiting for some sign from their lord and master, now he returned, as from a trance and walked from the room leaving the Empress and her attendants bowing in bewilderment.

The wedding feast and the ceremonial drinking of the 'Nuptial Cup' went according to plan, the court was in joyful mood, that is, all but one, the Emperor Himself, he was 'far away' dreaming of, what boys of sixteen will dream of, with one exception.

According to Manchu tradition the Emperor and Empress were to spend their wedding night in a bridal chamber some ten metres square in the Palace of Earthly Peace which was dominated by the 'Dragon Phoenix' bed which occupied almost a third of the red carpeted floor space.

> "When I at last entered this peculiar room I felt stifled. The bride sat on the bed her head bowed down; I looked around me, everything was 'red', red bed curtains, red pillows, red dress, red skirt, red flowers, her red face . . . . it all looked like a melted red candle. I did not know what to do . . . . should I stand or sit? . . . . what am I expected to do?" [4]

As his restless spirit coiled about inside him he could stand the awkward silence and his red-faced motionless bride no longer, he left the room and returned to his own apartments in the Mind Nuture Palace. Everything was quiet and he longed for Johnston to comfort and advise him. "How did she feel, abandoned in her bridal chamber? And what was that girl who was not yet fourteen who was now his secondary consort thinking?" These thoughts hardly entered his mind. What really consumed all his attention was the fact that he had come of age, and had it not been for the revolution he would now rule the Celestial Empire.

The following days were crowded with activity; worship of the Emperor's Imperial ancestors; court festivities of various kinds which breathed new life into the 'Great Within', life that had not been known since the Grand Dowager Empress had departed to the nine springs. Princes and nobles, old and loyal ex-officials poured their refined and warm congratulations over the awakening boy, Western uniformed republicans and frock coated government officials added their not ungenuine acclamation, if visibly dowdier than their court counterparts.

P'u-yi was 'Emperor', at least within *Forbidden City*, he had an Empress and *fei*, though he viewed them as somewhat unnecessary possessions at this time; his court was crowded with loyal supporters, he had Johnston to advise him; yes, he felt that he had really come of age. This fact was clearly demonstrated by the reception held for 'foreigners' two days after the official wedding and it represented a complete break with tradition, for the first time in the history of the dynasty foreign men and women were received at an informal joint reception presided over by the Emperor and his Empress. This was predictably Johnston's idea, and the young Emperor was most enthusiastic about it, he felt it was high time that he meet the important representatives of foreign countries, although they diplomatically, had to come as private persons, so as not to compromise their standing with the republic. But come they did, over two hundred of them. Not since the closing years of *Old Buddha* after the 'Boxer Fiasco' had foreigners been received en masse within the walls of the *Purple Forbidden City* and then, only formally with strict segregation of the sexes. These foreign guests were first conducted to the throne-hall of the Palace of Cloudless Heaven, there they were served 'Western' refreshments and received little silver boxes to commemorate the occasion. To further underline the informality of the reception the Emperor did not take his customary place on the dragon throne nor did he receive his guests in the throne-hall, but one by one they were ushered into a small apartment known as the *Hsi Nuan Ko*, (The Western Warm Pavilion), whose name also emphasized the spirit of the occasion. In this apartment the Emperor and Empress stood side by side attended by two princesses, two ministers of the Household and four others who introduced the visitors, (one of whom was Reginald Johnston), the foreigners bowed or perhaps shook hands. When the introductions were completed, the guests were ushered into the throne-hall where they were informed that His Majesty would address them. The huge doors swung noiselessly open and the young Emperor entered and ascended the steps to the throne, the hall was hushed in respectful silence; *P'u-yi* stepped forward, and with a winning boyish smile spoke the following words in slow precise English;

> "It is a great pleasure to Us to see here today so many distinguished visitors from all parts of the world. We thank you for coming, and wish you all health and prosperity." [5]

There was a rustling murmur of spell-bound approval from the assembly and the young Emperor turned and took a tall glass of champagne from a bowing attendant, bowed to the company on right and left, raised his glass in toast to his guests and put the glass to his lips, the unaccustomed bubbles tickled his nose and he sneezed, he self-consciously smiled at his enchanted guests.

Until this time the boy Emperor who dwelt within the *Forbidden City* had been a complete mystery to foreign residents of *Peking*, now, for the first time, they beheld a very charming young man, who was conducting himself in difficult and trying circumstances with all the graceful dignity inborn in the best princely families, demonstrating, by the simple frankness of his manners and bearing that he was every inch a monarch. His obvious pleasure in meeting the many foreign guests also endeared him to them, his curiosty veiled by his courtly manners, showed them that the old barriers between east and west had at last been swept away by this 'Modern' young Man.

The final cost of the Imperial wedding was, needless to say enormous, though on the credit side the gifts, which included over a million dollars in cash amounted to a very great sum. A 'red book' was compiled by the Household Department listing all the presents and the names of the donors, and it is interesting to note the absence of some prominent people such as *Sun Yat-sen*, and as might be expected, although the notorious 'Christian' general *Fêng Yü-hsiang* presented a *ju-i* of white jade, it must be doubted if the felicitations this gift symbolized were generated by real 'christian' motives. The list was extremely long and some indication has already been given of prominent well-wishers but there was on touchingly sincere entry which even more than the others, demonstrated the loving loyalty of an old *Ch'ing* veteran; it was given by an old and now poverty-stricken ex-offical and was the only treasure the old man possessed, a copy of the *Ch'ien Tzu Wen* (The Thousand-Character Classic) in the handwriting of the *Sheng Tsu* Emperor, (*K'ang-hsi*), which had been the most precious heirloom in his family for the last two hundred years.

In November 1924 all these 'personal' gifts along with all the other 'private' Imperial treasures were seized by a group of republican soldiers and politicians lead by the 'Christian' general, and 'stolen' in spite of the solemn undertaking made many times over guaranteeing that the private property of the Imperial House would not be touched. When the 'Christian' general made himself master of *Peking* by armed force and consequently master of the *Forbidden City*, he literally consficated everything in sight, and Reginald Johnston made the following comment;

> "Whatever may be said of this confiscation it can hardly be seriously argued that the wedding gifts given freely to the Emperor after he had ceased to be the ruler of China were also the rightful property of the Chinese Nation, and it would be interesting to learn the grounds on which he has been deprived of them. A few of the least valuable of the presents given to the Emperor on his wedding and on other occasions were presented by myself. They are included in the property that has been confiscated, though it was emphatically not my intention to present them to the Chinese people. I have no doubt that most of the donors of wedding gifts in 1922 would say the same in respect of their own intentions." [6]

For a few days during the chill *Peking* winter of 1922, it seemed that the grey clouds that had encircled the *Ch'ing* house for the last ten years had miraculously parted to let through, at least some rays of warming hope, but sadly this break in the heavens only heralded a deeper twilight, a prologue to a longer, colder, more desolate night, for both the young Emperor and China.

CHAPTER SEVEN

The Eunuchs
and
The Nei Wu Fu

With *P'u-yi's* marriage and coming of age the full realization of his precarious position occupied most of his thoughts, he knew that the 'Articles of Favourable Treatment' would not last forever, and he deeply resented the fact that he was a 'prisoner' of both the Imperial court and the republic. What he wanted more than anything else, was to go abroad as soon as possible, Johnston agreed with him but prevaricated, or so it seemed to *P'u-yi*, pointing out that this was not the right time for such a step. From the court's point of view, it was wholly undesirable on two counts, with the Emperor gone there would be no one to fill their rice bowls, and to those who hoped for a restoration, it was unthinkable for the Emperor to leave his ancestral home in the *Forbidden City*.

P'u-yi poured out his anxiety to his brother *P'u-chieh*, who shared the same ambitions and longing for freedom, and although *P'u-chieh* was a year younger than his Emperor brother, he knew far more about the outside world. They both agreed to escape as soon as possible and drew up a list of their priorities. Money was obviously necessary so, over the next six month *P'u-chieh* left the palace each day after lessons with all manner of things concealed about his person and in his school bag, the two brothers who had always been close, became closer, and enjoyed every moment of their 'secret' enterprise. Paintings, calligraphy, ancient books, precious stones, all slowly disappeared to their house in *Tientsin*.

On Saturday, 24th February 1923, Reginald Johnston was invited to a reception given by the president of the republic. There, during the course of the evening he met the wife of a foreign minister then resident in *Peking*, she told him that her husband had been prevented from attending because of a heavy cold, but that he was anxious to see Mr Johnston as soon as possible. Johnston made his apologies, left the reception going directly to the legation in question. On arrival he was informed that the Emperor's younger brother *P'u-chieh* had visited the minister during the preceeding three days and had informed him that the Emperor had made up his mind to leave the *Forbidden City* in secret, and had asked his assistance in first receiving him at the legation, then accompanying him to the British concession at *Tientsin*.

"Have either the Emperor or his brother discussed these extreme plans with you", the minister enquired.

"No, no they have not, although it comes as no surprise to me, this option has often been the subject of conversation between us. I suspect that on this occasion, they felt I might not approve of the timing, I have recently expressed my feeling to the Emperor that this is not the right moment for such a perilous undertaking." Johnston replied. "I know that a certain unnamed prince is a party to the scheme, and it is his house in Tientsin where they will reside, I am also informed that many valuable Imperial treasures have already secretly been transferred there." Johnston nodded but made no audible reply.

"I also know I must soon give my answer to His Majesty, I have given the matter much throught, I deeply sympathize with this young man who is kept a prisoner in the Forbidden City against his will and I have practically made up my mind to receive him here at the legation and personally accompany him to Tientsin, although you will fully appreciate that I can take no part in actually helping to bring His Majesty out of the Palace, I can merely act as host to him here at the legation."

Johnston then told the minister the whole background to the present situation, adding that in his opinion, it would be almost impossible for the Emperor to leave the palace without arousing the suspicions of either the eunuchs or the palace guards, someone was bound to raise the alarm. The next day, 25th February, Johnston wrote to the minister:

> "The more I think over what you told me last night, the more strongly I feel that your young visitors' scheme is extremely rash and that if any attempt is made to carry it out, the results may be very unfortunate for the person

whose interest we both have at heart. This being so, it is out of the question for me to be party to the scheme, especially as I am convinced that any such action on my part would meet with the strong of my legation and the British Government. If I am consulted on the subject by the person mainly concerned, I shall advise him not to take the action proposed, but I shall not take active steps to prevent the plan being carried out as I could not do so without betraying your confidence." [1]

These events took place during the holiday-period, which extended from the eve of the lunar new year, (which in 1923 fell on 16th February) and continued to within a few days of the Emperor's birthday, (the 13th of the first moon), 18th February. Because of this Johnston and his fellow tutors were not required, or expected to visit the palace, unless they received a special summons, and although Johnston wished to discuss the situation with *P'u-yi* he would have to go through the lengthy procedure of requesting a special audience.

The sympathetic foreign legation minister was none other than the Dutch Minister W J Oudendijk, whose steadfast desire to help the young Emperor had not in the least been dampened by Johnston's letter, and in the afternoon of the same day, (25th February) he replied to Johnston as follows:

> "My visitor, *(P'u-chieh)* informed me that the other one was bent on the execution of his plan, that he had carefully thought it over and that he meant to do it TONIGHT. . . . . . . I told my visitor that I had spoken to you, which did not surprise him. But if you feel as you do, please go and see our friend this afternoon, and if possible let me know the result of your conversation." [2]

Johnston immediately penned this reply:

> "I am much obliged to you for your letter. I have decided not to visit our friend this afternoon. I feel certain, from what I know of his character, that I could not now change his

191

purpose; especially as he knows perfectly well that I am in hearty agreement with him in his general attitude and have always been most strongly in favour of drastic changes being effected in his way of life. It is only the particluar plan which he has finally decided to adopt that I cannot approve of. All I can hope for now is that the plan will be successful and that my gloomy forebodings may not be realised. He is fortunate indeed in having enlisted the aid of so influential and sympathetic a friend as yourself." [3]

By the time these letters had passed between the Dutch Legation and Johnston's house, it was late afternoon and Johnston himself remained at home awaiting news, of what he knew in his heart, to be a dangerous escape. As he paced up and down, his mind was full of images of his young pupil, if only he could be free! If only he could take him to England and install him in the conducive calm of Oxford then, only then, could this intelligent and gifted boy begin to live his own life, free from the unnatural restrictions of the suffocating *Forbidden City*! Why, then he, Johnston could really begin to teach him what the world really had in store, he could. . . . . Johnston was brought back to reality by the sound of the telephone bell's shrill alarm; "Yes? What? You say the plan has failed? What? He has not arrived at your legation? But . . . . yes . . . . yes . . . . .alright . . . . I'll come to see you in the morning. . . . . . thank you. . . . . . thank you for letting me know." Johnston replaced the receiver and mopped his brow, what had gone wrong?

Next morning Johnston was abroad at an early hour, he had hardly slept and as he drove from his house to the Dutch Legation all manner of fantasies were attacking his weary mind.
"Come in Mr Johnston, come in . . . . I have much to tell you, please be seated." Johnston remained standing his tiredness and concern clearly visible on his usually calm and kindly face.
"I really know very little" the minister continued, "last night when the hour had passed at which I expected our friend, for as you know his brother was to bring him directly here from the City, my phone rang, it was the. . . . . . . our friend himself, he told me that something had gone wrong and would I send a car to one

192

of the palace gates to bring him away. Of course, as you know, I could not agree to do that, it would compromise both myself and my government but, I assured him that I would receive him here and accompany him to Tientsin as I had promised, I assured him that I had made all the necessary arrangement for the journey, I had secured tickets and reserved a private compartment on the night train, then as I was about to question him further the line went dead. . . . . ''

Johnston looked at the worried face of the minister, put his hand on his shoulder and left the room.

The following morning, the day before the Emperor's birthday, he received an urgent message from him to come to the *Forbidden City* at once, on arrival he was ushered into *P'u-yi's* private apartment, *P'u-chieh* was the only other person present on this occasion. The young Emperor looked suprisingly relaxed and assumed that this 'English tutor' had already been fully informed about the failure of the attempted escape. He politely excused himself for have not discussed the matter with Johnston, on the grounds that the unnamed prince had cautioned him not to allow anyone connected with the court to know of their plan, now, well it really did not matter, it had all failed because of one untrustworthy eunuch who, even though handsomely bribed, had betrayed his Imperial master's trust. *P'u-yi* related the details of the previous evening; an hour before the arranged 'escape' the Household Department had been alerted to the plan by the eunuch in question and Prince *Ch'un*, the Emperor's father, had issued orders to the palace guard that no one was to be allowed through any of the palace gates, within minutes the whole of the *Forbidden City* was in a state of siege. The brothers had been stupefied by the news as they prepared themselves for flight in the Mind Nurture Palace, within minutes Prince *Ch'un* was announced, and entered in a state bordering on hysteria, he stared at his two sons as he fought to regain his breath;

"I . . . . .I . . . . I. . . . . have been told . . . . .that Your . . . . .Your Majesty . . . . wa . . . . wants to leave the palace . . . .''
"Of course not . . . . .who can have told you that?'' *P'u-yi* replied trying hard to stifle the laughter that was bubbling inside him. He felt sorry for his severely perplexed father and disappointed

that the attempt had not succeeded but he could also see the humour of the situation.

"It would not be good for you to do so . . . . what can I do about it . . . . I . . . ."

"There is nothing to be done, I do not wish to leave."

Prince *Ch'un* glared at *P'u-chieh* who had been silent all the while and his father's stern countenance elicited a bow which broke the questioning gaze. "Everything is alright. . . . . I do not wish to go", *P'u-yi* repeated in an attempt to calm his father. The prince muttered some unintelligible words to himself and left taking the young Emperor's 'accomplice' with him.

Left alone to brood on the failure of that evening's great enterprise, he determined to find out the name of the eunuch who had betrayed him; he summoned the eunuchs of the presence but they either knew nothing or were expert in pretending they did not, *P'u-yi* suspected the latter. He could hardly ask the Household Department, so he made his mind up to let the matter rest for the time being, but eventually he would ascertain the name of his eunuch enemy and then, then, he would have him severely punished.

Johnston later claimed, as the foregoing correspondence shows, that he had no direct part in the Emperor's plan for escape, but this was assuredly 'face saving' on his part, and the Emperor emphatically chronicled his whole-hearted complicity in the incident. However, during their conversation the next day, after *P'u-yi* had poured out all his troubles to Johnston, whatever the degree of his implication, counseled that the matter should be forgotten as soon as possible, and that the Emperor should now turn his attention to the re-organization of the 'Great Within', something over which he did have absolute power. This did much to restore *P'u-yi's* good humour, for he was determined, now that he had come of age, to reform the iniquitous eunuch-system, by which he had so recently been dealt such an underhanded blow.

The next day was the Emperor's birthday, and if Johnston had been in any doubt about who the court blamed for the proposed 'escape' attempt, he very soon realized that he was the chief suspect. On other occasions he had been on the friendliest of terms with the princes and ministers, now, he was completely ignored by them, it was an unpleasant experience, for entwined in the broken thread of manners was more than a feeling of acute hostility.

The 'incident' was soon tabooed, and although it remained clearly in the minds of some, it was not openly referred to again, and the young Emperor enthusiastically launched himself into the task of reorganizing the Household Department and personally supervising the work of the committee which had been formed for this purpose. Johnston was ever present, and together he and his determined pupil set about the almost impossible task of investigating the finances and administration of the Imperial Household. The Household Department were less than enthusiastic at the proposed 'meddling' in their affairs, and soon received a severe shook, the Emperor informed them that the expenditure of the *Nei Wu Fu*, then running at about six million annually must be reduced to half a million a year, they had hardly recovered from this when he announced that an iventory must be taken of all the palace treasures, and that any item he mentioned must immediately be brought for his inspection.

Theft, either 'legal' or 'illegal' had always been the order of the day, even at the time of the young Emperor's wedding, almost as soon as the State ceremony was over, the large and valuable pearls which formed part of the Empress's bridal headress were stolen and replaced with copies. The Imperial 'treasure', still housed at this time within the *Forbidden City* was immense, including both *Ming* and *Ch'ing* collections, except for a small amount that had been looted by foreign soldiers in 1860 and after the Boxer incident in 1900.

Not that looting was confined to the foreign *devil faces*, it was almost openly indulged in by anyone who could manage it, from the highest to the humblest. The methods were as varied as the 'treasure'! Locks were picked or even forced on storerooms, items removed by stealth, or even in broad day-light, according to the confidence of the individuals concerned, many were sold quite

195

openly, others 'borrowed' for appraisal, and quite naturally never returned, it was a perpetual occupation which preoccupied all.

One day, almost by chance *P'u-yi* and Johnston discovered an almost hidden storeroom behind the Palace of Established Happiness (*Chien Fu Kung*); the doors were still thickly sealed with the strips of red paper and had obviously not been opened for many years; after convincing the eunuchs in charge that if they did not forthwith produce the keys to the heavy locks, they would be flogged until they did, the massive doors were at last opened. Inside were scores of dusty chests, and on examination their contents were discovered to be the personal collection of the great *Chien-lung* Emperor, packed away after his death and not opened until now. Johnston was so excited that in his eagerness to raise the lid of another 'treasure' chest, lost his balance and came crashing down on a pile of books and scrolls, much to his pupil's impish delight, his laughter echoed around the dark cobwebbed storeroom, Johnston, aware of his own loss of 'dignity', joined in, accepting the Emperor's out stretched hand, got to his feet brushing the 'antique' dust from his clothes, sneezing and laughing they re-emerged into the pale sunlight. Orders were given for the doors to be resealed and an inventory to be taken, under the strictest supervision within the following days.

Reginald Johnston was well aware of the urgency of the inventory for in *Ti An Men* street, where he lived, new antique shops were opening like prunus blossoms in high spring; some were said to be owned by senior eunuchs, others by officials of the Household Department or their near relations. As soon as the 'Imperial inventory' was announced thefts increased at an alarming rate; the *Yu Ching* Palace was broken into, as was the Cloudless Heaven Palace, it seemed that nothing was safe from the avaricious and daring thieves. The situation was getting badly out of hand, the eunuchs responsible for these palace storerooms were questioned and even tortured, but to no avail, after all, what was a flogging or two compared with the prospect of opulent retirement and wealthy old age?

The 'army of thieves' realised that time was running out, soon the Emperor's inventory would be complete, and that would bring an end to their highly rewarding occupation, so in a frenzy of 'terminal looting', plans were set and on the evening of the 26th June 1923 soon after the checking of the contents had begun, fire engulfed the principal storeroom and soon spread rendering to ashes everything, checked and unchecked, all were burnt to ashes. As these were the vaults where most of the *Ch'ing* treasures were stored the destruction was devastating; the pall of smoke had been sighted first by the Italian Legation who had immediately dispatched their fire brigade, but on arrival at the gates of the *Forbidden City*, were refused access, the guards not yet realizing the situation; soon other legation fire-fighting forces arrived and were at last admitted but, all to no avail for by now the whole area around the Palace of Established Happiness had been reduced to ashes.

Before dawn on the morning of the 27th June, Johnston was awoken by his servant, he was required to go to the palace immediately; hurriedly he dressed and not knowing what had caused him to be summoned at this early hour, he started his drive to the palace gates, the nearer he apporached the denser became the crowds, until at last he passed through the Gate of Spiritual Valour and saw to his horror, a large portion of the *Forbidden City* in flames; the beautiful Palace of Established Happiness had already ceased to exist, some neighbouring building had also caught fire, the scene was one of utter chaos and confusion, foreigners and Chinese shouting and getting in each others way with little real fire-fighting being done, it was a disaster and Johnston knew it had not happened by chance, it was obviously an act of deliberate and wicked destruction.

Next day the Household Department published a list of the losses, (how this was possible, considering the fact that the inventory had just been started and no other record was available, what their facts were based on still remains a mystery) their list included: 2,665 gold statues of Buddha, 1,157 pieces of painting and calligraphy, 435 'antiques' and tens of thousands of ancient books.

When Johnston finally arrived at the site he found the Emperor and Empress standing on a pile of charred wood viewing the devastation. Surrounding them, the crowd of Italian firemen being instructed by the officials of the *Nei Wu Fu*, which only added to the confusion for both the foreign helpers and the Chinese officials were in a state of high excitement. Suddenly, there emerged from the smoking ruins three Europeans, all in evening dress, their clothes, although proper for a state occasion, were now ruined with the soot and smoke; Johnston recognized them, Mr and Mrs Carson from the British Legation and Mr Gascoigne, after Johnston had greeted them they told him they had been dining at the Hotel de Peking and had seen the fire from the roof garden, they had at once driven to the *Forbidden City* to see if they could help. Johnston presented these three bedraggled representatives of the British Mission to their Majesties, who thank them for their courage in helping to fight the fire.

Apart from the historical and architectural value of the building destroyed the other losses were staggering, according to lists later submitted to the Emperor some 6.643 items of great value had been destroyed and in addition to those already enumerated were added 31 chests of state robes and furs, only 387 items had been saved according to the Household Department. The Peking Press were not slow to apportion the blame, citing the eunuchs, who they said had started the fire deliberately to cover their 'thieving' tracks; the following is an example of the press reports which the Household Department, usually so prompt in correcting erroneous press statements left on this occasion unchallenged:

> *Peking, 29th June*
> *"It now appears that an inventory of the property in the buildings of the Forbidden City destroyed by fire on Wednesday had actually been started. A close tabulation of the treasures had been ordered by the young Emperor but only two rooms had been gone over before the fire occured. This strengthens the view taken that culprits who had been gradually denuding the palaces of the property saw that they would soon be caught and adopted this desperate measure to cover their tracks."*

An 'official' enquiry was conducted into the cause of the fire but as that enquiry was undertaken by the officials of the Household Department, naturally no conclusive result was forthcoming.

The real cause of the fire was never discovered, although the officials made an attempt to persuade the Emperor that faulty electric wiring, installed at his insistence, was the reason for the outbreak, neither he nor anyone else believed this 'face-saving' attempt to apportion blame. Some of the eunuchs who had direct duties in the destroyed buildings were dismissed along with some of the electricians, but before long the *Nei Wu Fu*, unknown to the Emperor, reinstated them. The one question to which no satisfactory answer was made was; why had no fire-alarm been given until it was too late? The Imperial Household Department assumed the attitude that, since the damage was done, no amount of 'enquiring' could remedy the matter, it had best be forgotten as soon as possible.

But neither the Emperor nor Johnston had any intention of doing so, they both continued to ask 'embarrassing' questions, although within a few weeks the *Forbidden City* was outwardly calm, it was a calm that if the 'diviners' were really adapt at their art, would have foretold of a greater 'storm' to come.

An indication of the extent of the losses occasioned by the fire may be illustrated by the 'salvaging' of the ashes of the palace storeroom; when the rubble was carefully sifted through, there were no trace of the paintings or porcelain, which, in the case of the latter, was more than curious, but what there was ample evidence of, was a great deal of gold and silver. Various tenders were sought from the *Peking* gold merchants, the right to dispose of the ashes was finally secured by a bid of 500,000 dollars, and it was said that for this, he recovered some 17,000 taels of gold from the ashes. The rubble that remained after this was packed in sacks and 'distributed' to officials of the Household Department and, it is known that some time later one of them made a gift of four gold altars, one foot in height and diameter to the *Yung Ho Kung* Temple and the Cypress Grove Temple in *Peking*, made from his 'share' of the charred remains.

Just a few days later another fire 'mysteriously' flared up, this time in the No Idleness study in the eastern inner court of the Mind Nurture Palace, the Emperor's own apartments, luckily it was discovered before any real damage could be done and the cotton wad soaked in kerosene was extinguished; this, the Emperor knew was a direct attack on himself, he had been asking too many 'dangerous' questions, destruction of property, however valuable was one thing, but the attempted 'murder' of the Emperor was decidedly more serious.

An incident then occured that underlined the serious nature of the eunuch-ridden state of the 'Great Within'; the murder of a chief eunuch occured and the assailant was still at large; where would he strike next?

On the 15th of July the 'storm' the eunuchs had been dreading for centuries broke above their heads; on that day all eunuchs were expelled from the *Forbidden City*; the insidious institution that had endured since the time of the *Han* dynasty was finally no more. The plan was worked out in private, with the help of Johnston, who was in complete agreement with it, and who had always advocated the extinction of this court evil.

P'u-yi informed his father Prince *Ch'un*, that he wished to see him urgently and shortly after arrived at the family *Pei Fu* in the old Tartar City. When informed of his son's 'drastic' plan, the prince became hysterical, it was impossible, it could not be done! But *P'u-yi* insisted that he would not return to the *Forbidden City* until it was accomplished, his plan was thus; General *Wang Huai-ch'ing*, who was in command of his republican troops stationed between the summer palace and *Peking* was immediately summoned, for although a republican general, he had always been a staunch friend of the Imperial family. His troops were to go directly to the *Forbidden City* and there take up their positions, then the eunuchs were to be summoned to the main courtyard, there the comptroller of the Household *Shao-ying*, would inform them of their dismissal.

The Emperor's plan was successful, as the eunuchs assembled in the courtyard they were informed of their expulsion, which they received in silence, then they were escorted through the gate of Spiritual Valour by General *Wang's* soldiers. Within the coming days they were allowed back by two's and three's to collect their personal belongings and received what monies were due to them. The Emperor had proved himself master in his own house, much to the delight of the people and press of *Peking*, who gave the dejected eunuchs little sympathy in their 'exile'; the 'crows' suffered the heckling of the *Peking* wits, who more than demonstrated their dislike for these demi-men in the most basic way.

Of the thousand former court eunuchs only a handful remained, those in the service of the High Consorts, who pleaded with the Emperor not to banish their faithful servants, he gave in, but only after laying down the strictest rules for their future conduct. The young Emperor had quelled not only the eunuchs and the High Consorts, but his father as well, who now realized that his son was indeed 'master' of his own court.

The Press was uniformly eulogistic over the Emperor's abolition of the Eunuch-system:

> " . . . this action on the part of the ex-Emperor Hsüan-t'ung is welcomed by the vernacular press and the people in general. Hsüan-t'ung is now hailed as one of the very few progressive Manchu Princes of the present day, and probably there would have been no Chinese republic had he been born thirty or forty years earlier."

Johnston's part in the 'cleansing' of the palace was cited in a number of papers, notably the *Shun-t'ien Shih Pao*, and far from calling him a 'meddling foreigner' they applauded his 'progressive' influence on the young Emperor. Now, with the eunuchs gone, the Emperor could relax and with the more than ample space left by the destruction of the palace of Established Happiness he asked Johnston if some of this area could not be used for a tennis court; Johnston delightedly agreed. On 22nd of October the game of lawn tennis was played within the Walls of the *Forbidden City* for the first time, it was a game of doubles, the Emperor and his brother *P'u-chieh* against Johnston and the Empress's brother *Jun-ch'i*, the actual score is not known but the unbounded enthusiasm of the players was more then evident.

Having once gained ascendancy over the court by expelling the eunuchs, the Emperor, actively encouraged by Johnston, turned his attention to the corruption of the Household Department, with initially, less success. *Shao Ying*, the controller of the sinuous *Nei Wu Fu* frustrated the Emperors efforts to reform his omnipotent domain, and it was soon realized that no headway would be possible until he was replaced by someone honest and incorruptable, which ruled out, almost all the Manchus. Johnston again proved his value to the throne, for his searches for a new head of the *Nei Wu Fu* brought to light a Chinese who had held official office under the *Ch'ing*, which he had loyally resigned when the republic took over, and ever since had steadfastly refused all republican offers of appointment. *Cheng Hsiao-hsu*, (*Su-k'an*, as he was known in literary circles), was received in audience in the second half of 1923; his background was impeccable and he was undoubtedly one of the most learned and accomplished men of his generation, even at this time perhaps the most distinguished of Chinese poets and calligraphists, in fact that rare breed, a true Confucian gentleman. When *P'u-yi* questioned Johnston as to his opinion of *Cheng*, Johnston replied that in all his twenty-five years in China he had never met a Chinese for whom he felt a greater respect and admiration.

Although *Cheng Hsiao-hsu* had repeatedly refused to take office under the republic, at the Emperor's invitation, he agreed to assist the 'Lord of Ten Thousand Years' in reorganizing the *Nei Wu Fu*. In the beginning, he was appointed to the post of co-controller with *Shao Ying* merely in an attempt to save the latter's 'face', but it was soon more than evident throughout the *Forbidden City* who was really in control.

The corrupt fraternity of the 'Great Within' threatened directly and indirectly both Johnston and the new 'Co-controller' with assassination if they both did not resign their posts immediately.

Both men exchanged letters of threats they had received and tore them up, an act of no little courage in the circumstances. Soon the reformers were faced with a new ingredient emanating, not just from the disgruntled officials of the *Nei Wu Fu* but, voiced by a still powerful group of Manchu Princes within the court and rumbling from within the republican cabinet itself, it seemed the old roots of corruption nourished many an unknown branch.

Within just three months of taking office, *Cheng Hsiao-hsu* had reduced palace expenditure by many thousands of dollars a month, and try as they might, his enemies could not impune his high reputation, he worked on unperturbed, using a subtle and effective method of 'investigating' an official who had criticized him, thus making others more wary of taking a like course, lest he too come under 'official scrutiny'.

Unfortunately the web of 'established Malpractice' was too strong and widely cast for any one man to break, even if that man was the Emperor himself assisted by such men as *Cheng* and Johnston. There were too many well-lined pockets that had suffered from these 'reforms' and many of those were in the republican cabinet, so to frighten the young Emperor and his advisors, the government announced that it was to introduce a bill to abolish the 'Articles of Favourable Treatment', which was followed by another announcement of 'A Bill for the Protection of Old Books, Antiques and Ancient Relics", that was clearly intended to prevent the Imperial family from selling any of their own art treasures, making it all too clear to the 'reformers' that if they did not behave and allow the old system to resume they stood in danger of losing everything. The *Peking* 'Government Press' published numerous criticisms of the Emperor's policy, even citing the expulsion of the eunuchs, which had been so rapturously welcomed, now calling it a "callous act depriving many of their rightful livelihood"; that to make a *Han* controller of the *Nei Wu Fu* was illegal, (although the grounds for this statement were never forthcoming).

Cheng Hsiao-hsu had no choice but to resign, and the scheming *Shao Ying* reinstated, the *Nei Wu Fu* had won, just as they had against the last 'reforming Emperor' in 1898.

203

CHAPTER EIGHT

Eviction and Flight

Towards the end of 1923, Johnston was spending more and more time at the palace with *P'u-yi*, who not only relied on his sound advice and judgement, but in whose friendship he felt safe and secure. There were no longer any fixed hours of attendance, formal lessons having terminated after *P'u-yi's* wedding. They now spent the major part of each day in each other's company, Johnston only returning to his own house in the late evenings. To remedy this situation *P'u-yi* bestowed on his 'English Tutor' an honour without precedent in the history of the dynasty, he assigned him a private pavilion apartment within the Imperial Garden as his official residence where he could live and work, and where they could meet away from the formality of the inner court. Johnston's new Imperial residence was a large two-storied pavilion in the south-west corner of the garden which was only a few minutes walk from the Emperor's own palace, the *Yang Hsin Tien*, and was known as the *Yang Hsing Chai*, (Lodge of the Nourishment of Nature). *P'u-yi* had furnished "Johnston's Lodge" in the European manner, and had secretly even arranged for his books to be brought from his own former residence, much to Johnston's surprise. These idyllic surroundings were the scene of many an informal luncheon and dinner party, sometimes they dined alone, sometimes in the company of young Manchu Princes, and sometimes, though infrequently, they were joined by the Empress with her American friend and 'English Tutor' Miss Isabel Ingram.

These informal 'family gatherings soon developed into broader 'diplomatic' lunches, for Johnston was eager for his young protegé to meet prominent visiting Europeans, as well as resident ministers of the various foreign legations. Mr Yoshida, then counsellor at the

207

Japanese Legation was introduced to the young Emperor by Johnston at one of these informal gatherings and, although at the time, *P'u-yi* was unaware of the part these *dwarf barbarians* (as the Chinese always referred to the Japanese), were to play in his future, he intimated something of the sort to Johnston after their meeting.

During September 1924, a meeting took place between *Chu Yu-hsun* and the Emperor, again arranged by Johnston which, on the surface had nothing unusual to mark it out from any other audience, but Johnston had discovered, what he later described as, "a colourful historic fact", that made this meeting something out of the ordinary. The visiting card of this mysterious visitor read: "Chu Yu-hsun, descendant of the Imperial Ming House, Marquis of Extended Grace, (bearing the additional personal name of *Ping-nan*), dwelling in Yang-kuan Road, Little Street, north of the Tung-chih Gate." Johnston was determined that the last of the Manchu Emperors should come face to face with the last descendant of the *Mings*.

The surname *Chu*, was that of the *Ming* Emperors and his personal name, *Yu-hsun* translates as 'Shining Merit'; the hereditary title of Marquis had been bestowed on one of his ancestors by the *Shih T'ung* Emperor, (*Yung-chêng* 1723-1735) with the addition of *Yen-En*, (Extended Grace), which referred to the *Ch'ing* magnanimity of granting this title to a descendant of the dynasty they had overthrown. This historic meeting took place on 7th September 1924, two months later the last of the *Ch'ing* Emperors was to become a prisoner of a new order, or rather the prisoner of a few self-elected opportunists who called themselves the 'government of China', and the Marquis was to prove that his title was not without of meaning.

During September and most of October 1924, a quarrel broke out between the rival military leaders of the provinces of *Chehkiang* and *Kiangsu, Lu Yung-hsiang* and *Ch'i Hsieh-yuan* respectively. This in itself was not unusual, in the very beginning it occasioned little anxiety either in court circles or publicly, but it soon became obvious to intelligent observers that the strife would not be confined to central China because the Manchurian War-lord

Chang Tso-lin was an ally of *Lu*, whilst *Wu P'ei-fu* and *Ts'ao K'un*, (who had bribed his way to the office of Republican President in 1923) were both allies of *Ch'i*. What had begun as an armed skirmish between two *Yangtse* war-lords was now developing into a desperate struggle between *Wu* and *Chang*, and although the outcome was, at this early stage uncertain, what was certain was that this conflict could plunge the whole country into another civil war, this time more devastating than any that had preceded it.

Fêng Yü-hsiang, who was ironically known as the *christian General*, with a small *c*, held an important command under *Wu P'ei-fu*, although viewed as a potential menace because of his ruthless unpredictability, was thought harmless enough, as long as *Wu* was in direct control. *Wu* had come north with his 'punitive' army and spent several weeks in and near *Peking* making final preparation for his advance on *Shanhaikuan*, the pathway to Manchuria, at the point where the Great Wall meets the sea. He was confident of victory and openly boasted that he would be "master of Mukden" within a month.

Wu P'ei-fu had become a popular 'hero' in northern China, perhaps more than any other since the republic had come into being, if he did not embody all the ideals of "young China", he had at least the ability to inspire others with *national* feelings a good deal more commendable and less artificial than *Sun Yat-sen* had ever achieved. "Sunite", became an epithet, while the followers of *Wu*, who were nicknamed *Wu mi*, (infatuated with *Wu*), accepted their pseudonym with complete equanimity.

Wu has largely been replaced in modern Chinese history by *Sun Yat-sen*, quite without justification, for, during this period he was "the man of the moment" which *Sun* never was. *Wu's* most serious shortcoming was that he was a bad judge of character, he placed his faith in worthless associates who let him down time and time again, this coupled with an inordinate vanity, and in consequence an exaggerated notion of his own military abilities contributed to his downfall. He had been known to compare himself with Napoleon, which if only from a English point of view, was hardly a compliment. These failings, as well as a dangerous tendency to dismiss and despise his opponents, were inherent disadvantages from which he would eventually suffer.

On 17th October, Johnston found *P'u-yi* in pensive mood when he arrived at the Palace, *Tuan-k'ang* the surviving consort of the *Te Tsung* Emperor (*Kuang-hsü* 1875-1908), was very ill and near death, there seemed nothing anyone could do according to the doctors, and she died a few days later. After his meeting with the Emperor on the 17th, Johnston had gone to his retreat in the Western mountains outside *Peking*, 'Cherry glen'. There, alone amist some of China's most beautiful scenery, he rode and walked, reflecting on his part in the "Imperial Twilight"; storm clouds were gathering again over the tiny *Ch'ing* court, and he knew in his heart that his fate was irrevocably entwined with his young pupil and his family, they had become his family, and he resolved to stand by them whatever the cost. He returned a few days later on October 21st, and spent the night at the Summer Palace, where he received the sad news of *Tuan-K'ang's* death; he sat and mused by the margin of the lake, it was a clear autumn night, calm and beautiful, he likened its tranquility to that of the Scottish loch which Wordsworth had seen in his mind's eye, although on this occasion real wild ducks took the place of the poet's dream-swan. He drank in the peace that surrounded him like a cool draught of fine wine, little realizing that this was to be the last of the vintage, and although in the years to come, he was to try with all his might to find the fragrance of these past 'Imperial' years, it would be in vain, days not years were all that were now left.

Returning to *Peking* by car the next morning, he found the city alive with rumours, even his own servants were not immune from the nervous speculation that infected the northern capital. By the 23rd a mutiny of troops in the northern section of the old Tartar City was reported, and the street gate *Hou-men*, not a dozen yards from Johnston's house, was closed and guarded by troops, all the telephones in the area had been cut. The rumours of 'mutiny' were basically untrue,; what had in fact happened was that the *christian General*, who had not gone north as ordered, had brought off a highly successful *coup d'état*. The wealthier among the population were already flocking to the foreign legation quarter, (as they always had in time of danger), and were taking rooms in the Wagons-Lits Hotel. The railway station and telegraph offices had been occupied by *Fêng's* troops who had also suspended all telephone communications. *Fêng's* troops had surrounded the presidential palace, and by the time the slumbering encumbant awoke, he discovered to his horror, that he too, had been denied an escape route and was a prisoner of the *christian General's National* army.

Meanwhile Johnston, who was not at this time in possession of the preceeding facts, hurriedly drove to the *Forbidden City*;

> "The first ominous sign that I noticed, other than the deserted appearence of the streets, was the presence of armed men at the gate of the Chi An So, (a ceremonial building which belonged to the Imperial family). On reaching the open space between the Forbidden City and Prospect Hill I found futher cause for anxiety. The hill, which owing to its height and central position dominates the city of Peking, was not, as usual, silent and unpeopled but had become a scene of martial activity. Groups of men in uniform stood on the slopes and crowded the pavilions. At the gateway, which directly faces the Forbidden City, stood armed soldiers whose uniform was not that of the Imperial body-guard." [1]

By the time he had reached the Gate of Spiritual Valour everything seemed normal, his sedan-chair was awaiting him as usual and the guards presented arms. Johnston went directly to the Emperor's private apartments only to be told that he was awaiting him in Johnston's own pavilion within the Imperial garden.

P'u-yi was in the study attended by a few servants whom he immediately dismissed as Johnston entered;
"May I express my deep sympathy to Your Majesty on the death of *Tuan-k'ang*, it is to my sorrow that I was away from the *City* at the hour of her passing."
The young Emperor nodded and rose from the desk chair where he had remain seated since Johnston's entry. He slowly replaced the bcok he had been absentmindedly leafing through and looked

directly into the ice blue eyes of his friend and teacher;

"Do you know that there are armed troops occupying Prospect Hill, wearing neither republican nor Imperial uniform?"

"Yes, I saw them on my way here........"

"They went there without permission....... I do not know what they mean to do. *Shao Ying* has sent them food and tea, he seems to think that we must treat them as honoured guests."

"Did they give thanks for their refreshment?" Johnston enquired wryly, trying to ease the tension.

"No, they did not,......" *P'u-yi* added with the hint of the smile that Johnston had hoped for, "they merely asked for more!"

"Shall we go out and see them?" asked Johnston taking a pair of binoculars from a shelf, the Emperor nodded and they went out into the garden. On gaining a suitable vantage point, Johnston focused on Prospect Hill, it was literally covered with armed men, *P'u-yi* held out his hand for the glasses, put them to his eyes, and after a moment turned and walked back into Johnston's study. They lunched in the *Yang Hsin Tien*, and towards the end of the meal *Shao Ying* and other members of the *Nei Wu Fu* came in to discuss the situation.

"I must inform Your Majesty that this *New National* army has released from prison all political detainees and agitators, and the students are, even as I speak, distributing leaflets proclaiming some new form of political party called....... called communist." said *Shao Ying* in an unsuccessful effort to keep the tremor in his voice under control. Just then the arrival of the Emperor's father Prince *Ch'un* was announced;

"Your Majesty, have you heard the news? Do you know that...."

"Yes, Your Highness We have already been informed, please be seated." *P'u-yi* well knew his father's nervous disposition, and that if he did not make an effort early in the conversation to quiten him down nothing would be possible.

Johnston rose from his place at the Emperor's side,"If Your Majesty will permit, I think the most useful thing I can do in the circumstances is to go to the Legation Quarter and find out as much as I can, and to make what other enquiries might be pertinent at this time."

P'u-yi understood Johnston's thinly veiled meaning, for they had discussed the necessity of finding a safe refuge in case the worst should happen, which now, seemed inevitable. Prince *Ch'un* and the other officials were in a state of near panic when the Emperor informed them after Johnston had left, that he intended to take refuge in the Legation Quarter if it should prove necessary. They argued against this,

"Surely . . . . .surely, such an extreme step is not necessary" Prince *Ch'un* rapidly exclaimed, "Why, all the foreign powers recognize the Articles of Favourable Treatment and. . . . . .and, this *National* army or whatever it calls itself, would never dare to repudiate such a binding agreement . . . . .especially in the face of wide-spread foreign opposition . . . Your Majesty I implore you to. . . ."

"My mind is made up . . . . .there is nothing further to say, I thank you all for your advice." There was no mistaking the tone of the young Emperor, the meeting was over.

Meanwhile Johnston had gone to the Peking Club where, apart from a scotch whisky and water he gained little reliable information concerning the *coup d'état*. Theories were as numerous as the members, but few facts seemed to be known. The general ignorance of the club was reflected in the Legations. He decided to walk the two miles to his home feeling that he might yet glean some useful information, he was not to be completely disappointed. *Ts'ao K'un*, the republican President, had tried unsuccessfully to escape to the Legation Quarter and was now under house arrest within the presidential Palace; his close friend, the Republican Treasurer was in custody and soon to undergo a ten minute trial, all efforts having failed to force him to restore the enormous deficit in republican government funds; two days later he was summarily executed. Parliament was dissolved on the grounds of the gross corruption of its members, (who apart from other things had sold their votes in order to elect *Ts'ao K'un* president); salt was rubbed into *Ts'ao's* wounds when the *Nationalists* compelled him to sign the mandate of dissolution under the threat that if he did not, he might well meet the same fate as his friend the treasurer.

Having dissolved the parliament that had elected him, *Ts'ao* was also compelled to resign his presidency, and to append his signature to a number of other documents, one of which dismissed *Wu P'ei-fu* from all his posts. After these forcibly elicted actions, he was allowed to leave *Peking*. Naturally he lost no time in doing so, although he was determined to revoke all the mandates forced on him; to this end he carried off the presidential seals in his personal baggage and boarded the train for *Tientsin*. Unfortunately the disappearance of the seals was discovered before his train reached the safety of the port, it was stopped, and he was given to understand that his liberty, if not his life, depended on him handing over the seals immediately. Reluctantly he did so, and was allowed to continue on his jounrey to the foreign concession at *Tientsin*. The members of the dissolved cabinet followed *Ts'ao's* example as quickly as possible, realizing that they too, were in urgent need of a change of air. Notable among these dispossessed ministers was the foreign minister himself, Dr Wellington *Koo*, who eventually found refuge in the British concession of *Weihaiwei*, which ironically, in his official capacity, he had been negotiating for its return to Chinese administration some little time before.

The *christian General's* public announcement of his reason for the *coup d'état* was "To save the Chinese people from the horrors of another civil war". In this he completely failed, for these "horrors" increased, becoming more brutal and disastrous than ever before. His private reason, the ruin of Marshal *Wu P'ei-fu*, was perhaps the only successful outcome of his *coup*, and doubtless the only one he really cherished.

Thus from the end of October into the beginning of November, *Fêng's coup* seemed to have been completely successful; in an article in the *Peking Leader* published on October 26th it was described; "...unquestionably one of the most extraordinary coup d'états in Chinese history." Indeed it was. The *national* soldiers, under *Sun Yueh*, who were in occupation of Prospect Hill, became more and more insolent to the members of the Imperial Guard and household, it was evident, from their unmannerly action, that their one aim was to create an 'incident', which could allow them to commence real hostilities.

214

Top: P'u-yi on a tiled roof in the Forbidden
City, with Prospect Hill in the background,
(taken by Johnston C.1922).

The "christian General" Fêng Yü-hsiang, 1928.

At this time preparations for the funeral of the late dowager-consort *Tuan-k'ang* were in progress, although the usual ceremonies that accompanied a lying-in-state had to be severely curtailed.

Shortly after dawn on 2rd November Johnston was summoned to the palace for a conference with the Emperor, on arrival he found *P'u-yi* attended by his father-in-law, Duke *Jung* and *Cheng Hsiao-hsu*. They informed him that they had every reason to believe that the *christian general* was planning yet another *coup*, this time aimed at the *Forbidden City* itself. Plans were mooted for the imminent departure of the Emperor to the Legation Quarter, but now, every gate was guarded by *Sun Yueh's* soldiers, flight seemed impossible. The Emperor called Johnston aside and asked him to find a safe keeping place for a number of documents and other valuables, in preparation for an unimpeded escape from the 'Great Within'; Johnston agreed, and returned to the palace some time later informing *P'u-yi* that they were now safe in the vaults of the Hong Kong and Shanghai Bank.

During the next two days plans for the Emperor's escape occupied all their time, as the situation around them became more critical. On Wednesday, 5th November, Johnston received a telephone call whilst he was at breakfast from Prince *Tsai-t'ao: Fêng's* troops had entered the *Forbidden City* and seized all the gates, no one was allowed in or out, the palace telephone had been cut and there was no way of knowing what had happened to his Imperial Majesty.

The two men were soon speeding towards the Gate of Spiritual Valour which on arrival they found heavily guarded by *Fêng's* forces, Johnston's passenger was quite terrified when their car was approached by sentries;"Tell them I am your servant. . . don't tell them I am a Manchu Prince. . . . . "
The prince was torn between two conflicting emotions; apprehension of the fate that might await him if he ventured inside the *Forbidden City* and, loyalty to his Emperor for whom, there is little doubt he would have gladly risked his life. This degrading dilemma that the prince, who was the brother of one Emperor and the uncle of another, now found himself in presents, perhaps, more than any major instance could, the plight

in which the once proud Manchu now found themselves. He was prepared to humble himself and take the part of a common servant, and of a foreigner at that, in order that he might escape the notice of the soldiers and enter the *Purple Forbidden City*, the home of his dynasty, were he was a prince of the blood and in former times one of the 'ten', who ruled the Celestial Kingdom.

However, his intense uneasiness was soon calmed, for the sentry returned and informed Johnston that on no account was he to be allowed to enter the palace, these orders eminated from the high command and he particularly was named in them. Johnston turned the car around and drove away. By now Prince *Tsai-t'ao* was in tears.
"What are we going to do, what can we do?"
"There is only one thing to be done", Johnston replied calmly, "we must go to the Foreign Legation Quarter at once and ask the foreign ministers whay they can do to protect the Emperor and his family." The Prince nodded his agreement drying his tears on the long sleeve of his gown.

On arrival at the Legations they went directly to the Dutch Minister, Mr W J Oudendijk, who had tried to help the Emperor and his brother on the occasion of their former unsuccessful escape attempt. As luck would have it the British Minister, Sir Ronald Macleary, whom Johnston knew well, was just leaving, he immediately informed him of the invasion of the *Forbidden City* and the imminent danger to the Emperor, which neither minister knew about. A few moments later, the four men were seated at the large round table in the Dutch Minister's study. After a lengthy discussion it was agreed that the two ministers would that afternoon would call on Dr *C T Wang*, (the new Chinese Foreign Minister), and make firm representations, in an attempt to save the Emperor from any threat of personal violence; it was further agreed that the Japanese Minister Mr K Yoshizawa should be informed of the situation and invited to join them, which he willingly did.

All this time, rumours were circulating in the 'outside' City of *Peking*; 'There had been a massacre; the Emperor and Empress were dead and all the remaining members of the Imperial family were being put to the sword!' The panic that this, and other horrific rumours generated, was more than enough to send the remaining Manchu nobles and their families in terror to the Legation Quarter where they found, at least temporary sanctuary in an empty building belonging to the German mission. It was here that Johnston visited them and tried to calm their worst fears, whilst they awaited the outcome of the foreign ministers' meeting with the Chinese foreign office.

Earlier that morning, (5th November) *P'u-yi* was seated in the Palace of Accumulated Elegance (*Chu Hsiu Kung*), busily attending to a pile of urgent documents, glancing at the clock every few minutes anxiously waiting word from Johnston. As the clock chimed nine, filling the room with a musical rippling of bells, the ministers of the Household Department were announced, at their head *Shao Ying*; he stood almost breathless before the young Emperor holding a document in his outstretched hand;

"Your Majesty. . . . . Your Majesty . . . . " He panted, vainly trying to control the tremor in his voice, "General *Fêng Yü-hsiang* has sent soldiers and an envoy, saying that the republic is going to annul the Articles of Favourable Treatment." He stepped forward and handed the papers to *P'u-yi*, "He insists that you sign this at once". *P'u-yi* quickly rose and took the papers from the trembling official, unrolling them on his desk read:

By order of the President;
Lu Chung-lin and Chang Pi have been sent to arrange with the Ch'ing House the revision of the Articles of Favourable Treatment.

5th November, 13th year of the Republic of China
Acting Premier Huang Fu

The Revision of the Articles of Favourable Treatment
Whereas the Emperor of the Great Ch'ing Dynasty wishes to enter thoroughly into the spirit of the Republic of the Five Races and is unwilling to continue any system which is incompatible with the Republic, The Articles of Favourable Treatment are revised as follows:

218

1   The Imperial title of the Hsüan-t'ung Emperor of the Great Ch'ing is this day abolished in perpetuity, and he shall henceforth enjoy the same legal rights as all citizens of the Republic of China.

2   From the time of the revision of the Articles the Government of the Republic will grant the Ch'ing House an annual subsidy of 500,000 dollars and will make a special payment of 2,000,000 dollars for the founding of a factory for the poor of Peking in which impoverished bannermen will have the first priority for admission.

3   In accordance with the third clause of the former Articles of Favourable Treatment the Ch'ing House will leave the Palace this day. They will be free to choose their own palace of residence, and the Government of the Republic will continue to be responsible for their protection.

4   The sacrifices at the ancestral temples and the mausolea of the Ch'ing House will be continued for ever, and the Republic will provide guards for their protection.

5   The Ch'ing House will retain its private property, which will enjoy the special protection of the Government of the Republic. All public property will belong to the Republic.

        November 5th, 13th year of the Republic of China.

As *P'u-yi* perused the documents, which he had fully expected to confirm his worst fears, he felt slightly relieved, although the clauses concerning 'private' and 'public' property were dangerously ambiguous. His musings were interrupted by *Shao Ying*;
"They have ordered us to leave the *Forbidden City* within *three* hours." *P'u-yi* gazed at the terrified official in blank amazement; "Three hours? . . . . Three hours? How is such a thing possible? What about the High Consort? . . . . . How can We possibly collect all Our property . . . ."
He paced behind his desk and then turning to *Jung Yuan* he said; "Telephone Johnston, he will know what to do."

"The telephone lines have been cut Your Majesty" his father-in-law answered. "Send someone to bring His Highness." for although *P'u-yi* well knew that his father would have no practical contribution to make, it was necessary for him to be present, "I knew there was going to be trouble eventually but,. . . . .*three* hours?. . . . . they mean to rob Us of all Our property if not Our lives, get His Highness. . . . .!"

"Your Majesty we cannot" a voice from the huddled officials informed, "they have posted soldiers at all the gates and outside every building, they will let no one in or out."

"*Shao Ying*, go and talk to them in my name, find out what they *will* allow".

"Yes Majesty" *Shao Ying* replied bowing, as he hurried away.

The situation was grimly serious, *Tuan-k'ang* had only died a few days before and the two remaining High Consort adamantly refused to leave the palace. *Shao Ying* used this as his main excuse in his negotiations with the Republican envoy *Lu Chung-lin* and succeeded in gaining a little extra time before the proposed 'eviction', they had until 3 pm to gather up their belongings and leave their Imperial home. *Shao Ying* was also able to persuade the republicans to admit the Emperor's father Prince *Ch'un*, and the Imperial tutors *Chi Yi-fan* and *Chen Pao-shen*, only Johnston was denied access. Some short time later Prince *Ch'un* was announced, as he entered *P'u-yi* almost shouted, "What are we going to do?"

The prince stopped dead in his tracks, as if these words from his son had cast a spell over him. He stood and gazed at his son, he moved not a step closer, nor did he answer the question, but in a voice trembling with despair he hoarsely said; "I obey the edict . . . . I obey the edict . . . ."

P'u-yi turned away sickened by his father's incompetence and left the room returning to his private study. Once alone, he gazed around in numb despair, what was he to do? Why was the one person who could save him denied access? What was their real plan? Would he be 'accidently' killed in the chaos that would inevitably follow? Would he never again see the *Purple Forbidden City* which he had, in recent months tried so unsuccessfully to leave? The confinement he had hated, but the *City* itself he loved, he had known no other home, all his memories were rooted here. Then, he realized that he was no longer the *Hsüan-t'ung* Emperor of the Great *Ch'ing* Dynasty, what would he call himself? *Mr P'u-yi*? Or even *Henry P'u-yi*? Where would he go? Where, where was Johnston, in this hour of utter darkness? True, he had known the pain of loneliness all his life, as long as he could remember he had been alone, and now, he had one true friend, that friend was denied access. As these thoughts cried in his head, a knock on the door swung him around and *Shao Ying* stood trembling in the doorway; seeing the Emperor he fell to his knees trying vainly to hold back his tears: "The . . . . .the republican envoy *Lu Chung-lin* . . . . is, is urging us to go . . . . he has threatened that if we do not leave within twenty minutes he will order his soldiers on Prospect Hill to open fire with artillery on Your Majesty's City, and all remaining within its walls." The official was now weeping convulsively and *P'u-yi* gently helped the old man to his feet and led him into the council chamber where the others were still waiting.

Prince *Ch'un* was pacing up and down murmuring to himself, "It is all over . . . . it is all over now," he took his hat with the three-eyed peacock feather from his head and murmuring, "Well, I will not ever need this again." Threw it across the floor, it came to rest at the feet of his son as he entered. *P'u-yi* looked at the discarded hat, then at his father, who could not endure his shaming gaze, turning away burst into floods of tears.

P'u-yi slowly walked to the desk, took a brush from the jade stand, signed his name on the revised articles which he handed to *Shao Ying*; "Take this to the republican envoy, tell him we agree to leave, enquire what transport is available." He then turned to his father, "Your Highness, the moment of departure is near, I shall leave the home of our ancestors in a short while never to return; please go ahead to your house and inform them that I will be your guest, at least for the next few days." The prince nodded his hatless head, bowed and left the chamber.

The authorities had laid on five cars for the transport the ex-Emperor and his dispossesed family; the first in the motorcade was occupied by the Republican envoy whilst *P'u-yi* followed in the second, the three remaining cars accommodating the other ex-Imperial family members and the chief officials. The air was chill and the darkening sky, cloudless, as the strange, sad convoy wended its way to the *Ch'un* family mansion in the Old Tartar City. By the time they arrived the long fingers of darkness were clawing the last glimpse of light from the late autumn sky.

The cars came to a halt and *Lu Chung-lin* alighted from the leading vehicle and opened the Emperor's car door, hesitantly shook his hand with just the hint of a bow;
"Well, *Mr P'u-yi*, do you intend to be an Emperor in the future? Or will you be a good and ordinary citizen?"
P'u-yi looked the envoy directly in the eyes and in a clear calm voice said; "From today onwards I will be assuredly a citizen, but whether a good one, will be for my betters to judge."
"Good, then we will do our best to protect you and your family" replied the sheepishly smiling envoy quite unconscious of the ex-Emperor's innuendo.
"After all we can hardly have someone going about calling himself 'Emperor' in the Republic of China, can we?" as no reply was forthcoming he awkwardly continued, "but now, Your M . . . . *Mr P'u-yi*, can do your best for your country as a free citizen, you will have the right to vote in elections, why, you might even stand for election yourself, and if you work hard enough, who knows, you might even become president one day."
The word 'president' fell like a whip-lash on *P'u-yi's* ears, he flinched momentarilly but quickly regained composure;
"I have long regarded the Articles of Favourable Treatment as being obsolete, I am pleased to see them annuled and I agree with your kind words, as Emperor I knew no freedom now, as you so rightly inform me, I am *free* at last and I intend to live as a 'free citizen'. I thank you for your advice and your courtesy."
A group of republican soldiers who had been standing nearby broke into spontaneous applause at the end of *P'u-yi's* words. The delighted envoy bowed and then remembered himself shook hands again, *P'u-yi* turned and entered his father's house with the word *freedom* fluttering around in his head like a dying butterfly.

Once inside the family mansion, *P'u-yi* set about finding out exactly how dangerous the situation really was; before leaving the

Forbidden City he had secretly sent messages to his most loyal ex-ministers urging them to find a way of releasing him from the clutches of the unpredictable 'National Army', but as yet had received no reply. He desperately needed someone to talk through the situation with, his father was, as he had expected, a big disappointment. The prince was more flustered than anyone, from the moment *P'u-yi* entered the family mansion his father scarcely stood still for a single moment. When he was not walking up and down and muttering to himself, he was rushing in and out in near panic making the already tense atmosphere even more so. *P'u-yi* could stand it no longer;

"Your Highness, ...Your Highness! . . . . . .please come and sit down and let us talk this over. We must decide what to do, but before we can do that we must have some news from outside."

"Decide what to do? . . . . from outside? . . . . .Very well" he murmured as he seated himself in the chair his son had indicated. Whether he actually heard, let alone understood the words his son was speaking is debateable, for in a moment he leapt to his feet again and exclaimed with come vehemence;

"*T'sai Hsun* has not appeared either . . . . where can he be?"

"Your Highness, calm yourself . . . . . .we must have news of what is happening."

"Yes . . . . yes. . . . .I must get some news . . . . ." and with this he hurried from the room only to re-emerge a few moments later exclaiming in indigeant amazement;

"They . . . . . they, they won't let me out. There are soldiers at the main gate, and, they will not let me out! Can you believe such a thing?" "Then try using the telephone" *P'u-yi* counselled with visibly failing patience.

"Telephone? Yes. . . .yes . . . I shall telephone" again he hurriedly made for the door, then paused and turned to his son and asked;

"But whom shall I telephone?"

P'u-yi clasped his hands, and if he mumbled a few unfilial words, his father did not hear them.

All the other officials, except for *Shao Ying*, who was in much the same state as Prince *Ch'un* and therefore as useless, were away from the mansion attending to the Emperor's belongings which were still within the *Forbidden City*, as were the two High Consorts who had adamantly refused to leave until the proper ceremonies were performed for the departed *fei* whom they watched over. Within two hours the tutors arrived in the company of some princes and officials of the Household Department followed closely by Johnston. All this time Johnston had been waiting at the Legation Quarter for the return of the three foreign ministers to learn the outcome of their meeting with Dr *Wang*. The news they eventually brought was circumspect, but at least slightly reassuring. The republican foreign minister had assured them that the Emperor was in "no imminent danger" and that the "drastic" revision of the Articles was "the will of the people" and that the Emperor was now in his father's family mansion. Johnston thanked them for their efforts and took his leave to drive the three miles or more to the Tartar City. On the way as he drove through the dark street, for it was now late at night, he wondered if he would be allowed access; on arrival he found that the outer gates were closed and guarded by a strong force of *Fêng's* unruly soldiers. He stopped his car, two officers came forward and he handed them his official card and announced that he had an appointment with Prince *Ch'un*. After a short delay the gates were opened and he drove into the large inner courtyard. He was recognized at once by the family servants and escorted to a large reception hall, where the Emperor, surrounded by his officials, awaited him. *P'u-yi* rose smiling and warmly welcomed him.

"We are pleased to see you *shensen*, what news have you brought from the ministers of the foreign legation? Have they seen the republican minister?"

"They have Your Majesty."

Johnston then recounted the details of the meeting, all were attentive and still, all that is, expect for Prince *Ch'un* who, while Johnston was speaking moved nervously around the room and every now and then quickened his pace and rushed up to Johnston uttering a few incoherent words and then resumed his pacing. After he had repeated this four or five timed, Johnston's patience began to run out, the next time he rushed up and said, "Tell *Huang Shang* not to be frightened" Johnston more than slightly irritated replied; "His Majesty is, here, standing beside me. Why not address him direct?" The prince was far too preoccupied to either hear or understand the slight rebuke in Johnston's remark and merely nodded and resumed his aimless wanderings. *P'u-yi* took

Johnston by the arm and then went to his private rooms where they could talk quietly about the days events away from the alarm and bewilderment that surrounded them in the reception hall.

The *Pei Fu*, (the *Ch'un* family mansion), was by no means the best refuge that could have been chosen at this critical stage, being situated in the extreme northern section of *Peking* over three miles from the Foreign Legation Quarter which, at this time offered the only hope of secure sanctuary. The authorities were no doubt aware of this, for when Johnston at length left the Emperor, his car was painstakingly searched by the sentries before he was permitted to proceed on his way.

As he returned, through the now deserted streets, he felt anxious and despondent. From one view point, this old enemy, the corrupt *Nei Wu Fu* had collapsed at last, and the Emperor was now at least free from the catastrophic and unwholesome atmosphere of the *Forbidden City* yet, he was still a prisoner, only now of the unpredictable *national* army. For all the 'self-appointed' republican cabinet's assurances that "Mr P'u-yi was a free citizen", it was ominously clear that he was not, all that was needed to turn the already serious situation into a major tragedy was for *Fêng*, or some other powercrazed war-lord, to take matters into their own hands, and destroy all possibility of a future *Ch'ing* restoration. Johnston remained in his study into the early hours, remembering, reliving what was to him, the most important era in his life; dreaming of the Summer Palace and all the plans he had for its renewal as a home for the Emperor and his family, plans that would now sadly never be. His sense of loneliness was intense, but in no way was his resolve weakened; he would serve 'his' Emperor whatever the danger.

The next morning, when he drew up outside the *Pei Fu* he was curtly informed that he was not to be granted admittance on any pretext whatsoever and the following day, (7th November) he received the same refusal, he was not to see *P'u-yi* again for almost three weeks.

Few if any outside government and court circles knew what had happened to the deposed Emperor and his family; the country was still alive with a thousand and one rumours. Slowly, carefully 'edited' extracts filtered into the Peking Press all without exception ranging from the suspect to the down-right-unbelievable. A massive 'face-saving' propaganda campaign was set in motion by the fragmented government.

The Far Eastern Times
6th November 1924

"A Monarchist plot, as great as any formulated two hundred years ago in Europe on behalf of 'Bonnie Prince Charlie' was frustrated yesterday afternoon in Peking. Attempting to take advantage of the unsettled state of the country, several groups of Manchus and their adherents were plotting for the return of the youthful Hsüan-t'ung, as Emperor . . . . 'in fact' instead of 'in name only'. Final details awaited settlement, details regarding the proper costumes to be worn at the enthronement ceremonies, precedence, titles to be bestowed and other trivialities. . . . . . Now comes the amazing part of the stroke and possibly the inner reason. There is little doubt that Wu P'ei-fu was set on a restoration had he been successful in his war-fare, with himself as guardian of the throne. Certain very curious details which are still veiled in secrecy, go to prove that he was making dispositions in that sense."

In the same paper on the 10th November:

"It is no longer disputed in Manchu circles that a high emissary was sent to Loyang before the present civil war to sound Wu P'ei-fu on the subject of a restoration. The reply given by Wu P'ei-fu was considered sufficiently encouraging to report to the ex-Emperor Hsüan-t'ung that Wu P'ei-fu was certainly favourable to the idea and that all would depend on the march of events. . . . . The very careful steps taken to surround and sandbag the Palace entrances since November 1st prior to the clearing of the Palace and the handing-over of all the Imperial seals, were dictated by these considerations,

the ever present possibility of a 'coup' in what is after all a Manchu city, being one that cautious men could not ignore."

This was official 'face-saving' on a monstrous scale; there had been no planned restoration and the smearing of *Wu* came clearly from one quarter only, the *christian General* who had publicly sworn to destroy his rival. Without the trumped-up 'restoration' plot what other justification did either *Fêng* or the 'cabinet' have for invading the *Forbidden City* and tearing up the 'Articles'. However the balance was soon restored, the following day (11th November) the *North China Standard* gave voice to the lie of a monarchist restoration for which the *Far Eastern Times* had made itself foolishly responsible: *"As everybody knows, a swindle pure and simple!"*. This repudiation was taken up by the *Peking and Tientsin Times* of November 17th:

> *"There has been no monarchical plot in which the Emperor has been in any way implicated. The alleged restoration conspiracy was a fake invented with the object of justifying a wanton outrage. Try as he may Mr C T Wang can find no plausible pretext for tearing up the Abdication Treaty. And it is now obvious that the virtual imprisonment of the Emperor is designed to prevent his public repudiation of the agreement forced upon him by the unscrupulous men temporarily in power in the capital."*

The article continued:

> *"Mr Wang scoffs at the idea that the abdication agreement can be regarded as a treaty. Yet, Marshal Tuan Ch'i-jui, whose memorial to the throne was the decisive factor in securing abdication, is our authority for the statement that 'the People's Army' had undertaken 'if the throne accepts its terms, to register that latter with the Hague Tribunal.' Is it customary, we would like to ask, to register agreements which are not in the nature of treaties, at the Hague Tribunal? Is it possible to construe this undertaking in any other way than as revealing an intention on the part of the republicans to give the abdication agreement a treaty status? The terms*

of the abdication themselves reveal that the intention of both parties was to enter into a binding pact, which could be altered or modified only by mutual agreement . . . . . . not, as in the present case, by a handful of Bolshevik upstarts temporarily in power in Peking."

Fêng yü-hsiang, the so called *christian General* had received his most enthusiastic foreign support from Christian missionaries in China, foremost among whom was a Rev Mr Goforth who was described by a canny contemporary as *"A evangelist and revivalist of 'fundamentalist' views."*[2] His selfconscious efforts in marketing his peculiar brand of christianity had already been the subject of withering comment in Johnston's book of 1911 [3] and when, so the anecdote goes, the Rev gentleman was informed that the *christian General* had gone *red*, he replied in his best pulpit manner, *"yes, he is red . . . . red with the blood of Christ"*; but shortly after this it was the reverend gentleman's face that was *red* for the *christian General* was reported in the press to have *"gone on a pilgrimage to Moscow"*. What *Fêng* did in Moscow is not completely clear, although it was reported that he spent a great deal of his time drawing portraits of Lenin with a Chinese brush and signing his name to them in large characters.

The Articles of Favourable Treatment have never, not even to this day, been legally and constitutionally abolished. Any real sympathy that the so called 'national parliament' may have enjoyed, evaporated almost completely with *Fêng's* deplorable treatment of the Emperor and his defenceless family; the applause that was beginning to ripple stopped, and the self-appointed cabinet soon found to their dismay that they were called *Chu tsai*, or 'piglets' by both the people and press.

"The arbitrary cancellation of the abdication act by the government caused widespread consternation. The impression of it was even greater than the stabbing in the back of Marshal Wu P'ei-fu. . . . . . . Only a few approved the action of the government . . . the Chinese politicians who were in lively communication with the Soviet embassy, and Dr Sun Yat-sen."[4]

The leading foreign newspaper in northern China, the *Peking and Tientsin Times* declared that *Fêng Yü-hsiang's* second *coup* was like everything else he had done, *"Rooted in dishonour"*. Its editor went on, *"one of the most unsavoury chapters in the whole chequered history of the so-called Chinese republic."*

A leading Shanghai paper, *The North China Herald* confirmed this view in its issue of 29th November;

> *" . . . . . this flimsy tale*, (referring to the fictitious restoration plot), *was developed, not at the instance of monarchical plotters and schemers, but as a reaction against a political experiment which instead of a republican authority has produced so far only competiton among a congress of military cliques. Many Chinese are coming to believe in monarchy for no better reason then they believe in bridles for undisciplined horses."*

On the 15th November a government controlled paper the *Shih Chieh Wan Pao*, (The World's Evening News) blatantly announced that the source of almost all the anti-government pro-Manchu propaganda emanated from but two 'evil' men . . . . Dr Wellington *Koo* and *Chuang Shih-tun*, (Reginald Johnston). Their evidence was as flimsy as their charges were 'fantastic'; *Koo* had lost his 'rice bowl' because of recent events, and Mr *P'u-yi's* 'English Tutor' Johnston had been *"given great dissatisfaction by the Ministry of Foreign Affairs"* and these two villians had decided to join forces in *"upsetting the newly-established regime"*. They met in secret daily in *"a certain room"* in the Wagons-Lits Hotel, (in the Legation Quarter) and there concocted their plots in collabration with an unnamed English news agency and other 'low' press representatives. Of course hardly anyone took it seriously, least of all Johnston, but it did tilt the spotlight in his direction at a time when darkness and anonymity were far more desirable.

A grim story was then currently circulating in the Foreign Legation Quarter, a certain prominent communist was asked what he thought of the expulsion of the Emperor from the *Forbidden*

City, he had replied with a sinister smile, *"Why draw the line there? We in Russia know how to deal with Emperors!"* One aspect, that could, and was generally overlooked by Western Observers at this time was, from a Chinese point of view highly emotive; this *coup* and *eviction*, had taken place at a time of Imperial mourning for the dowager consort *Tuan-k'ang*, according to the traditional social code of China, observed by all people, it was a "wicked intrusion" on family grief, especially as the funeral ceremonies had not yet taken place and the two remaining consorts, who had refused to leave the palace, had become popular examples of "Honourable behaviour". Certainly this aspect was a severe embarrassment to the authorities and caused much public animosity towards them. *Fêng* had quite literally gone *red, red* in the face at least, two old ladies had defied both him and his troops and the whole so-called government, they had even threatened to commit suicide if they were not allowed to stay within the *Forbidden City* and attend to the funeral rights. An appeal was even made to the "ex-Emperor" to persuade the consorts to leave without any undue fuss, but he felt little inclined to assist the very man who had 'evicted' and disinherited him at one cowardly stroke. All this time the two imperturbable old consorts went about their duties, assisted by their few remaining servants and eunuchs, oblivious to the 'propaganda' they were causing. The funeral ceremonies in the *Forbidden City* ended on 19th November, on the afternoon of that day a modest little procession, robbed of its appropriate Imperial splendour passed slowly through the Gate of Spiritual Valour to a temple near the Drum Tower in which the coffin of the departed consort found a temporary resting place, before its final journey to the Imperial Mausolea. Two day later the two surviving Imperial dowagers passed through the same gateway leaving the *Forbidden City* for ever. Their new home was in the eastern part of the Old Tartar City, there, attended by the last few of their faithful servants, they lived out the remaining few years of their lives. What mental suffering these two courageous old ladies had endured will never be known for they are reported to have never referred to their 'eviction', not even in private.

On the 25th November both the Chinese and Foreign press carried the following announcement:

> *"Yesterday Marshal Tuan Ch'i-jui assumed the post of provisional executive. One of his first acts was to remove the restrictions over the Manchu Emperor which have caused such an outcry and to inform Mr R F Johnston, his tutor, that he could visit him."*

On another page was printed;

> *". . . . . by order of Marshal Tuan Ch'i-jui, Fêng Yü-hsiang's men were withdrawn from prince Ch'un's palace yesterday and replaced by guards provided by the headquarters of the metropolitan police."*

Almost the same hour that Johnston had read with great relief these press statements, he received two visitors, the first an official from the chief executive's office informing him that he was now quite free to visit the Emperor, the second was a messenger from *P'u-yi* informing him that the hated *Fêng's* soldiers had indeed departed and would he please come at once to the *Ch'un* family mansion. Johnston lost no time in complying with this happy Imperial command and drove to the *Pei Fu* with more than usual speed. On arrival he was admitted at once.

P'u-yi was anxiously waiting for him in the courtyard of his own apartments, at the first sight of Johnston he ran towards him and flung his arms around him. Both were so overcome at their reunion after what seemed a lifetime, that they remained silent for some minutes. Then *P'u-yi* led Johnston by the hand into his private rooms where they remained alone for most of the day.

Towards dusk, a messenger arrived from Marshal *Chang Tso-lin* asking Johnston to visit him that evening, as soon after dark as possible. He remained with the Emperor until it was almost dark then, just before leaving, *P'u-yi* handed him a signed photograph of himself and a large smoky-topaz ring set with diamonds. "Give these to Marshal *Chang* with my compliments and send him my respects". Johnston smiled and nodded, after a long moment he left for his mysterious appointment.

Darkness falls early on *Peking* in November and by six o'clock it was quite dark as Johnston drove to Marshal *Chang's* headquarters in the west of the city. On arrival he passed through a series of courtyards which were all occupied by the Marshal's body-guards, then finally on into a large reception room where Marshal *Chang* greeted him in a friendly and informal way. The Marshal was wearing Chinese civilian dress and after a few moments of general conversation in front of his staff officers he escorted Johnston into his private office. During their hour-long discussion the door remained closed and not even the inevitable tea-attendents entered. "The Emperor", Johnston said deliberately, "sends you his felicitations and these tokens of his respect." Johnston handed Marshal *Chang* the photograph and ring. He looked at the photograph in a thoughtful manner and after but one glance at the ring handed it back, motioning Johnston to be seated.
"I wish to help the, 'Emperor' and try to undo some of the evil that has been done by the overhasty and ill-advised action of others who had no authority to act as they have. But, you must understand I can do nothing that might give rise to suspicion in republican circles that I am aiming at another 'restoration', " Johnston looked directly at him, " . . . . I am not."
"I have a plan whereby the 'Emperor' might be reinstated and his privileges restored", he continued, "this could be accomplished without it seeming to be the outcome of Manchurian pressure, which, I am sure you realize, at this time would be disastrous." Johnston nodded. "If, and I only say *if*, the Articles of Favourable Treatment are to be continued I must know the attitude of the ministers in the Foreign Legation to my proposals. This is where you come in; will you convey my proposals to the foreign diplomatic representatives?"
"Naturally Marshal, I shall be glad to do what ever I can to secure the well being of the Emperor and his family." Johnston replied.
"Good, I though I could rely on you. Will you please come and see me within the next few days and tell me the outcome of your visit to the Legations?"
"Gladly, Marshal Chang." The Marshal rose and shook hands with Johnston. The interview was over.

For a brief few days all seemed more hopeful; Johnston visited *P'u-yi* every day and they dined and laughed together as they had in those now lost days before the humiliating eviction. But even as they talked, the skies above *Peking* were growing black with ominous clouds. Strange rumours were becoming current foretelling yet another, even more serious *coup d'état*.

The *christian General* had been sulking after his monumental loss of 'face' and he retired to a Buddhist monastery in the Western Hills and was mumbling about resigning, which was a sure sign that he had no intention of so doing. It was also common knowledge that Marshal *Chang* owed his victory in the civil war entirely to *Fêng's* betrayal of *Wu P'ei-fu* and now, these two uneasy allies, who disliked and mistrusted each other, obviously their 'alliance' could not be a lasting one. Sooner or later there would be yet another armed power struggle.

On paper, *Fêng* was still in military control of *Peking*, Marshal *Chang* had only his bodyguard. "What" said the rumours, "what if Chang and his small bodyguard were surrounded and disarmed and the 'Marshal' invited to a 'tea-party' in his own headquarters, then a seemingly innocent 'walk'. . . . . . . .a 'walk' during which a little accident would remove the 'Marshal' once and for all from the battlefield of Chinese politics?"

When Johnston expressed his and the 'evicted' court's apprehension at the rumours to the ministers at the Legations, he was thought to be over-reacting to the situation. The diplomats assured him that the present political atmosphere in *Peking* was perhaps a little confused, but quite stable. The Emperor's friends and advisors did not share this optimistic view, from their intelligence sources it was evident that *Fêng* was slowly reinforcing his troops within Peking and was even now deep in conference with his senior staff officers at his temple retreat in the Western Hills.

On November 29th, the day after the national soldiers had been withdrawn from the *Ch'un* mansion and the *christian General* had issued his telegram of threatened resignation, a somewhat ill-advised communication was sent from the 'evicted' court in the name of the Household Department to the republican Home Ministry:

> "......... *According to the provisions of the principals of jurisprudence as applied to criminal law, all those who use violence to compel others to do things against their will may be held guilty of assault; and according to the principals of civil law anything that is extorted through violence or terror has no legal validity. We wish to make it known through this letter that the Ch'ing House is unable to recognize the legal validity of the five revised 'articles' imposed by the provisional cabinet ....*"

On the same day *P'u-yi* gave an interview to the *Shuntien Times*, which was Japanese run, with direct support from the Japanese Legation and which, for reasons that will soon become apparent, gave full support to the Emperor's cause. This was against the direct advice of Johnston who, at the time of the interview was absent from the *Ch'un* mansion. The resulting article was a highly coloured basically fictitious account of "atrocities" committed against the court at the time of the eviction from the *Forbidden City* by *Fêng's* national army. It ended with a quote which reportedly had come from the Emperor; " .... of course I did not freely assent when I was forcibly compelled to sign the document by the soldiers of the national army who were pretending to act in the name of 'the people' ...."

These public protestations, though justified, had the immediate effect of raising republican blood-pressure and Johnston said so, it seemed to him that every time he was absent from the Emperor's side his other advisors, all of whom had a different 'solution' to the problems, influenced him in a dozen conflicting ways, all of which were inept to say the least. One of these advisors *Chin Leang* wrote in his private journal at this time;

> "After Tuan Chi-jui and Chang Tso-lin entered the capital they appeared to be very friendly to us but their friendship extended only to words, not deeds. Everyone was deceived into believing that a return to the palace was imminent; when it did not take place people were of various opinions.

234

Some said that we should not allow a word of the original articles to be altered; some that the Emperor should return to the palace with his title restored; some that he should change his title to 'Retired Emperor'; some that annual expenditure could be cut, but foreign guarantees should be obtained; some that the court should move to the summer palace; and some that a house should be bought in the eastern part of the city. But as real power was in the hands of others all these plans were dreams; I do not know what led them to think as they did." [5]

Prince *Ch'un*, as might be guessed, led the faction that was in favour of the Emperor staying put in the family mansion and, for a time his insistence on this point held sway, but, *P'u-yi* had no intention of exchanging a large *Forbidden City* for a small one; he was determined to leave and it seemed that for the moment, the Foreign Legation Quarter offered the only possible refuge. All this time whilst the tiny court was twisting and turning in the Northern Mansion, Johnston was busily making practical preparations and sounding out opinions in the Foreign Legations, he knew that the situation was daily becoming more untenable and that if the reinforcements to *Fêng's* national army continued at their present rate a new and more disastrous *coup d'état* must be imminent.

On the evening of the 28th November, Johnston was in consultation with *Cheng Hsiao-hsu* and *Ch'en Pao-shen*. They had come to Johnston's house by appointment realizing, as he did, that the Emperor must be found a place of safety and quickly. Johnston pointed out to them that the Foreign Legations seemed to be still blissfully ignorant of the impending danger, which did little to erase their fears. They agreed that to remove the Emperor directly to the Legation Quarter would be too dangerous. Another 'residence' was necessary that would not give rise to suspicion; the *Nei Wu Fu* had recently acquired a large house in *Soochow Hutung* street quite near the *Hataman* city gate, which was very close to the eastern entrance to the Legation Quarter, this would be ideal they concluded.

235

The next morning, 29th November Johnston arrived early at the *Pei Fu*, he was meet by *Ch'en Pao-shen* who had been anxiously, awaiting him with news that the *christian General's* troops were flowing into the capital in ever increasing numbers and, it seemed likely that at any moment he might replace his soldiers outside the *Ch'un* mansion, if only to regain 'face' as a preliminary gesture of defiance to Marshal *Chang*; if this were to happen the last chance of escape would have vanished.

Johnston agreed, the 'escape' must be made at once, but when *Ch'en* proposed to inform *Wang yeh*, (Prince *Ch'un*), Johnston vehemently disagreed, on the grounds that the prince would make such a fuss that the whole enterprise might flounder, *Ch'en* reluctantly agreed. They then went directly to the Emperor's private rooms and acquainted him with the imminent danger and the need for an immediate 'escape'. After Johnston had fully explained the urgency of the situation *P'u-yi's* immediate reply was; "I understand, I am in your hands and I will do whatever you think is best."
"No one must know of our plans Your Majesty, least of all your father." Johnston cautioned with one of his customary half smiles which *P'u-yi* understood all too well.
"I agree" he said, returning his friend's smile.
"To avoid arousing any suspicion you must make no visible preparations for travel, you must take nothing with you, you. . . ." Johnston paused as his young Emperor handed him a bundle of pearls and other jewels which he had taken from beneath a large cushion and taking them, his smile growing broader, he thrust into the recesses of his fur coat. "We will not order the car until we reach the courtyard, now we must go."

Johnston lead the way through the Emperor's private courtyard, through the two main central halls, and out into the main courtyard where, as luck would have it, the car was already parked. The three figures assumed an air of false nonchalance and moved slowly towards the vehicle; just as the Emperor was seating himself, Prince *Ch'un's* chief steward *Chang Wen-chih* suddenly appeared from the house and asked;
"Where are you going, Sirs?"

"Oh, just for a short drive, nowhere in particular, we shan't be long." Johnston calmly reassured the steward.

"A short drive? May I come too?" the three were silent, which *Chang* took as confirmation of his request, and settled himself in the back seat next to *Ch'en*. The chauffeur, fortunately was one of *P'u-yi's* most devoted servants and both he and Johnston took their places besides him in the front seat so that Johnston, could more easily give the changes of direction which might be necessary during what was going to be a difficult journey. The main gate was opened and the car slowly passed through onto the public road where the police guard was stationed; three of the five passengers almost held their breath as they waited to be challenged, but no, the police saluted and did not attempt to interfere with the exit the vehicle. Just as the tension relaxed two armed constables mounted the car on each running-board with the intent of accompanying the 'escaping' car.

Johnston's main object was to avoid all the main streets where they were most likely to encounter *Fêng's* troops, he had already instructed the loyal chauffeur to drive through the eastern section of the city, as they intended to inspect the new house of the Household Department in *Soochow Hutung* street. It soon became a tedious and dangerous journey as Johnston constantly instructed the driver to change direction; the distance that, in normal times was no more than three miles, took over five. Fortunately, except for two occsaions, when they had quickly to turn down a side street to avoid meeting *Fêng's* troops headon, the drive was uneventful. When they at last came to the corner of *Soochow Hutung* and *Hatamen* streets Johnston leaned forward and told the driver not to turn into the former street but to turn right, (west), and drive on until he came to a certain photographer's shop where His Majesty wanted to inspect some photographs.

"I know the shop" said the driver in a clear voice, "it is in the Legation Quarter." Johnston and his fellow conspirators stiffened and the steward sat bolt upright.

"Just drive straight on to the shop and then stop," ordered Johnston glancing at the two armed constables who to his great relief made no visible response. In a few moments they had passed the eastern entrance to the Legation Quarter and came to rest outside the shop. Johnston and *P'u-yi* dismounted and casually entered. They were greeted by the German proprietor Herr Hartung; "*Guten Tag* gentlemen, may I be of service to you?"

"We would like to see some of your views of Peking." Johnston replied. "Ah, good, here you will find an wonderful selection" motioned the proprietor. "Please take your leisure gentlemen."

Johnston nodded his thanks and began to absentmindedly examine the views of the city he knew so well, it was then that he committed one of his rare blunders; turning to *P'u-yi* he said; "Would you care to look at this *huang shang*?" (which mean your Majesty), the three Chinese in the shop looked at *P'u-yi* in startled silence and one immediately rushed into the street. The Emperor moved closer to Johnston, who, trying to gain the upper hand of the situation, said to the hovering proprietor;

"We will take these, thank you." Handing a bundle of randomly chosen photographs to the shopkeeper who quickly wrapped them and handed them back with Johnston's change. When they emerged from the shop they were confronted by a crowd of silent Chinese; thankfully they were merely curious to gaze on their Emperor for the first time, and were in no way aggressive. *Ch'en Pao-shen* and the prince's steward were still seated in the back of the waiting car;

"Why have we come here?" the steward questioned in a tone of mounting excitement, "Why did we not go to *Soochow Hutung* street?"

Johnston left these enquiries unanswered and turning to the Emperor said; "Dr Dipper resides close by. He is an old friend of mine and I know he would much like to meet you, shall we call on him?" *P'u-yi* nodded and the two returned to their seats in the car and the driver started towards the German Hospital which was only a minutes drive from where they had stopped. This seemed the longest journey of all, both *P'u-yi's* and Johnston's hearts were pounding as they drew up in front of the Hospital where the Doctor had his consulting rooms. He was well known to the Emperor for during the past two years he had been frequently summoned to the *Forbidden City*. They alighted and Johnston sent his card in with the request for a immediate interview; the doctor emerged seconds later and recognized both Johnston and the Emperor and summing up the situation lead them upstairs to an empty ward. Johnston told him what had happened and what they proposed to do, the good doctor understood perfectly and offered to help in any way he could.

"Meanwhile" Johnston informed him, "I am going to see the Foreign Ministers. I must leave the Emperor in your charge. Please see that he is well protected." The doctor's heels clicked together in assent. Johnston then approached the lonely figure seated on the crisp white linen of one of the beds, reaching deep into his pockets he restored the jewels to *P'u-yi*;
"I shall not be long, be patient, you are quite safe here." He turned and left the little ward and returned to the street; the moment Prince *Ch'un's* steward saw that Johnston had returned alone, he hurried away, and Johnston had no doubt that he would soon be reporting the events of the morning to a horrified and hysterical Prince *Ch'un*. *Ch'en Pao-shen* was still seated in the car and Johnston asked him to join the Emperor in the upstairs ward and to await his return from his meeting with the Foreign Ministers.

It was now almost one o'clock in the afternoon as Johnston hurried to the Japanese Minister; he was not at home, he was out at a lunch. The Netherlands Minister was also absent. Johnston now hurried to the British Legation where fortuitously Sir Ronald Macleary was at home. He recounted to him as briefly as possible what had happened, suppressing his own part in the 'escape' knowing the British attitude to interference in Chinese internal politics. He told the British Minister that the Japanese had indicated, through Mr Yoshizawa, their willingness to protect the Emperor which eased Sir Ronald's anxiety and he added that if this were so, Johnston was welcome as a guest at the British Legation, where he could be near the Emperor as the two Legations were almost face to face. It was nearly three o'clock by the time Johnston returned to the Japanese Legation, but the Minister had still not returned. Just as Johnston was about to leave and return to the German Hospital he arrived; hurriedly Johnston explained the situation and begged him to extend to the Emperor the hospitality of his Legation. He did not reply but commenced to pace up and down considering the matter, then, finally he gave the anxious Johnston his answer:

"We would be honoured to receive the Emperor, but . . . . but it is necessary to prepare suitable accommodation for him, therefore Mr Johnston you will be good enough to return to the German Hospital and await my message."

Johnston was less than reassured, what did the Japanese Minister mean by "suitable accommodation?" He thanked the Minister and returned to the hospital.

He entered the door and bounded up the stairs to tell the Emperor the news.

"You Sir! Where do you think you are going?" a German voice asked him.

"To see the Emperor" Johnston replied swinging around to view his questioner.

"What Emperor!" continued the voice which belonged to a German male nurse, "There is no Emperor here."

"Nonsense" Johnston replied impatiently, "I brought him here myself."

The German looked at Johnston closely, "The Emperor was here, but he has gone."

"Gone? Gone where?" Johnston gasped.

"I haven't the faintest idea" came the prompt reply.

"But I have just now made arrangement for him to go to the Japanese Legation" exclaimed Johnston in bewilderment.

"That must be where he has gone" assured the young nurse. Johnston's alarm was slightly relieved but he was still extremely worried. "Where is Dr Dipper?"

"He has gone home, he told me if any strangers came and asked for the Emperor I was to say that we had no Emperor here," he smiled and disappeared into a ward, for a moment Johnston stood alone in the corridor trying to make some sense out of the off hand information he had just received. Then he descended the stairs and made for the Japanese Legation.

Unknown to him after he had left the Emperor at the German Hospital *Chang Hsiao-hsu* had arrived at the *Ch'un* mansion, only to be told that he had left for *Soochow Hutung* street, he had proceeded there in his carriage and had found no trace of them, pondering what to do, he had seen the prince's steward hurrying by and, on enquiring was told that the Emperor had 'fled' to the German Hospital. *Chang*, on arriving found the Emperor and *Ch'en* upstairs in the ward, he told them that very morning he had made arrangements for the Emperor to be sheltered in the Japanese Legation and had the military attache's, Colonel Takemoto's word, that he would be welcomed. All this had happened at almost the same time that Johnston had been with the Japanese Minister. Takemoto had told *Chang* that he would acquaint his Minister with the decision, but had never done so. *Chang* had then returned to find the Emperor vanished and had at last traced him to the German Hospital. Once there, he had explained the arrangement with Colonel Takemoto, and the Emperor had consented to accompany him to the Japanese Legation. Their journey there was to prove hair-raising, for *Chang's* coachman, either through ignorance, or stupidity, drove his royal passenger out of the Legation Quarter along *Ch'ang-an* street which was a few dozen yards outside Legation territory. The only thing that had saved the Emperor was the dust laden wind which helped to conceal the carriage and it occupants from the gaze of the increasing number of soldiers in this part of the city. Within a few minutes the carriage had turned south again into the Legation Quarter and drove along the side of the creek that separated the British from the Italian and Japanese Legations. The Japanese Commandant had been awaiting his Imperial visitor at the gate of his Legation and they had not long been ushered inside when Johnston finally arrived.

It had been only after their arrival that the Consul had communicated the news to his Minister and the door was opened to Johnston by the Japanese Minister himself Mr Yoshizawa who, had installed his illustrious guest in his own private apartments, which he deemed "suitable accommodation", for the young Emperor and where he was to remain a guest for some months to come.

The *escape* of the Emperor caused a sensation in *Peking* which rivalled his *eviction* from the *Forbidden City*. The Press had a field day, though most of the reports were fallacious, being based on either rumours or inadequate information, or a combination of both. The main object of the printed rebukes fell heavily on the

Japanese Minister and to redress this he gave an interview which was printed in a number of papers on 2rd December, in which he gave an entirely truthful account of the incidents that had resulted in the Emperor becoming his "honoured guest". Nor did Johnston excape censure from the press, particularly in the *Ching Pao*, which was well known for its support of the communists, and in the *Ch'en Pao* which supported the Peking students who, if not bright red at this time, were decidedly pink. The two unfortunate policemen who had accompanied the Emperor's car into the Legation Quarter begged to be allowed to stay as they were fearful of being held responsible for the Emperor's escape; their petition was granted and they became courtiers, if only temporarily of the 'exiled' court within the Legation Quarter, which, it should be remembered, was wholly under foreign control.

Within a little over an hour of the Emperor's installation in the state rooms of the Japanese Minister's residence, Prince *Ch'un* arrived at the head of cluster of Manchu Princes and officials of the *Nei Wu Fu. P'u-yi's* new reception room was crowded with a chattering crush of nervous and excited officials, foremost among whom, was a distracted Prince *Ch'un* who tried every excuse he could think of to persuade his son to return to the family mansion, an invitation that was not, unnaturally declined.

During the confusion and anxiety of the last twenty-four hours the Empress and the secondary consort had been completely forgotten and when Johnston mentioned the fact to *P'u-yi* he stared back in amazement, for he too had completely forgotten the 'wives' he had chosen from photographs. Johnston made a telephone call, and the next day the two overlooked ladies were ready to leave the Tartar City but, at the gate of the *Ch'un* mansion their car was stopped by the already embarrassed police, and politely told them they must remain where they were.

Some hours later the Emperor received a note begging him to devise some means of rescuing them; he showed the note to Johnston who suggested that they approach their host the Japanese Minister for his advice. Immediately the subject was broached Mr Yoshizawa dispatched one of his diplomatic secretaries, (Mr *Ch'ih Pu*), to the *Pei Fu* with strict instructions to bring the Empress back to the Legation and, "Not to return without her." Within an hour the secretary telephoned from Prince *Ch'un's* house saying that the Empress was ready and anxious to leave but that the police at the gate would not allow her out.

Without a moments hesitation Mr Yoshizawa ordered his car and drive straight to the office of the Chief Executive *Tuan Ch'i-jui*, and requested politely but firmly that instructions should immediately be issued to the guard at the *Pei Fu* that no restrictions should be placed on the movements of the Empress and her ladies. The effect was indeed immediate for within an hour the Empress arrived at the Japanese Legation.

That evening, 30th November, Johnston set out for his second visit to *Chang Tso-lin* as he had promised some days previously. It was going to be a delicate meeting to say the least, just how 'delicate' Johnston was soon to find out. On arrival he was ushered into a large hall, not a private office as before, and the suave, sympathetic Manchu gentleman, that Marshal *Chang* had posed as on the previous occasion was gone; in his place he found an "arrogant, ill-mannered and tempestuous Manchurian bandit." [6] Without the customary greeting or any show of courtesy *Chang* plunged into a vehement denunciation of Johnston and his "unlawful" plot in taking the 'Emperor' to the Foreign Legation Quarter. Although Johnston at this time was not aware that the crafty officials of the *Nei Wu Fu* had carefully placed the whole responsibility for the 'incident' on his shoulders, he was now faced with a torrent of abuse. He tried vainly in his calm gentlemanly manner to explain the 'true' facts to the shouting Marshal, but he would not listen to one word Johnston had to say. Pride seemed to be the main pebble in the Marshal's spleen; "Tell me . . . . tell me Englishman, what harm could possibly have come to the Emperor in the house of his father? None . . . . . . none as long as *Chang Tso-lin* is in Peking! You have meddled in Chinese affairs over and over again . . . . you a foreigner, a guest in our country . . . ."

Johnston stood and took all the abuse, he could do little else as the tirading bandit-marshal seldom paused long enough to allow him to speak; it seemed that part of the 'performance', if not all, was for the benefit of the numbers of his staff who were now openly listening at the four open doors that lead off the hall. When Johnston tried to reintroduce the subjects that they had previously discussed in 'private' the Marshal shouted even louder, clearly this was a 'public' performance. It seemed even then that much of *Chang's* indignation came from the realization that his own position was far from safe and that he might at any moment be forced to follow the Emperor's example and seek refuge in the Legation Quarter as the *christian General* tightened his grip in *Peking*. The 'Manchurian' storm ended as quickly as it had begun, Marshal *Chang* turned and left the hall without a word of farewell and Johnston was left standing for a moment, looking at the blank space where the angry Marshal had stood; the curious faces were still at the doors and as he turned to leave, he felt their eyes uncomfortably following him to the door. The epilogue to the incident followed in just a few days; Marshal *Chang Tso-lin* left *Peking* in his own special train in the grey dawn of a December morning. *Peking* was now in the undisputed military control of *Fêng Yü-hsiang*, the *christian General*.

The Emperor remained an "honoured guest" at the Japanese Legation from 29th November 1924 until 23rd February 1925. He was still in residence when Dr *Sun Yat-sen* arrived in *Peking* for the last time, a dying man both mortally and politically.

During those months the Emperor never left the safety of the Legations, he either remained in his quarters at the Japanese residence, or he dined with Johnston, who now had rooms in the British Legation. There was to follow a long and lonely 'exile' in the dreary Japanese concession in the treaty-port of *Tientsin* which lasted from February 1925 until November 1931.

CHAPTER NINE

The Dragon Departs

During *P'u-yi's* three months at the Japanese Legation he celebrated two important events; the Chinese New Year, when he received former *Ch'ing* officials in his small drawing room there, which he later described as, "a room brimming with pig-tails". He sat facing south, in true Imperial style, although seated on a Western chair draped in yellow for the occasion. Thirteen days later, he celebrated his twentieth birthday, (by Chinese reckoning, nineteenth by Western), being an "honoured guest" and not wanting to cause his host any more inconvenience he did not mention the fact, but the Japanese Minister insisted on his receiving the congratulations of his guests in the main reception hall, furnished especially for the occasion with fine Chinese carpets and an improvised throne-dais backed by a yellow draped screen. Here *P'u-yi* received his five hundred guests, *Ch'ing* officials, members of the diplomatic corps, princes and high dignitaries who all observed the court usages as if they were still in the *Forbidden City*.

It was a very moving occasion for the young ex-Emperor, the sight of his depleted court in its temporary 'palace' filled him with heartbreaking melancholy, at times he could hardly hold back his tears, especially when he saw the loyal old *Ch'ing* veterans painfully perform the nine-fold *kowtow*, some having to be assisted to their feet after the obeisance by their fellows.

After the last congratulation had been made *P'u-yi* rose and made and impromptu speech to the assembly;

"As I am only a young man of twenty it does not seem right that I should be celebrating 'long life' and the present

difficulties make me even less inclined to do so. . . . .
many of you have come a great distance and I wish to take
the opportunity to meet and talk with you. . . . .It seems that
in the 'modern world' there is no longer any place for an
Emperor . . . . . my life inside the 'Great Within' was virtually
that of a prisoner and I took little delight in my lack of
freedom. I have long cherished the ambition of going abroad
to study and to this end I have studied the English language
but, up to this present time there have always been too many
difficulties in my path to make this 'dream' a reality.
The continuation or abolition of the Articles of Favourable
Treatment seem to me no longer a matter of any importance.
Had I been allowed to end them voluntarilly, that would have
been acceptable but, it is intolerable that I have been forced
to do so through compulsion. The 'Articles' are a bilateral
agreement and may not be altered by one party alone any
more than can an international treaty. The 'invasion' of the
palace by the troops of *Fêng Yü-hsiang* was a violent act,
especially as the matter could have been settled easily and
calmly by negotiation. I have long harboured the sincere wish
not to continue using an 'empty title', but then, to have that
title taken from me by armed force causes me much pain.
The Republic should realize that such barbarous acts do great
damage to our country's name and its reputation for good
faith . . . . Of the motives behind my 'eviction' from the
palace I will not dwell, the details are probably well known
to you. As both I and my family were completely powerless
it was shameful of *Fêng Yü-hsiang* to act against us as he did,
and the humiliation and intimidation we suffered even
continued after we had been forced from our home . . . .
I would accept a settlement, an honourable settlement
without demur. I have one more important announcement to
make: I will never agree to any proposal that would mean
foreign intervention in Chinese domestic politics."

The young Emperor paused, the guests, many of whom were
dabbing their eyes, remained silent, then, the sound of applause
slowly rippled through the room, the foreign diplomats and guests
had begun it in admiration for the young dispossessed monarch

who had, by his directness and humility won their hearts, and it was enthusiastically taken up by the Manchus and Chinese and, perhaps over enthusiastically by the Japanese.

About this time, the press began to attack the ex-Emperor and his tiny court with unabated fury; the Household Department of the *Ch'ing* court had been "wickedly stealing national treasures for years", these were the "rightful property of the people" . . . . the ex-Emperor's meddling Japanese "protectors" were trying to restore the 'Articles of Favourable Treatment' in league with the *Ch'ing* sympathizers. A 'League Against the Articles of Favourable Treatment of the *Ch'ing* House' suddenly sprang from the depths republican movement, had began to take vicious action against the little court. This so-called "public disapproval", was expressed in the press in various ways; innunedo, accusations, and well-meaning advice to the court and Japanese Legation. One report, is in retrospect, pertinent:

The Peking Daily

" . . . . . . The darkest part of their plot, (the Japanese), is to keep him until there is an incident in a particular province, when a certain country will send him, (the ex-Emperor), there with armed protection and revive the rank and title of his distant ancestors. The province will then be separated from the Republic and will receive that country's ,(Japan) protection. The second step will be to deal with it in the same way as another country that has recently been annexed was dealt with, Korea . . . . .P'u-yi's terror and flight were the result of deliberate intimidation by certain people. He has fallen into their trap, which was a part of the pre-arranged long term plan. . . . In their present treatment of him they are willing to go to any expense to provide him with everything. The country in question had bought the friendship of each of his fellowers, who have come under its control without realizing it and will be its tools in future."

At the time these vitriolic words seemed, the mere rantings of fanatics, but, they were to prove prophetic.

249

During this time, Johnston remained close to his pupil, and they often walked together in the evenings along that short section of the city wall which, being the southern boundary of the Legation Quarter, was excluded from Chinese control. From this vantage point could be seen the wooded park surrounding the great Altar of Heaven; the great white marble altar which, in happier days he would have officiated at. The gleaming yellow tiled roofs of the *Forbidden City* were also visible, and the sight of them reduced *P'u-yi* to tears, and he buried his head in Johnston's chest; while Johnston was soothing him a solitary dark figure could be seen coming towards them, after he had passed *P'u-yi* asked who it was, "he looked so frightening".

"Karakhan, the Soviet ambassador," Johnston replied in a whisper. *P'u-yi* shivered and they returned to the British Legation where they dined privately together.

During that evening, both were in pensive mood, for they realized that soon their paths would inevitably lead them in different directions, their time together was coming to an end. Johnston, because the British Foreign Office had more than hinted, that through him they could not be seen to be influencing internal Chinese politics, and that his 'official' association with the ex-Emperor must soon cease. *P'u-yi*, also felt the cold breath of change on his cheek, a change that seemed predestined; his one wish was to go to England with Johnston, but he knew in his heart, that this was but a dream that would never be realized.

The scandalous reports that were appearing in the Chinese Press and the rumours being spread by the *Fan Ch'ing T'ung Meng* (the Anti-Manchu League), made allegations that the Japanese would use the youthful ex-Emperor to further their aggressive Imperialistic ambitions in China, and would shortly spirit the willing, or unwilling "puppet Emperor" to Japan. No official Japanese hint of this was ever forthcoming, and indeed Johnston was "officially" told by the Japanese Minister, that the presence of the *Ch'ing* Emperor in either Japan or the Japanese leased territory of *Kuantung* in Manchuria would "seriously embarrass" the Japanese Government.

The smug protestant missionaries who had taken such obvious pride in their most distinguished convert, "the christian General", and had hailed him as a sincere and pure hearted "soldier of christ", now mentioned him, if they did at all, with greatly diminished enthusiasm. *Fêng*, who had been lauded as "an old testament christian", or "the great christian general, the Cromwell of China" was now spoken of as "a crafty secret wolf", which was still something of an understatement.

Nor did Johnston escape from mischievous press attacks, the following first appeared in the Chinese press, *Min Pao* and was translated and published in the English press on 11th August 1925:

> *"Ever since the arrival of the former Emperor in Tientsin, Mr Johnston has been making overtures to all the Ministers and consuls of the European imperialist countries in China in the name of his pupil. He did his best to win their support in a restoration movement by offering various concessions. As a result of his intrigue, the British Chargé d'affaires has come under his influence. Since the Shanghai outrage of May 30th, Mr Johnston has been taking a more prominent part in this Monarchical plot together with the British chargé."*
> (the British *Chargé* at this time was Mr C M Palairet, Sir Ronald Macleary being temporarily absent.)

The Anti-Manchu League a few weeks later published an open letter to the British Minister in *Peking* demanding Johnston's expulsion from China; the immediate execution of all Chinese monarchists and as Johnston's "crimes were unpardonable", he too, should meet the same drastic punishment! The league claimed to represent four hundred million Chinese, which they clearly did not, even ten per cent of that figure would have been over generous to them.

However, the republican government intimated to Johnston that it would be grateful if he would make a public reply, it would facilitate their own efforts to curb the anti-Manchu agitators. He willingly agreed and his letter was published in the *Peking and Tientsin Times* and other foreign and Chinese papers.

The last paragraph is the most pertinent:

> *"Even in his retirement in Tientsin, the nineteen-year-old Emperor is not free from the bitter and unchivalrous attacks of his enemies. Not content with having deprived him by force of the rights and privileges accorded to him in the original abdication pact, they are now attempting by every possible means to deprive him of such privileges as remain to him under the revised pact imposed upon him at the time of the coup d'état last November. Charges are incessantly being made against him of intriguing for a monarchist restoration. In this morning's Chinese press, for example, it is stated that he is surrounded at Tientsin by active members of the monarchist party; that he has established close relations with the various foreign counsels in Tientsin; that he has recently applied to a certain foreign power for protection, and has promised 'when restored to the throne' to grant that power various valuable privileges in China; and that he is allying himself with a certain military party, also with a view to a monarchist restoration. It is hardly necessary to say that not the smallest fragment of evidence is produced to support these wild assertions."*

At 7pm on the 23rd February, *P'u-yi* took his leave of the Japanese Legation and his generous host and hostess. He left accompanied by the Japanese police chief from *Tientsin* and several plain clothes policemen who escorted him from the Legation's rear entrance to the *Chienmen* Railway station. At every station the train stopped several more Japanese plain clothes policemen got on, and by the time they finally arrived, the carriage was literally crowed with Japanese protectors. He was welcomed by the Japanese consul-general in *Tientsin*, Yoshida Shigera with a strong contingent of offficers and men from the Japanese garrison. Some little time before this, he had dispatched an official to find a suitable house in the Japanese concession in *Tientsin*, as the one he already owned was situated in the British concession and, for political reasons was not "favourable" to the interests of either party.

The *Chang* Garden, was not in a sufficient state of readiness to receive him and he was obliged to spent his first day in the Yamato Hotel. However, the next day his hastily furnished house was almost ready and he moved in and was joined the same day by the Empress and secondary consort. The *Chang* Garden was set in large grounds of about three acres and in fact belonged to a former *Ch'ing* general who, insisted that the Emperor reside there rent free, the old man even swept up the garden leaves to demonstrate his loyalty to the Imperial house in exile. *P'u-yi* was to be the old general's guest for five weary years before moving to 'the Quiet Garden' on the death of his kind landlord whose son, within a few days of the old man's death, demanded an enormous rent from the impoverished exiles.

P'u-yi had merely thought of *Tientsin* as a temporary resting place before he set out for his studies abroad; sadly that was never to be, and his life from this time was enveloped in the darkening clouds of a tragic classical drama.

P'u-yi's sense of isolation and despair were deepened when Johnston was summoned back to England in 1926 in connection with the administration of the British share of the 'boxer' indemnity. It was his second trip during twenty-eight years of residence in China. He returned early in the following year to take up his new post as British Commissioner at *Weihaiwei*, the British leased territory were he had previously served as district officer and magistrate; he was to remain there for four years until the British government carried out its long-standing promise to restore the territory to China. During those four years, he made a number of visits to *Tientsin*, the first, was on his arrival back in China in February of 1927, just a few days before *P'u-yi's* birthday, which that year, fell on the 14th. It was a happy reunion, *P'u-yi* was his former happy self for those few brief days before Johnston had to leave to take up his official duties at *Weihaiwei* on 31st March.

During these dangerous and confused days, the long red hand of bolshevik Russia was reaching out and gaining in influence under Stalin's direction. At the second *Kuo-min tang* conference of January 1926, although the *kuo-min tang* held the balance of power, it continued the alliance with the Chinese Communist party who made up some twenty per cent of the central executive committee. This arrangement was publicly endorsed by the leader of the left, *Wang Ching-wei*, and the rights new principal 'war-lord' *Chiang Kai-shek*. *Chiang's* "Whampoa Cadets", had already defeated all opposition in the Canton area, but the alliance between the two leaders and their parties was delicate to say the least. Moscow favoured collaboration; Stalin needed his alliance with *Chiang* as part of his struggle against Trotsky, just as *Chiang* still needed a united 'revolutionary' front with the Chinese Communist Party and Soviet support for his proposed "great Northern Expedition".

Chiang Kai-shek shared the same intellectual limitations of his master *Sun Yat-sen*, but his determined political ambitions, coupled with the military skills he had acquired in Japan and Russia placed him above his fellow war-lords, whom he manipulated by any means that would keep him on top. For this, and his military ambitions he needed Western money, his marriage to *Soong Mei-ling*, a Wellesley graduate and sister of *Sun Yat-sen's* widow, provided him with the contact with the West he needed. These new relatives, with their American background, he used in top financial posts; his wife's brother *T V Soong*, a Harvard graduate, and her brother-in-law *H K Kung* an Oberlin graduate; whilst his Japanese trained minions, he used in military posts. He was to be responsible for more human misery and bloodshed than all the other opportunist war-lords put together, *Yüan Shih-k'ai* would have been proud of him.

Peking was alive with rumours concerning this new "Nationalist" war-lord who was surging northwards at the head of a "murderous army"; they had sworn to kill all monarchists especially the Imperial family; *Chiang Kai-shek* was slaughtering every communist in sight like a "raging flood of wild beasts", the rumours ran; *P'u-yi* feared for the safety of his own life and those of his family and again urgently put forward his hopes of going abroad, but this had the effect of merely terrifying his miniature court, who he well knew would be destitute without him.

P'u-yi with some of his brothers and sisters in
exile in Tientsin.
The Chang Yuan, (Chang Garden), P'u-yi's
temporary home in Tientsin.

In 1928 *Chiang Kai-shek*, *Fêng Yü-hsiang* and *Yen Hsi-shan*, (the war-lord ruler of *Shansi* province), announced their intention of co-operatiing in a concerted attack in northern China. Sweeping around the Japanese troops who were supporting *Chang T'sung-chang* along the *Tientsin-Pukow* Railway they swallowed up *Chang's Shantung* base and forced him to retreated northeast.

Northern China was alive with "mad-dog armies", fighting each other and plundering anything of value, even killing each other, if the division of loot was not to their liking. But by far the most serious devastation took place in early July 1928. The descration and looting of the Imperial Tombs, (the *Tung Ling*, east of *Peking*). The Emperor and the whole Manchu court was plunged into deepest mourning; the whole Chinese nation was shocked by this catastrophe, the magnitude of which could hardly be estimated, except by those who know how deeply the cult of ancestor worship was venerated by both Manchu and Chinese alike.

Whether the culprits are described as "soldiers", or "bandits", is of little importance, there was no clear dividing line in those days of internal strife and disorganization. The mausolea, in the *Malan* Valley situated in *Tsunhua* county of *Hopei* province housed the tombs of the illustrious *Ch'ien-lung* Emperor and the Grand Empress Dowager *Tz'u-hsi*.

Sun Tien-ying a former gambler and opium dealer, and one time subordinate of *Chang T'sung-chang* was now a favoured commander under *Chiang Kai-shek* and whether, directly on the orders of the "Generalissimo", or on his own initiative, which is hardly likely, he ordered his troops to the area of the *Ch'ing* mausolea and began to carry out a planned and systematic robbery. He posted notices that he and his army were going to carry out military manoeuvres, cut all communications and sealed off the whole area.

Tung Ling, in fact comprises seven separate Imperial cemeteries, each stand in its own vast grounds and housing palatial structures after the style of the *Forbidden City*, nestling majestically at the foot of rolling hils which curved into a fourteen miles formation

256

following the natural landscape of a picturesque valley. Each cemetery had its own mile long road converging into a common avenue, the 'Ten Li Spirit Pathway' lined on both sides with ten foot high granite statues of warriors, officials and animals. Of all the tombs that were built, the one for the Grand Dowager Empress *Tz'u-hsi* was the most magnificent and costly. The main structure, which was built on a marble terrace, was in the style of a temple and termed 'the Spirit Hall'; stuccoed in the traditional pinkish-red colour, which symbolized the Northern Star rays representing wisdom. The roof top was tiled with highly glazed yellow tiles which glittered in the sunlight like a canopy of pure gold; this was supported by massive columns thickly lacquered with gold-leaf. The fourfold massive doors were bound with thick brass and heavily reinforced, giving strength and sturdiness to this hall which contained the 'spirit tablet', resting on a stand fashioned from incense wood, carved with flying phoenixes around the border and decorated with gold lacquer. The face of the tablet carried the name and titles of the deceased and in a secret sliding panel in the back, a paper inscribed with the date and hour of both birth and death together with other important particulars concerning the departed, whose spirit is believed to be embodied within the tablet, therefore it is accorded the same honour that the departed enjoyed during life. It is because of this belief, sacrifices were held there three time a year celebrating birth, death and at the festival of *Ching Ming*, (the annual 'sweeping of the tombs'). All the major buildings face south in true Imperial tradition representing, prosperity, light and harmony. The grounds were landscaped with rockeries, springs and wonderful fountains which mingled with the giant and ancient pine trees. The actual place of interment, the sepulchre , was situated at the back of the 'spirit hall', not visible from the approach road, which only affords an inspiring view of the massive 'Spirit Hall'.

The tomb itself was twenty years in the building and cost an estimated eight million taels. Prince *Ching* and minister *Yung-lu* supervised the construction, consulting constantly with the Dowager Empress who was most particular about every detail, making regular tours of inspection to examine every aspect of the building, even down to the materials used. In 1897, when the tomb was almost completed she ordered the teak pillars to be changed as they were not massive enough.

Chiang Kai-shek's subordinate, *Sun Tien-ying* and his fifty soldiers had many problems to overcome before they could plunder the entombed treasure of the Imperial dead. First they had to dispose of the Imperial guards, stationed around the building; then with the use of dynamite blast their way into tombs through walls of solid granite, many feet thick, sealed with concrete blocks. Under the cloak of moonless darkness, *Sun* deployed his men, within half an hour, not an Imperial guard remained alive, the thieves were then free from interference, and went about their ghoulish work unhampered. Kerosene torches were lit casting eerir shadows over the now silent scene, *Sun's* men became more nervous as the flickering shadows revealed here, a bloodsoaked murdered guard, and there, a fiery dragon sculpture peering from the blackness of the night. *Sun* shouted and raged at their foolish fears and set them to work drilling the holes that would soon be filled with hundreds of sticks of dynamite. The tomb walls proving too thick to be effectively drilled, the roof was inspected, and drilling recommenced there; finally the explosive filled holes were sealed and the wires run out, the soldiers withdrew without any urging from their commander and took shelter behind the low wall that surrounded the tomb, the wires were connected to the battery box, wound up and *Sun* plunged the lever down. The resulting explosion shook the surrounding countryside, and echoed around the deserted valley. *Sun* and a few less apprehensive of his troops rushed forward and climbed the ladders to inspect the damaged roof, a hole had been made in the granite large enough to permit two men to descend at a time and when the dust had settled sufficiently, a ladder was gingerly lowered into the blackness of the tomb and finally, to the relief of the soldiers, came to rest on the marble floor below. *Sun*, seeing the nervous state of his men shouted "Bu par", (fear not) and taking a torch started to descend the ladder into the gloom below. Even by the light of his flickering torch he could see the outlines of the contents; in the centre of the magnificent chamber stood the Dowager Empress's massive coffin resting on a rectangular marble platform. The coffin was twice the normal size, carved from heavy catalpa-wood, the lid secured with thick long nails of soild gold, the whole covered with an elaborate canopy of imperial yellow silk-satin heavily embroidered with blue and green phoenixes; at its foot stood a cinnabar carved lacquer table displaying a set of solid gold incense burners and candlesticks. As *Sun* looked around him in shivering amazement, he became aware of a bubbling sound, looking up, his torch partly illuminated the head of a huge dragon and he stumbled back in fright, then when it did not move he stepped forward to examine it; its month spouted water which fell into a semicircular pool and drained around the entire chamber through a narrow marble channel before disappearing through an outlet in the floor, designed to keep the tomb cool and thus preserve the earthly body of the departed Empress. The four walls were decorated with Buddhist paintings in vivid colours.

A voice from the ladder-top brought him back to reality and he shouted for his men to come down and begin the looting of the richest tomb in China's long history. Slowly and nervously his men complied with his commands, once within the chamber he set them to work; two snatched the gold incense-set from the table and threw it into a waiting sack which was hauled up to the roof; axes were sent down and others dragged the yellow canopy from the huge coffin and began to hack at its heavy lid. The first thick outter lid soon succumbed to their frantic battering and fell to the floor; they edged forward holding their flickering torches aloft, these revealed an inner lid; which was soon removed and a gasp of amazed terror came from the grave-robbers, for there laying, as if in sleep, was the still awesome figure of the Great Dowager Empress surrounded by a glittering mass of gems which sparkled in the light of their torches. The rouge on her cheeks looked freshly applied and her lustrous hair shone beneath her sparkling headress. Some of the soldiers stood stiffened with fear, others hurriedly picked up their rifles and aimed them at the magnificent lifeless figure, most just stood and trembled. Slowly regaining their courage some moved closer, the Empress' hands were covered with what looked like inch long white hairs which quivered in the moving air, some, unable to control their terror stumbled back from the lifelike figure lest she should rise and place a curse upon them. One drew his bayonet and poked at the eerie white hairs, he soon realized were only mildew. As they gazed a transformation began to take place; the bright rouge on the Empress' cheeks having come into contact with the fresh air for the first time in twenty years, began to fade, the iridescent brightness of her silk robe began to turn to a shabby yellow. The stern voice of their commander brought the men to their senses, they rushed forward as ordered and began despoiling the coffin, it slipped from its marble platform spilling a shower of jade and precious stones across the floor of the chamber and with them the body of *Tz'u-hsi* tilted forward and fell to the floor. The looting went on well into the next day, and for two days thereafter. The tomb of the great *Ch'ien-lung* Emperor was also robbed and his still well preserved body hacked to pieces in a frenzy of guilty fear.

Some four days later a young nephew of one of the Imperial guards journeyed to the tombs to visit his uncle; what he saw turned his blood cold, all the guards had been massacred including his uncle and the devastation caused by the explosions and looting had turned the area around the tombs into a rubble covered desert. He rushed away to raise the alarm. As the tomb site was remote, it was several days before any official investigation could take place and during this delay the tombs were looted by a second wave of soldiers who gathered up what their fellows had overlooked; these were followed by a swarm of curious peasants who picked the site clean well before the investigators arrived. When *P'u-yi* received the news four hundred miles away in *Tientsin*, he was so overwhelmed with grief that he could not speak and wept convulsively as did the other Manchu Princes who had gathered around him.

Details were scarce, and for nearly ten days mystery surrounded the desecration. The Republican government, whose legal responsibility the tombs were, showed no willingness to either investigate the matter or to apprehend the culprits; their dishonest excuse was, that they did not wish to be reminded of the Manchu yoke that had lately been cast off, there was no other word from them. No arrests were ever made, none of the stolen property ever recovered; the customs service, after a number of weeks did, half-heartedly check travellers baggage at the northern ports and railways stations, but they "officially" recovered nothing.

P'u-yi, faced with this monstrous situation, called together his remaining Princes and officials to decide what action they should take; the tomb site must be immediately guarded, a survey of the damage carried out, and an estimate arrived at for the reinterment ceremonies. How was the latter to be achieved? His only income was from the Republican 'articles', which had never been honoured, even when they were in force, and now, he had been keeping his family by selling what few treasures he had been able to secretly take to this new home in *Tientsin*. A body of Manchu clansmen lead by Princes *Pao-hsi, P'u-lun* and *Tsai-chih* travelled with all speed to *Tung Ling* to inspect and secure the tombs.

What they saw on arrival was the most heartrending sight they had ever beheld. On entering the Dowager Empress' tomb, they found her half naked body thrown diagonally across the splintered coffin lid, it showed no visible signs of decomposition, except a faint purplish tinge. The body had not been embalmed. The once proud and lustrous hair lay dishevelled across the floor; the Princes stood in stunned horror, then, unable to bear the heartbreaking sight Prince *P'u-lun*, who had deeply loved *Tz'u-hsi* fell to his knees and wept bitterly; his whole body shook as he moaned, "Oh, my dear Old Buddha, what have they done to you . . . . what have they done to you?".

The reinterment ceremony would cost more than the impoverished members of the disbanded court could possible raise; new coffins and clothing, burial gifts and religious ceremonies as befitting such an august members of the *Ch'ing* House would run into tens of thousands of dollars, where was it be found? It was pointless to appeal to the Republican government, who were very probably involved in the crime themselves, one of their bright new military leaders certainly was. The problem, seemed to the Princes, beyond solution; then, one of the Manchu clansmen tried to console the sorrowing Princes; perhaps the fine Lama paintings which adorned the chamber wall could be sold to foreigners and the necessary money thus raised. It seemed an unwarranted thing to do, but what other choice did they have? One of the Princes walked over to a painting and lifted if from the wall to make a more critical appraisal, the others gasped in amazement, for there in a niche

261

behind the painting stood a ten inch high gold Buddha! Quickly one of them examined it, it was marked on the base with a 'pure gold' chop; on removing the other paintings a similar gold Buddha was found behind each, nine in all!

A week later the Imperial reinterment took place, and nestling behind each of the paintings was a beautiful porcelain Buddha replacing the gold ones that had made the ceremony possible. The Dowager Empress's remains were shrouded in a new yellow phoenix robe and her long hair, of which she had been so proud, was redressed, a new coffin provided, and the tomb cleaned and repaired. There, as she lay in State the mourners gathered a second time about her in a quiet but impressive funeral ceremony. *P'u-yi* was the chief mourner and he wept unrestrainedly, as did many, for this bitter ceremony represented not only the desecration of an Imperial grave, but the death of the Great *Ch'ing* House.

The funeral rites ended, the tombs were sealed on the Dowager Empress and the *Ch'ien-lung* Emperor. The sorrowing band of mourners left the desolate site that had once been the nobelest mausolea in all world history.

The Chinese and foreign press meanwhile voiced its general indignation and condemnation at this appalling act of vandalism and robbery and as the tumult reached its height one Peking paper carried a very interesting article. *Chang Mo-ling*, the grand nephew of the late chief eunuch *Li Lien-ying, Tz'u-hsi's* favourite and confident, had come across a diary his grand-uncle had kept, on examining it he discovered that it contained the list of treasure that had been interred with the Dowager Empress; he considered it his duty to communicate this information to the press and chose the *Chao Po* who, no doubt made it worth his while. The following is an extract from the published article:

> *"Before the Dowager Empress was laid in her coffin, the bottom was spread with a mattress of gold thread, seven inches thick, in which were interwoven an embroidery of pearls. On top of the mattress was laid a silk embroidered coverlet sown with a thick layer of pearls. Over the pearl*

layer was spread a lace sheet of pearls into which was woven a figure of Buddha in precious gems. At the head of the casket, there was placed a green jade plate-like ornament resembling a large lotus leaf and at the foot several ornaments of jade, the size of coconuts in the shape of louts flowers. These were arranged in their places, symbolizing purity, and then the body was placed in the coffin. The head of the Dowager Empress rested on the large jade lotus leaf and her feet upon the lotus flowers. She was dressed in a ceremonial yellow robe on which pearls and emeralds were embroidered in gold thread, and over that, an embroidered jacket with a rope of pearls around her neck. A cape of cherry sized large pearls, nine loops deep that she had often worn in life covered her shoulders. Eighteen pearl images of Buddha were laid by her arms many of which were not included in the official lists of valuables. When these ornaments had been properly arranged, the body was covered to the shoulders with the sarced Tolo pall on which were written prayers in the Manchu script. A chaplet of pearls was then placed on her head and by her sides were laid gold, jade and gem Buddhas to the number of 108. On each right and left side to the feet were placed volley-ball sized emerald green jade water-melons with a slice cut out revealing a natural pink centre with black specks representing seeds. Ornaments made from precious stones, in the shape of peaches, pears, apricots to the number of two-hundred were wrapped in silk and placed alongside the body. Near the left shoulder was placed a rare jade ornament shaped like a lotus root with leaves and a flower sprouting from the top . . . . .all from one natural stone. Near the right shoulder a small coral tree in a gold pot in which the interstices were filled with loose pearls and other gems until the whole was level and then covered with a network of more pearls. Before the casket was closed, a princess entered with a set of jade ornaments of eight galloping horses in different colours three inches in length, and another set of mutton-fat jade Lo-han wearing yellow shoes from the same piece of nautral stone, and placed these by the side of the body. Then all the crevices that remained were filled with many baskets of loose pearls. Thus concluded the ceremony of encoffining."

The meticulous *Li Lien-ying*, had engaged three experts to value the contents of the coffin and their itemized appraisal which has been miraculously preserved in the Household Department's records is astonishing, as apparently he overlooked nothing in strict accordance with his Imperial mistress' wishes. The prices in Chinese taels were, at their market value in 1908, when the tael had an equivalent value of roughly fifteen new pence, in 1928 the tael in money terms was 1.33 ounce of sycee silver, the treasure entombed with the Great Dowager Empress would in todays terms represent a massive fortune.

	Taels
The mattress of gold thread in which were woven 100 pearls of 8 *fên* in weight, and the gold thread wires:	84,000
304 pearls of 3 *fên*, 500 pearls of 1 *fên*, 1200 pearls of 6 *li*. Seed pearls 20,000. Other gems used were rubies, sapphires, hyacinths, emeralds and white jade which numbered over a thousand pieces.	
Pearls	854,200
Other gems	42,000
The layer of round pearls weighing each 5 *fên* numbered 2400	320,000
Coverlet with image of Buddha; 1 *fên* pearls 1320 and precious stones	22,200
Jade lotus leaf of emerald green, the viens of which were natural and not carved	850,000
Jade lotus flowers of emerald green each weighing 36 ounces	750,000
Pearl shoulder cape; pearl necklace; gem ornaments and phoenix robe	1,200,000
A movable mirror inset with 860 pearls and 35 gems	190,000

The Tolo pall embellished with 820 large pearls (Gift of Dalai Lama)

160,000

Various Jewelry such as rings, bracelets, necklaces and pendants in rubies, diamonds, pearls and emeralds

10,500,000

Chaplet of pearls on head. One large center pearl alone weighed 4 ounces

2,000,000

Golden Buddhas each weighing 8 ounces; Jade Buddhas and 27 gem Buddhas

620,000

2 Jade watermellons, emerald green rind, natural red pulp, specked with white and black spots, representing seeds

2,200,000

Four sweet melons, two placed on each side of the feet. They had emerald green rind and yellow pulp

600,000

Ten apple green peaches with natural red tips. 100 jasper pears, 600 sapphire appricots, 40 ruby dates

95,000

Two jade cabbages with green leaves and white hearts. On the heart of each cabbage was a cricket in natural yellow exquisitely carved, and on the leaves two wasps also in natural yellow, being gifts from Mongolia

100,000

The gem lotus root placed at the left side of the body was three sections long (18 inches) and all carved from one piece of rare natural jade. The root itself was pink in colour and had green lotus leaves sprouting at the top and a white flower with a black corolla. The bottom was in natural gray giving the illusion of earth adhering to it

1,000,000

One red coral tree placed at the right side of the body that had a circle of red cherries in rubies, and leaves of green jade. The tree trunk itself was of coral with darkish red roots, a multi-coloured jade bird perched on one of the branches. The interstices were filled with loose pearls and gems; 500 large pearls of 8 *fên* each, 1000 pearls of 6 *fên*, 2200 of 3 *fên*; 2200 sapphires   2,230,000

The network pearl coverlet with phoenix design was woven with six thousand pearls, each two *fên* in weight   228,000

Forty eight Tibetan Buddhas two inches tall and carved in mutton fat jade with the Buddha's white feet encased in natural yellow jade shoes   52,000[1]

The amount of the items listed above comes to some fifty million taels, but added to this total, must be the deluge of unlisted gifts from the Manchu princes and nobles, of which no record existed.

The 'Spirit Tablets' of both *Tz'u-hsi* and the *Ch'ien-lung* Emperor were temporarily set up at *P'u-yi's Tientsin* residence, the *Chang* Garden, where he provided tables of incense and kneeling carpets for the never-ending stream of shocked *Ch'ing* veterans who daily came to *kowtow* and pay their respects to the defiled dead. Open telegrams were published to *Chiang Kai-shek* and his so-called government demanding the immediate punishment of his guilty underling *Sun Tien-ying. Chiang*, to 'save face', set up, what was to be a completely ineffectual 'special court', and *Sun* was at last arrested, but released a few days later for "lack of evidence", nothing else was ever done.

Some months later *Chiang Kai-shek's* new and wealthy bride was observed in a famous *Peking* Hotel wearing on her shoes, the pearl and phoenix ornament that had come from *Tz'u-hsi's* burial crown. The more the *Chiang Kai-shek* administration were questioned or urged to redress the crime, the more frigid they became, and the more 'unfavourable' the situation became for the desposed court in *Tientsin*.

As the months passed reparation or even the admission, that a serious crime had been committed, was never forthcoming. It was said at the time that although the culprits were known, *Sun Tien-*

The "christian General" Fèng Yü-hsiang, (left)
with Chiang Kai-shek.

ying and his fellows suffered no reprisal or punishment, that is, except one; it was known, from a reliable source, that the most precious and valuable of the stolen treasures had been crated in three large cases and sent to *Shanghai* to await dispersal, and were in the care of *Sun's* most trusted officer. *Sun* duly arrived with two interested foreign dealers and proceeded to the secret hiding place where the treasures had been safely lodged. When the trunks were at last opened they were found to contain nothing but bricks, the real treasure was missing, one of the robbers suffered a heart attack and *Sun* was discredited; only one man had won, and even to this day, none of the looted Imperial treasure has ever "officially" been identified but, after the ultimate Communist victory in the late 1940's there mushroomed perhaps the best endowed museum in Asia on a small island off the Chinese coast and a private collection of its then leader, which could not be equalled. The Chief architect of one of the most callous and wicked acts of barbarism in all of China's history is long dead and the whole episode almost completely forgotten, but the shame remains.

P'u-yi's heart smouldered with a hatred that he had never before experienced; hatred for this former *Sunite war-lord*, as he stood within the dark and gloomy defiled funerary hall he swore an oath before his weeping clansmen;

> "If I do not avenge this wrong I am not a true Aisin-Gioro. As long as I live, the Great *Ch'ing* will never perish!" [2]

As *Chiang Kai-shek* tightened his grip on northern China and appointed new officials throughout the provinces official attitudes hardened considerably towards the ex-Emperor and his clansmen, even Prince *Ch'un*, who had been determined to stay in *Peking*, now moved with his family into the Japanese concession at *Tientsin*, afraid to remain any longer in his family home in the old Tartar city under *Chiang's* new belligerent administration. *P'u-yi's* mood changed from indignation to deep depression, all the inmates of the *Chang* Garden understood the unfavourable implications of *Chiang Kai-shek's* wedding to *Soong Mei-ling*, the daughter of a family of former compradors who had made their fortune in the service of British and American companies, now this former stock-broker war-lord who had many unsavoury accomplices in the Chinese underworld was in a stronger position than any of his republican predecessors. By the end of that year their worst fears were confirmed when *Chiang's* "National Government" in *Naking* was recognized by all countries, including Japan, making him the most powerful man in China.

As *P'u-yi* searched for an answer to his problems, he realized that with the present political climate, being manipulated by one powerful and ambitious man, it boded ill for his dreams of a *Ch'ing* restoration. He burned with ambition and longed for revenge, but decided that the 'will of heaven' was not enough, he must try to alter the times himself. What had been the secret of *Chiang's* success? Military might and foreign capital, well, if this bandit chief and former gangster could achieve ultimate power, why not the rightful Emperor? He decided there and then to send two of the most trusted members of his family to military school in Japan, his brother *P'u-chieh* and his brother-in-law *Jun-chi*. He then arranged to have his two "future Generals" tutored in the Japanese language and the accommodating Japanese consul in *Tientsin* selected Toyama Takeo, who was incidently not only a good teacher, but a member of the Japanese Black Dragon Society. In March 1929, *P'u-yi's* two "future Generals" left for Japan, just seven months after the desecration of the Eastern Mausolea.

It was becoming increasingly clear to both *P'u-yi* and his advisers, that the only hope of a *Ch'ing* restoration lay with Japan. In consequence, discreet negotiations were initiated, and much to *P'u-yi's* delight, he found himself more and more in agreement with his protectors, they had after all been indispensable to both he and his court after the 'eviction' and he had little doubt that, had it not been for their strong political and military support, he and his followers would not have survived the 'angry seas' that first republican, and now nationalist war-lords, had whipped to a fury around them.

The Japanese attitude towards the ex-Emperor and his tiny court was never less than courteous, he was always addressed as, "Your Majesty", and shown due deference. The Japanese now, after talks had commenced, became ever more accommodating; *P'u-yi* was invited to visit the primary school for Japanese children in *Tientsin*; they lined the road and welcomed him shouting *"Banzi!"* (ten thousand years), and waving *Ch'ing* and Japanese flags.

At Chinese New Year, and his birthday, the senior consular and military officials lined up to congratulate him and show their respect for this last of the *Ch'ing* Emperors, and invited him to be their guest of honour at the impressive military parade on the Japanese Emperor's birthday. When *P'u-yi* took his place on the parade ground dais, the commander robe directly over to him and saluted in a most Imperial fashion. During this time the staffs colonels of the Japanese Legation kept him fully informed on all current affairs, not just in South East Asia, but world-wide; maps and summaries were specially prepared for him, together with all available literature. One of these high-ranking officers, Yohsioka, who later became "Attaché to the Imperial Household" and who was to remain a close adviser to *P'u-yi* for some ten years, was particularly helpful and anxious to please; "The root cause of China's disorders, is that she lacks a real leader and has no longer an Emperor". He pronounced in his deep guttural manner. *P'u-yi* inclined his head modestly.

> "The Japanese Imperial Government is strong and healthy because all people honour the Emperor. The hearts of the Chinese people can only be won by the Hsüan-t'ung Emperor. These poor bandit armies in China are no match for the might of the Japanese armed forces; the great bear of Russia has learnt that lesson well, so will many others in time!" [3]

He bowed briskly and took his leave. *P'u-yi* gazed after him and remained some time in deep thought; true the Japanese were the strongest nation in Asia, they had demonstrated their support for him over and over again. . . . . . . could they be the way back to his ancestoral Dragon Throne?

One incident perhaps demonstrates the Japanese attitude towards the young Emperor at this time; one day when he was out for a walk beside the *Pai* River, he saw a Japanese naval vessel, the Fuji, moored there; although he saw the captain on board he did not think for a moment that he would recognize him but, suddenly the officer hurried ashore and bowing deeply invited "Your Imperial Majesty" to come on board and inspect the ship. Delightedly *P'u-yi* agreed. As he came aboard, on what he knew was an impromptu visit, all the officers saluted him and received him with great courtesy and, although a language barrier existed they communicated via the written word quite happily. Some days later the hospitable captain and a few of his officers paid a return courtesy visit to the *Chang* Garden and when, at the end of the visit *P'u-yi* gave them signed photographs of himself, there was no mistaking the deep honour they felt at this gift.

The sense of security generated by the highly 'favourable treatment' *P'u-yi* received from the Japanese, coupled with his first real taste of personal freedom filled him with a new 'modern' confidence, which was not without its lighter side. He purchased what he considered to be the 'most fashionable' western clothes from the foreign shops in the concession, which included stores such as Whiteway, Laidlaw & Co etc and dressed himself in strict conformity that the thumbed pages in his old copies of 'Esquire'; thus attired, he would set out for the very grand 'Country Club' in the British quarter where, he was the only exception to the strict rule of "No Chinese allowed". He carried a "civilization stick", wore tinted Zeiss spectacles, and exuded a fragrance of Max Factor lotion, eau de cologne and moth-balls, the latter he had first smelt on Johnston's clothes and he now felt it an essential extra, and always carried some 'perfumed moths-eggs' where ever he went, although the size puzzled him. He was generally accompanied by attendants with three or four large Alsatian dogs, a very oddly dress 'Empress' and concubine who, at their Lord's insistence dressed in a muddled mixture of Chinese, Manchu and Western costume.

He became a regular visitor to the theatres and cinemas in the area and drew many a word of censure from his conservative advisers for his "loss of Imperial Dignity". But the young Emperor felt completely alive and free for the first time in his life and he was not going to return to the "bad Old days" and submit to strict *Forbidden City* discipline. The *Ch'ing* veterans were rigid with disapproval when some time later their Emperor became friendly with the talented and notorious *Peking* opera star *Mei Lan-fang* who was reportedly the finest female impersonater of the day, both on, and off stage.

P'u-yi was intoxicated by his first real draught of freedom, and without Johnston to keep a constraining hand on him he became, by contemporary standards, just a little outrageous. Johnston had been at pains to introduce his pupil to the 'best people' in *Tientsin* society before he was forced, by his official duties, reluctantly to leave. Now unrestricted *P'u-yi* surrounded himself with an odd assortment of guests in the *Chang* Garden, much to the displeasure of the old *Ch'ing* veterans.

The Emperor's two 'wives' became bitterly resentful; they were used as ornaments on public occasions, but nothing else. *P'u-yi* can hardly be blamed for this, he had, after all been forced to marry them, but had no intention of being forced to be a real husband, it was completely against his nature, a nature that had been shared by a number of his Imperial ancestors.

There is little doubt that the greatest emotional crisis of his young life came with the news that Johnston had been ordered back to England after he had successfully completed the rendition of the British concession of *Weihaiwei*. He received a letter informing him that Johnston was coming to *Tientsin* to bid him farewell, possibly for ever.

P'u-yi arrived at Johnston's hotel in *Tientsin* very early in the morning of 15th September 1930, and remained with him all day. Their meals were served in the room where they remained together until the very last moment before setting out for the steamer. They drove to the wharf in silence and *P'u-yi* accompanied Johnston on board and remained in his cabin until a few moments before the gang-plank was raised, then walked across the wet

P'u-yi playing golf at Tientsin.

Birthday celebrations at the Chang Garden, (P'u-yi seated centre).

quay-side and resumed his seat in the back of the open car. Johnston stood at the rail. It took nearly half an hour for the steamer to manoeuvre around for its journey down stream, all the while the two friends looked towards each other recalling the many happy times they had shared and both realizing that this was probably the last time they would ever see each other. *P'u-yi* replaced his dark spectacles to hide his tears, Johnston was waving as the steamer began to move downstream and *P'u-yi* stood up in the back of the car and returned this final gesture of farewell. Soon the tall figure on the deck was little more than a speck in the distance but both continued to wave on out of sight.

Johnston could just make out the young Emperor's car leaving the quay-side and with a deep sight he turned and slowly walked to his cabin. Once inside he poured himself a generous scotch and caught sight of the small paper parcel *P'u-yi* had left. He unwrapped it carefully, this precious farewell gift; it was a fan on which his ex-pupil had written a version of an ancient Chinese poem:

The road leads ever onwards,
And you, my friend, go this way, I go that.
Thousands of miles will part us —
You at one end of the wide world, I at the other.
Long and difficult is the journey—
Who knows when we shall meet again?
The Tartar horses breathe the northern winds,
The birds of Yüeh build their nests in the southern trees.
Our farewells are said, we are far apart;
Already I grow weak with pining.
The sun is hidden by drifting clouds,
The traveller journeys on, turning his head no more.
Thinking of you, I seem to have grown old.
The months have swiftly passed, a whole year gone.
It is all over. There is no more to be said,
I must make myself strong for the strenuous days to come...
Out of the city's eastern gate I go on foot,
To gaze longingly at the road that leads to far Kiangnan.
On that day of storm and snow,
Here it was that we parted, and my friend went away.
I want to follow him across the river,
But the river is deep and has no bridge.
Oh that we were a pair of herons,
That we could fly home together.

CHAPTER TEN

Emperor of Manchukuo

P'u-yi was at the confluence, the current that was to sweep him away, even against his will, was gaining momentum.

In July of 1929, *P'u-yi* and his tiny court had moved residence to a house they renamed "the Quiet Garden", it was from this seemingly peaceful setting that the secondary consort *Wen Hsiu* set out one morning to go shopping, and never returned. Some days later a communication was received asking for a divorce to be granted her. This request was denied, on the grounds that such an unheard of thing would reflect discredit on the Emperor and his whole court. Until the Communist Government's Marriage Law of 1950, divorce by consent had always been possible, the two parties merely signing a document to this effect before two witnesses. Some months later, the startled officials of the Quiet Garden received news that she was commencing divorce proceedings in the *Tientsin* District Court. Reluctantly they gave in, and agreed to make her an allowance. The grounds on which the divorce was granted, were not made clear, but she got her wish and fifty thousand dollars, the greater part going to her greedy lawyers and avaricious family. She was officially demoted from her former rank to that of a 'commoner' and passing from the pages of history, she became a primary school-teacher and died in 1950.

The popular theory for her actions, was that the Empress had made life in "Quiet Garden" impossible, and the Emperor was so preoccupied with politics, that he did not realize what was really happening within his own household. However, it must have taken much courage on her part to quit the security of the court and face up to the rigours of the outside world at a time when uncertainty, was the only constant daily factor.

The northern war-lords had proclaimed their allegiance to *Chiang Kai-shek's* National Government in*Nanking,*and he was now leader of the new regime. The question was; what would his attitude be to the *Ch'ing* House? There seemed little doubt, judging from his past record, that it would be aggressively hostile. The anxiety this precipitated within the 'Quiet Garden' did not, however last long. Ruinous civil wars continued under the National *Kuo-min tang* government just as they had under the war-lords, there was really very little change. What slight unification *Chiang Kai-shek* claimed to have achieved, became more and more illusory.

The Emperor's younger brother *P'u-chieh*, had all this time been studying in Tokyo, and was preparing to return to China for a holiday, when he received an invitation from a battalion commander named Yoshioka, asking him to stay for a few days before undertaking his journey. Yoshioka had previously been a staff officer with the Japanese forces in *Tientsin* and had frequently visited the Emperor with summaries of current events. *P'u-chieh* was treated with great hospitality by his host who, on bidding him farewell drew him to one side and said in a grave tone; "When you return to Tientsin tell your elder brother that Chang Hsueh-liang has been, in our opinion, behaving disgracefully in recent months and 'something' soon might be going to happen in Manchuria. Please ask the Hsüan-t'ung Emperor to look after himself; tell him that his situation is by no means hopeless."
P'u-chieh imparted this strangely prophetic message to his brother on his return to *Tientsin* on 10th July. Two week later, on 19th July the Japanese viscount Mizuno Katsukuni paid the Emperor an unexpected visit. It was an informal and friendly meeting, and before the viscount took his leave he presented *P'u-yi* with a somewhat extraordinary present, a Japanese fan on which was written a couplet: *"Heaven will not let Kou Chien fail. The age does not lack a Fan Li."* (*Kou Chien* had been a king of the State of *Yüeh*, who had been defeated by the nieghbouring State of *Wu* and, *Fan Li* was the able minister who was instrumental in helping *Kuo Chien* avenge his defeat and destroy the State of *Wu).*

The significance, in Japanese terms, of this couplet, referred to a story during the fierce civil war in Japan between the northern and southern dynasties: The Emperor, Godaigo, who was then under the control of the Kamakura shogunate brought about his own fall, was captured and exiled to Oki. During the term of his exile a soldier carved this couplet on the trunk of a cherry tree as a subtle hint to the dispossessed Emperor. Some time later this Japanese 'kuo Chien' overthrew the shogunate with a band of 'Fan Li's' and returned in triumph to Koyoto thus beginning the 'kemmu restoration'. What viscount Mizuno had ommitted to mention, was that less than three years later, the Emperor was toppled by a new military leader, Ashikaga Takauji!

P'u-yi was delighted to be given this veiled indication from the Japanese, for it confirmed his belief in their support. He did not have long to wait for a decisive illustration of Japanese power, on 18th September 1931, the Japanese army launched an attack on the Chinese forces at *Shenyang*, in Manchuria, close to the capital *Mukden*. By October the Chiness press was full of rumours that the ex-Emperor was about to ascend to the Manchurian throne.

Before that, on the afternoon of 30th September *P'u-yi* received the first 'official' news of the Manchurian situation. He was informed by an interpreter from the Japanese garrison, that the Commander, Lieutenant-General Kashii Kohei, would like to see him concerning an "important matter". He gladly complied and arrived at the Japanese barracks full of anticipation. He was greeted warmly by the commander and ushered into the main drawing room. There were two others respectfully awaiting him, *Lo Chen-yu* and a Japanese in Western dress, General Kanshii introduced him as Keaisumi Toshiichi who had been sent by colonel Itagaki of the *Kwantung* general staff. *Lo Chen-yu* greeted him formally and handed him a large envelope? It was from a distant relation who was now chief of staff to *Chang Tso-hsiang* and deputy head of public security in the northeast, *Hsi-hsia*. He had, in the absence of *Chang* opened the gates of *Kirin* city to the Japanese troops and he "begged" the Emperor to come at once to the "land where your ancestors rose", he continued that with Japanese support, he could win the whole northeast and then the rest of the country; "restoration", could be a fact within just a few short days! His "subjects" were longing for his return and the whole *Kwantung* army had 'joyfully' agreed to his "restoration". Everything was arranged, *P'u-yi* had only to set out on a waiting Japanese naval vessel, which had orders to take him to *Talien*. He was then handed a copy of the *Talien* paper of the day before, where he read; " . . . . *all walks of life in Shenyang are ready to greet the Great Ch'ing Emperor".*

The Peking Press was already full of reports of the retreat of Chinese forces in the northeast and the way that Britain was "covering up" for Japan at the League of Nations.

P'u-yi left the barracks and on the way back to the "Quiet Garden", his mind was bounding through the prospects that had just been revealed to him. Japan supported him, and so did Britain it seemed, albeit obliquely. His excitement was soon calmed by his pessimistic old ministers who, counselled him that the present situation was far too volatile, what if he went only to be disappointed, then, any possibility of a cherished restoration would be lost forever. The next day Brigadier F H Burnell-Nugent, the commander of the British troops in *Tientsin* called on the Emperor and offered his personal congratulations for the opportunity that the "September 18th incident" had presented. He went on to say that he would be proud to serve as a soldier under the Dragon Flag if *P'u-yi* took the throne of Manchuria.

The press soon learnt about *P'u-yi's* visit to the Japanese garrison, some papers even said that he had already gone to the northeast, rumours were beginning to circulate that the Chinese authorities were planning to "take action" against him. Clearly he had no choice, he must go.

The Chinese authorities tried to make out that the Emperor had been kidnapped by the Japanese and carried off against his will. It was believed by many, but it was completely untrue. It seemed that any lies would be used to 'save face'. A wholly fictitious telegram was published addressed to *Chiang Kai-shek* purporting to be signed by the "Emperor and Empress", asking for "sanctuary" and threatening to "commit suicide" if the "generalissimo" did not come to their aid. It is certain, that if the report had been true, which it was not, war-lord *Chiang*, would have been the very last person to whom they would have made an appeal.

The situation in the northeast was still confused and the exact time for *P'u-yi's* departure was discussed for some days, which to the young man, seemed like years. During this time he received many messages from Manchuria, one from the *Ch'ing* veteran *Chin Liang* was typical: *"Everything in Fengtien is ready and we are only awaiting the arrival of Your Majesty"*.

The main reason for the delay, was the friction between the Japanese civil and military authorities, who seemed unable to agree on a suitable date. Whilst arrangements were being made, *P'u-yi*, after some consultation, agreed to see an emissary from *Chiang Kai-shek*, albeit with some apprehension. He was informed by the emissary that the *Nanking* Government was prepared to revive the Articles of Favourable Treatment and to pay an annual allowance or a lump sum, provided that he should not live either in Japan or the northeast, and he might retain his Imperial title. It took little intelligence to realize that this was merely another one of the *Chiang's* 'face saving' plays, if the Emperor agreed, he would find himself at the war-lord's mercy, he had no intention of putting his head on that particular block. His answer to the emissary was suitably noncommittal, when the authorities "called" again, *P'u-yi* had gone.

The day of his long awaited departure was set for the 10th November 1931. To draw attention away from the Imperial exit, the Japanese secret agents arranged a number of diversions; Chinese agents were paid to make trouble in that part of *Tientsin* under Chinese administration; a state of emergency was announced and communications were cut between then Japanese concession and the rioting Chinese quarter. Japanese armoured cars surrounded the "Quiet Garden", and marshal law was brought into force. Three days later, when the disorder was at its height, *P'u-yi* prepared to leave his house with his most trusted personal assistant 'Big *Li*', *Chi Chi-chung* and a loyal driver; *P'u-yi* hid in the luggage boot of the big convertable and drove out of the main gate, but the driver was so nervous he hit a telegraph pole causing muffled shouts of protest to issue from the luggage compartment, which only increased his anxiety. A little way from the house the Japanese interpreter was waiting in another car and followed at a discreet distance. When they reached the Japanese road-block they were waved through and although the driver's skill did not improve, they reached the appointed rendezvous, a Japanese restaurant safely. Inside Japanese officers were waiting and helped *P'u-yi*, still stiff from his concealed ride, into an army greatcoat and cap. On leaving the restaurant they seated themselves in a Japanese army car and drove directly to the dock on the bank of the *Pai* River. As they drew up, *P'u-yi* was alarmed to discover that they were no longer within the Japanese concession, but Yoshida assured him that he was quite safe as they were now in the British section.

They hurried along the wharf until they came to a small unlit motor launch. *P'u-yi* was relieved to find, on entering the cabin, that his old official *Cheng Hsiao-hsu* and his son *Cheng Chui* were there to greet him in company with three more Japanese officers. The captain came in and assured *P'u-yi* that in addition there were ten soldiers on board for his protection, and the boat, though small, had been specially fitted out with armour plating for this important mission. The order was given to cast off, slowly the launch edged away from the wharf and turned on its lights, as it was now almost dark. (Some twenty years later there appeared in the Japanese magazine, Bungei Shunju, a 'memoir' by one of the officers who had taken part in this secret mission; he recalled, that on board the 'Imperial launch' there had been hidden a large drum of petrol, if they had been discovered by Chinese forces, he had orders to set light to the boat and destroy it along with its 'Imperial passenger'.)

Happily, *P'u-yi* knew nothing of this on the night in question, and he sat gazing out of the windows dreaming of his anticipated restoration. The calm was soon to be shattered, about two hours into their journey a voice shouted from the riverbank; "HALT!"

One of the officers pushed *P'u-yi* face down on the cabin floor; the soldiers hurried on deck, the officers giving orders in harsh whispers. Soldiers were now visible behind sand-bags along the bank . . . . . . the boat began to slow down and turned towards the shouting voices . . . . then, the aunch lights went out quickly followed by the crack of rifle fire and at the same time the powerful engine of the launch accelerated and the boat leapt forward and away from the river-bank . . . . .the rifle shots and shouting grew fainter and fainter. . . . . . . the plan had succeeded.

Some minutes later the cabin light came on again and the passengers all congratulated themselves on their narrow escape, not least of all *P'u-yi*. By the middle of that night they reached the mouth of the river at *Taku* and dropped anchor to await the arrival of the merchantman, Awaji Maru to meet them. Food was produced, and the relieved passengers and crew enjoyed a meal washed down with generous helpings of saké.

The Awaji Maru arrived at the South Manchurian Railway dock at *Yingkow* on the morning of the 13th. *P'u-yi* was puzzled, why had they docked at *Yingkow* in *Liaoning* province in order to go to *Shenyang*? He went on deck, expecting to see the wharf crowded with loyal flag-waving supporters, but there were no such welcoming signs to be seen; finally, when he did go ashore, the only welcoming committee was made up entirely of Japanese.

With little, or no explanation, *P'u-yi* and his two followers were taken to the railway station, and on arrival ushered into a private carriage, still without explanation. The trains set off and an hour later drew to a halt, they were asked to change into yet another private carriage, for no obvious reason. Finally, they arrived at the hot springs district of *Tangkangtzu*, and it was with mounting suspicion he entered the *Tuitsuike* Hotel. The hotel was owned and operated by the Japanese South Manchurian Railway Company, a luxuriously furnished Western style building, strictly reserved for high ranking Japanese officers and officials. He was ushered up the impressive marble staircase to an equally impressive drawing room on the first floor, there he was at last warmly greeted by delighted ex-*Ch'ing* officials *Lo Chen-yu, Shang Yen-ying* and *Tung Chi-hsu*. He was enthusiastically informed that the officials were even at this moment in the middle of discussions with the *Kwantung* Army about his restoration, and cautioned him that news about his presence should not be discovered until their negotiations had reached, what they assured him, would be a joyful conclusion.

That evening *P'u-yi* sat down to an exotic Japaense dinner full of hope and relief. The sunset gleamed through the long first floor windows and seemed to fill the whole room with gold, which he took to be the best of omens for his family name, *Aisin-Gioro* means gold; he had returned at last to the land of his ancestors and was soon to be the 'Great *Ch'ing* Emperor' again; the radiance of the setting sun was only rivalled by the shafts of sunlight he felt within. He retired early and slept a calm peaceful sleep, the first for many months.

The next morning he awoke with the same intense feeling of well-being, and was almost finished washing when his attendant *Chi Chi-chung* came in to help him dress.
"Help me to dress quickly, I want to go out for a morning walk and see My country. . . . . hurry now."
"It is not possible Your Majesty . . . . they will let no one out" responded *Chi-chung* with his head bowed.
"Why not?" *P'u-yi* asked, turning to him in bewilderment, "Who has given such orders? Go downstairs at once and tell them I wish to go out."
"I cannot" protested the uncomfortable young man, "they won't even let us go downstairs."
P'u-yi subsided into a chair, "So" he said to himself, "I am to be as isolated here as I was in *Tientsin* . . . . . . will it never end . . . . . . can I never be free? Not even for a day?"
Unknown to him at that moment the *Tuitsuike* Hotel was prohibited to all except the Japanese officers involved in the restoration discussions, even other officers and officials were forbidden access to the first floor which had, in its entirity, been reserved for the Imperial party.
"Go and bring the senior Japanese officer to me" *P'u-yi* at last said, he wanted an explanation and intended to have one. *Chi-*

chung bowed and left the room. Some moments later, the beaming face of Major Kaeisumi appeared around the door;

"Your Majesty" he begain bearing his glittering teeth in the broadest of smiles, "this is only a safety precaution, merely a safety precaution" he apologized in Chinese which was almost obliterated by his thick Japanese accent.

"Just how long am I going to be forced to stay here?" enquired the Emperor.

"Well. . . . . that really depends on Colonel Itagaki Your Majesty."

"Where are the others, *Hsi Hsia* and the rest of my party? They were going to take me to *Fengtien.*"

"That too, depends on Colonel Itagaki Your Majesty."

"What has happened to *Lo Chen-yu?*" Demanded *P'u-yi,* his temper rising with every word that the major massacred.

"He has gone to *Fengtien* . . . ."

"Why?"

" . . . . . to see Colonel Itagaki . . . . . " *P'u-yi* slumped back into his chair, "they are still discussing the new State, and no doubt when they have reached agreement. . . . . . *Lo* will then return and escort Your Majesty to *Fengtien.*"

An exasperated moan escaped for *P'u-yi's* lips as he covered his face with his hands.

"I was told . . . ."

"Yes? Your Majesty . . . . . ." Kaeisumi prompted.

"I was told in *Tientsin* that everything was settled . . . . . . that all was in readiness for me to ascend the throne. . . . . why do you now tell me that the matter is still under discussion?"

"Your Majesty. . . . . . .to carry through such a great undertaking is much easier said than accomplished . . . . . . be patient Your Good Majesty. When the time is ripe you will assuredly be invited to go." He explained, his smile wavering just a little.

"To go, to go where? To *Fengtien?*" *P'u-yi* prodded.

"That . . . . . . .that will be decided by Colonel Itagaki" came the inevitable reply.

P'u-yi jumped to his feet in exasperation, the now not so broadly smiling Manjor snatched at his cue and made a hasty exit, just turning briefly at the door to say, "Thank you, Your Majesty" he bowed and disappeared.

Quite unknown to *P'u-yi* at the time, the Japanese were in a state of desperate confusion. Japan was internationally isolated, and from within there were still grave differences of opinion as to what form of rule their new colony should adopt. Naturally the *Kwantung* Army could not yet allow their chief actor to take the stage, the scene was far from set.

P'u-yi at this time detected a change in the Japanese attitude towards him; they were not as respectful or accommodating in their manner as they had been in *Tientsin*. Finally, after a week of uneasy waiting, he received a telephone call from the all powerful colonel Itagaki, who informed him that he would soon be on his way to *Lushun*.

Why *Lushun*? *P'u-yi* puzzled, why was he not going to *Shenyang* as arranged? The Major informed him of the reason;
"Oh, Your Majesty, you will have all your answers after you have spoken to Colonel Itagaki" *P'u-yi* had anticipated this answer. "You see Your Majesty, it is not really safe here in *Tangkangtzu*, we are in constant danger from bandits, you will be much better off in *Lushun*, it is a big city, and far more convenient in every way." He bowed and advanced towards the door turning just to add, "You leave this afternoon."

Once in *Lushun*, much the same arrangement awaited him as he had just left behind. The whole of the upper floor of the Japanese Yamato Hotel was given over to the Imperial party. Again, no one could venture downstairs and only those directly concerned were allowed up.
"It would injure Your Majesty's celestial dignity were you to show your face; if you will but be patient and wait until your ministers have arranged everything then, Your Majesty can ascend the throne at the appropriate time, and receive all the homage with decorum and Imperial propriety."
P'u-yi had no choice but to content himself with this answer and wait. The Japanese at this time were under pressure, not only from the Western powers, but their own domestic opinion, but having once started the game they were determined to continue, they had diplomatically lost a few moves, but they had a "New King" up

their sleeve, and they were not going to be rushed into playing him, not even by the "King" himself.

P'u-yi endured this tedium for more than a month before being moved to a mansion owned by the son of the former Prince *Su* where he was at last joined by the Empress *Wan-jung* and his second and third sisters who, up to this time had not even been allowed to see him.

On February 19th 1932, the Republic of Manchukuo came into being and the "Administrative Committee of the Northeast" issued a "declaration of independence" on the same day. *P'u-yi* was formally invited to become provisional head of the new government under the title of *Chih-cheng* (this is a somewhat vague term, which is perhaps best translated as "Chief Executive", it was intended to be merely temporary, as the aim of the new administration was to establish a monarchy), as such he was sworn in on 9th March at *Ch'ang-ch'un*, which was renamed *Hsinking*, (New Captial). The new title of the Republic, *Manchukuo*, translates to 'The Country of Manchuria' the *Kuo* appendage being Chinese for country. This new style was made necessary, according to the 'administrators' because its people included Chinese, Manchu, Mongol, Korean and Japanese and the five colours of the new flag reflected this.

P'u-yi disappointment at becoming "Chief Executive" came to the boil in an interview he had with the shadowy Colonel Itagaki Seishiro on the 23rd of February. Itagaki, a short man, even by Japanese standards, his head was completely shaved and the dull pallor of his skin was in sharp contrast to his bushy black eyebrows and small moustache. He was immaculately dressed, his cuffs and collar stiffly starched and dazzling white, his uniform pressed and tailored to perfection, yet though he affected the air of an elegant and cultured man, his lack of height severely reduced the desired effect. At the meeting with the new "Chief Executive", he commenced by thanking *P'u-yi* for the gifts he had sent him and began to explain the functions of the new State.
"I have come 'Your. . . . . Excellency'," (the new title made *P'u-yi* start) on the orders of General Honjo commander of the *Kwantung*

287

Army, to report to 'Your Excellency' on the formation of the new State of Manchukuo." He began pacing up and down in front of the far from happy "Chief Executive".

"The actions of the Japanese army have been fully justified, for it is our sincere wish to help the Manchurian people to establish a paradise in a 'kingly way'," he emphasised, looking side long at his audience of one, before continuing.

"Naturally, under the Republic, all the five races will enjoy equal rights, all will, for example, have the opportunity of holding office in the government and administration of the new State." He then took from his brief case a document, the 'Declaration of Independence of the Manchu and Mongol people' together with the new flag and placed them on the table in front of *P'u-yi*, who, by this time, was beginning to tremble with indignation; rising, he faced the smug Colonel;

"I did not return to the land of my ancestors to become "Chief Executive" of a Republic!" *P'u-yi* exclaimed clutching the new flag and using it to emphasis his words, "I returned to restore the *Ch'ing* Dynasty in the land of its origin. . . . that is what I was led to believe by your emissaries. . . . ."

"Of course, this is not a restoration of the Great *Ch'ing* Empire . . . how could that be? . . . .This is a new State. The Administration of the Northeast has passed a unanimous resolution proclaiming Your Excellency head of the new State. You are "Chief Executive", is that not enough?"

Every time the *dwarf-barbarian*, (for so the Chinese have always called the Japanese), pronounced "Your Excellency", *P'u-yi* felt the blood surging to his face, at one stroke, or so it seemed to him, he had lost his Imperial title and become "Your Excellency";

"I am not prepared to tolerate the abolition of my Imperial title, not even in exchange for the two million square miles and thirty million people of the Northeast, not even the rebel war-lords could take my name from me and I. . . . ."

"Names? I do not understand your preoccupation with names . . ."

"The people of Manchuria were not longing for me as an individual, but as the Emperor of their own dynasty, if you abolish my title their loyalty will also be abolished. . . . . I must ask you to consult your superiors and ask them to reconsider this. Japan, after all, has an Imperial system, so how can they agree to the founding of a Manchurian 'Republic'?"

"If Your Excellency does not like the name *Republic*, then we will not use it." Soothed the imperturbable Colonel, "This new State will be built around the "Chief Executive system", if you so wish."

"Do not think I am ungreatful for all the enthusiastic help I have received from your country but, I cannot accept a 'Chief Executive system'." said *P'u-yi* trying to control himself, "My Imperial title has been handed down to me by my ancestors, and if I were simply to abandon it, I would be both lacking in loyalty and filial piety . . . . please try to understand . . . ."

Itagaki became ever more conciliatory, smiling and nodding his head at every point the young 'Chief Executive' made.

"The office of 'Chief Executive' will only be temporary. It is perfectly well known that 'Your Majesty'." *P'u-yi* looked at him in surprise, "That, 'Your Majesty', is the twelfth Emperor of the Great *Ch'ing* Dynasty, I am quite sure, that after the formation of a 'national assembly' a constitution will be adopted that will restore the Imperial system."

The interview lasted over three hours and finally the Colonel picked up his brief case and bowed;

"'Your Excellency' looks tired, perhaps we had better continue our discussions tomorrow", he turned and strutted towards the door, all trace of the ingratiating smile gone, and his last words seemed to carry flakes of frost on them. *P'u-yi* sank into an armchair and closed his eyes in deep despair.

That evening, he had to face the Colonel again, for he had arranged a banquet in his honour. The occasion passed off smoothly enough, and all mention of the days' topics were carefully avoided.

The next morning *P'u-yi* received a message from Colonel Itagaki, "The demands of the *Kwantung* army cannot be altered in the least. We will therefore regard their rejection as evidence of a hostile attitude and act accordingly. This is our last word."

The bluntness stunned him, a cold shiver went through his body. *Lo Chen-yu* who had relayed the message remained silent for a time then quietly began to urge him to accept the Japanese ultimatum; "The Japanese always do what they say they will, Your Majesty must not risk their displeasure; besides Your Majesty will be head of State which is really the same as being Emperor, it is only the name that is different. This is the opportunity of today and it must be taken, tomorrow, who is to know what possibilities may show themselves? This is the reason that I have been working for Your Majesty all these years; if you now insist on refusing, I must pack my poor belongings and return to my old home."

The words made *P'u-yi* feel even more desperate.

"If Your Majesty agrees to the Japanese army's demands", added his son *Cheng-Chui*, "you will be able to strengthen your position for the future, then you will be able to order things the way you wish."

"Although one may regret the present situation, there is nothing we can do about it," *Lo* added in conclusion, "Our only course would seem to be to set a time limit of one year, then, if the Imperial system is not restored, Your Majesty can resign."

Father and son waited for *P'u-yi's* reply;

"Very well", he agreed reluctantly, "please go and tell Colonel Itagaki that I consent."

Some little time later, the old minister returned, his face beaming with delight, "Colonel Itagaki is very pleased that you have agreed and this evening has invited you to a little banquet to celebrate your becoming head of State."

In March 1933, Japan withdrew from the League of Nations and immediately increased her military activity against China, pushing south of the Great Wall and even encircling *Peking* and *Tientsin*.

Chiang Kai-shek's Nanking government, preoccupied with its murderous civil war against the Communists, made many further concessions to Japan, embodied in the 'Tangku Agreement'. In July, Komai, head of the General Affairs Office of the State council of Manchukuo resigned, in order to work secretly for the 'independence' of northern China and quietly pointed out to the 'Chief Executive' that this meant working for the restoration of 'Your Majesty's' rule throughout the whole country. *P'u-yi* was overjoyed. It seemed at last that his dream would soon become a reality. This was further heightened by the news that the military authorities were now in favour of a monarchy. This was officially confirmed in October 1933. Hishikari Takashi, the new commander of the *Kwantung* Army, informed him that the Japanese Government was about to recongize him as the "Emperor of Manchukuo".

P'u-yi was overjoyed; when the others had left him, he danced around the room, pausing to bow to himself infront of the long mirrors which filled the room. He paused again, "I must send to *Peking* for my Dragon Robes and court regalia, I cannot be enthroned without them", he mused to himself. These magnificent robes duly arrived, they had been in the safe keeping of the High Consort *Jung-hui*, and had been carefully preserved for some twenty-two years, for they had belonged to the *Kuang-hsü* Emperor. But the Japanese authorities objected to them; "Japan does not recognize you as the Great *Ch'ing* Emperor, but the Emperor of Manchukuo, you must wear the uniform of the Supreme Commander of the Land, Sea and Air forces of Manchukuo", he was informed. However a satisfactory compromise was arrived at; the 'Emperor' could wear his *Ch'ing* regalia to perform the ceremony of "Announcing the accession to heaven", this seemed to satisfy all parties. Thus, the Republic was transformed into 'The Empire of Manchukuo' and *P'u-yi* found himself Emperor for the third time in his young life.

On March 1st 1934, *P'u-yi* robed in his predecessor's Imperial twelve symbol *lung-pao* (Dragon robe), officiated at the ceremony of "announcing the accession to the ancestors", at a make-shift 'Altar of Heaven', especially erected for the occasion in the eastern suburbs of *Ch'ang-ch'un*. After the brevity of this 'concessionary' ceremony, he was driven back to his official residence, which had now changed it's name from 'The Chief Executives Residence' to 'The Emperors Palace', there he changed into his prescribed uniform for the enthronement ceremony which took place in one of the large halls. The floor had been covered with crimson carpet and part of the north wall had been draped with silk, in front of which stood a high backed chair. There the uniformed *P'u-yi* stood flanked by 'palace' officials; the civil and military officials then entered, bowed and arranged themselves in rows in front of the 'throne'. Then, Hishikari, the commander of the *Kwantung* Army stepped forward and presented his credentials as Japanese Ambassador. The Japanese formalities over, members of the Household Department and a number of former *Peking* courtiers came forward and, as if to shame the austere Japanese, performed the nine-fold *kowtow* before their restored Emperor. Congratulatory memorials poured in from all over China, one was even received from the notorious *Shanghai* underworld boss *Chang Yu-ching*, proclaiming his loyalty as an obedient subject.

On 6th June, Prince Chichibu (Chichibu-no-Miya Yasuhito), came to congratulate the new Emperor on behalf of his brother the Emperor of Japan and invested *P'u-yi* with the Grand Cordon of the Chrysanthemum, and the Empress with the Order of the Crown.

Prince *Ch'un* arrived to salute his son a month later and was met at the station by a group of palace officials and driven to the 'Emperors Palace', there *P'u-yi* and Elizabeth were waiting for him at the main gates; Elizabeth dressed in full Manchu court costume and *P'u-yi* in his resplendent uniform, to which he had added many *Ch'ing* decorations to augment the Japanese and Manchukuo ones he already wore. Prince *Ch'un's* car drew up and he clambered out as his daughter-in-law knelt and his son saluted, the Prince was quite taken aback and realizing that a return courtesy was expected from him fell to his knees without looking where he was, the poor flustered Prince had come to rest in a large puddle of muddy water, when he tried to rise, he slipped and fell full length sending a shower of muddy water over the assembled company.

That evening, a great banquet was held in the Emperor's palace, a family banquet; the menu was Western or what passed for it, *P'u-yi* and Elizabeth sat at the head of the table as host and hostess. An orchestra had been engaged, which played rather loud Western music, *P'u-yi* loved anything with trumpets and the ensuing cacophony though, not always tuneful, disguised the dropping of knives and forks as the guests did battle with the unaccustomed cutlery. When the worst of the music and constricted eating was over, champagne was served, and the Emperor's brother *P'u-chieh* rose, as rehearsed, to propose the toast; he stood and raised his glass and almost shouted: "Long live

P'u-yi in the uniform of Commander-in-Chief of the Manchukuo Army.

A group photograph of the enthronement of P'u-yi as Emperor of Manchukuo. The Commander of the Kwantung Army, Hishikare Takashi is fifth from the left.

His Majesty the Emperor" to which the guests responded, although Prince *Ch'un* almost choked and had to be assisted to regain his breath and composure, "Good. . . . good, good. . . ." He croaked as he displayed to the assembly his complete recovery by drinking another glass, which had almost the same effect.

The next day, *P'u-yi* was informed by his senior official *Pao-hsi* that the *Kwantung* Army had sent an officer in the name of the Japanese Ambassador to make a formal protest at the sending of an armed guard to the station to receive his father, this was directly in contravention of an agreement between the former Northeast authorities and Japan, which the new Empire of Manchukuo had undertaken to observe. Under this agreement the land on either side of the railway lines was the territory of the Southern Manchurian Railway Company, no armed men were allowed there except by the special permission of the Japanese Army. The Japanese Ambassador therefore wanted a firm assurance that no such incident should reoccur!

P'u-yi, apart from being mildly surprised, thought little of it, had he done so, he might have realized that his 'power' was really non-existent and that the Japanese wanted a figure-head, not an intelligent and ambitious young ruler.

The many official ceremonies kept *P'u-yi* extremely busy; two 'Imperial progresses' each year to other parts of his 'Empire'; four major ceremonies in the capital each year; the fourth of which was the annual meeting of the 'Concordia Association'. The motorcade was indeed truly Imperial; first the police cars followed by the Chief of police followed by a Roll Royce flanked by four motorcyclists that contained the 'Emperor and Empress', followed by dozens of cars containing all manner of officials. The route was cleared of all unsightly citizens or suspicious characters by the over zealous police, no one was allowed to either enter or leave any buildings along the route which was peppered with police and soldiers.

Before the motorcade set off, the radio station would broadcast to the whole city in both Chinese and Japanese; "The carriage of

His Majesty the Emperor is leaving the Palace". Immediately the officials of the "Concordia Association", filed out in readiness to greet him bowing low to the strains of the Manchukuo National Anthem. He was then ushered inside to meet 'His ministers' and after a brief interlude they would enter the main hall in procession and with the band still booming away the Emperor would mount the dias, which was the signal for the music to stop, and to the assembled officials to bow. The Emperor then read his address to the association, all of whom stood with their heads still bowed, as they were not permitted to look at their sovereign; this done the Emperor would leave the hall and start his short journey back to the palace, which was again heralded by an appropriate radio announcement. From this time, the Empress 'Elizabeth' was seen less and less in public. She had her own apartment within the palace and her own staff and annual allowance to maintain them. There were many rumours; she was ill and could not attend public gatherings; she had offended the Emperor and was thus confined and so on, but, the truth was far worse, she had become an unreclaimable drug addict, almost all her money was spent on opium or, 'ointment for the increase of longevity', as the Chinese poetically termed it. There was nothing poetic about the Empress's addicition. Accounts show that during one year alone she purchased seven hundered and forty ounces, about two ounces a day, together with thirty thousand four hundred and thirty cigarettes, which averages out to eighty-five a day! In consequence, she was rarely in a fit state to see anyone, and soon took to her bed suffering from the severe symptoms of both opium and tobacco addiction.

P'u-yi can hardly be blamed for the decline of this highly strung women, he had, after all been forced to marry her, and even if he had never been a husband to her in the real sense, she did not lack male companions, for many an illicit incident with either a servant or guard had to hushed up. Later she became almost paralysed in the legs and there was nothing any of the many doctors could do.

In April 1935, arrangements were made for a State visit to Japan so that the new Emperor might demonstrate personally 'Japan-Manchukuo Friendship'. This was stage-managed to perfection by the Japanese; he was to travel there on the battleship Hie Maru, with an escort of other warships, on arrival at Yokohama he was greeted by a flypast of over one hundred aircraft. Sadly, he saw little but his luxurious State room onboard, as he became horribly seasick for the whole four days of the passage. He managed to emerge on landing in Japan, dressed in the uniform of Supreme Commander of the Manchukuo Army and exhibited no signs of his discomfort when Prince Chichibu greeted him on landing. An hour later they arrived in Tokyo to be meet by the Mikado.

The cherry blossom was in full bloom, and as the two Emperors reviewed the combined military parade from the comfort of a carriage and pair, it seemed to *P'u-yi* that he had at last shaken off the dark days of despair and anxiety, there was no doubt now he was truly Emperor again.

Johnston would have been deeply proud of his pupil; he behaved every inch as an Emperor and made a profound impression on all who met him. Even the Pope sent a representative to offer his respects to "God's anointed" and his recognition of the new Manchukuo Empire.

The three weeks of official receptions, audiences and sightseeing soon passed, and it was time for *P'u-yi* to begin his homeward journey. He arrived in *Hsinking* on 27th April.

His head was full of the rapturous reception he had received in Japan, he immediately issued the 'Admonitory Rescript on the Occasion of the Emperor's Return', which he filled to overflowing with his impressions of the 'Imperial Journey'. The next day he was an enthusiastic participant in the birthday celebrations of the Japanese Emperor Hirohito, and the day following, he summoned all his officials, whether Chinese or Japanese, to gather and hear his reflection on his visit. The speech was extempore and concluded thus:

> "The Friendship between Japan and Manchukuo had led me to hold the firm belief that if any Japanese acts against the interests of Manchukuo he is guilty of disloyalty to His Majesty the Emperor of Japan, and if any Manchurian acts

against the interests of Japan he is being disloyal to the Emperor of Manchukuo. Disloyalty to the Emperor of Manchukuo is the same as disloyalty to the Emperor of Japan. . . . ." [1]

A month later he was forcibly made aware that he might be Emperor in name, but not in power, for when he was informed by the Commander of the *Kwantung* Army Minami, that the, "Premier *Cheng Hsiao-hsu* wishes to retire as he is exhausted by his efforts", and advised *P'u-yi* to grant his request and replace him with a new prime minister, *P'u-yi* gladly agreed, as he too, had been far from satisfied by *Cheng's* performance in this high office. "I agree, and suggest that he be replaced by *Tsang Shih-yi*" *P'u-yi*, now sure of his own authority, said loftily.
"No. . ."the word hit *P'u-yi* in the face, "No . . 'Your Majesty' . . . the *Kwantung* Army has already considered the question, and chosen a most suitable man. There is no need for 'Your Majesty' to worry about politics in the slightest; all Your Majesty has to do is to endorse *Chang Ching-hui* as the new prime minister, that is all." The commander bowed and left the room leaving a very unnerved Emperor gazing after him.

During this time, northern China was in ferment as the Japanese continued their 'fragmentation of China policy'. *Chiang Kai-shek's Nanking* government made more and more concessions to the *dwarf barbarians*. Secret treaties were signed as *Chiang* gave away, what was not his to give, in a failing effort to keep the Japanese war machine at bay so that he could pursue his fight for power against the communists. The 'Ho-Umezu Agreement' in 1935, the 'Chin-Doihara Agreement', and other such treaties virtually gave the Japanese control over northern China, without a shot being fired. *Chiang's* administration also permitted the functioning of the 'Autonomous Military Government of Inner Mongolia', the 'Anti-communist Autonomous Government of Eastern Hopei', and a number of other 'puppet' States; it also cringingly assured the Japanese that. . . . ."not only do we engage in no anti-Japanese activities or thoughts, but we do not even have any cause of being anti-Japanese". This was backed up by the publication to the sorrowing people of China, of the 'Harmony with Our Neighbour

Order', any anti-Japanese activities were punished by the severest penalties. Of all the crimes of the *Whampoa War-lord*, and he had committed many against his own people, this sell-out of the five northern provinces of China was the most disgusting by far. As a direct consequence, the Japanese sunk their claws deeper into northern China, and tightened their grip on Manchukuo, all the while increasing their military strength for the inevitable conquest of the whole Middle Kingdom.

From 1937 onwards, Japanese war preparations increased dramatically for the planned full-scale invasion of China. The Japanese secret police became much more active, especially in Manchuria, thousands of Chinese vanished overnight, in an effort to purge the puppet state of anti-Japanese elements, the same was happening in the other areas under Japanese influence, and it soon became clear, even to *P'u-yi*, that he stood potentially in as much danger as any of his 'subjects'.

Early in this same year an extraordinary rumour, eminated purportedly from the palace; *P'u-yi* was about to take another wife! The speculation was intense, but when it was 'officially' confirmed and a date, (25th March) announced for her 'patent of appointment', it had to be taken seriously. Prince *Ch'un*, the Emperor's father, had selected the new secondary consort and, as the rumour goes, insisted on his son accepting her with the backing of the Japanese administration. Thus, *T'an Yu-ling*, who was just seventeen and the daughter of a Manchu family whose surname had been changed from the Manchu *Tatala* to the Chinese rendering *T'an*, entered the palace. Jade Years, (the English rendering of her name), became the secondary consort, under much protest from the thirty-one year old Emperor of Manchukuo. The Empress Elizabeth, by this time, was hardly ever seen through her haze of opium smoke, and made no recorded protest at this addition to the Imperial household.

As a wedding present the *Kwantung* Army presented the court with a 'Law of Succession to the Throne', which provided that on *P'u-yi's* death he would be succeeded by his brother *P'u-chieh*; if the Emperor had no male issue. This was part of an elaborate

Japanese scheme, that was not realized by the court until all the parts of the puzzle were in place. The document of succession went against all the Manchu and Confucian laws in naming as heir, one of the Emperor's same generation in the person of *P'u-chieh*. And, it almost blatantly emphasised the Emperor's childless state, and the conviction that it would remain so. *P'u-yi* felt the 'insult', for so he interpreted it, severely, his childless state could be blamed directly on the Japanese, who had been secretly doctoring his food to deprive him of the ability to breed! His Empress was barren, and deep in the 'hell of opium', his new secondary consort was, although not a drug addict, incapable of bearing children. Anything but the real truth. Shock was soon added to his insult with the news that his brother was to take a Japanese wife, for the sake of the 'friendship between the two countries'.

The young woman in question was Hiro Saga, a second-cousin to the Mikado. Her grandmother's sister had born a son to the Meiji Emperor who succeeded him as Emperor Taisho who, in turn was the father of the present ruler, so there was no mistaking the political intent implicit in such a union. The wedding took place on 3rd April 1937. Invitations were kept to a minimum, only one distant relative of the Japanese Emperor was present, and participation by the palace was not encouraged.

It was not until October, when *P'u-chieh* had finally graduated from military school as a fully fledged officer, that he took his new wife back to pay a visit to his brother in *Hsinking*, his wife was already heavy with child. *P'u-yi*, not unnaturally, considered the whole sequence of events as nothing less than a plot against him, and the news of his brother's pregnant wife filled him with horror. However, he realized what was officially expected of him and determined to put a brave face on things, and received his successors with all the majesty he could muster. His brother's wife was also prepared to show how 'Chinese' she could be, and to allay all fears that she was, as rumour now had it, a 'Japanese spy'.

A dinner party was planned to receive the Emperor's officer brother and his pregnant Japanese wife, *P'u-yi* determined to show all present that there was nothing amiss, naturally the Empress would have to be present, which posed some difficulty, as by this time she was never seen outside her own apartments. *P'u-yi* and his tottering Empress greeted their guests in the main reception hall, perhaps to underline to them that he was still Emperor, Hiro had donned a Chinese split-skirt which had been a wedding present from her bridegroom's father and, even in her condition insisted on observing the traditional obeisance to both Emperor and Empress. *P'u-yi* was impressed in spite of himself, and they went into dinner accompanied by three of the Emperor's sisters and their respective husbands. The Empress had not sat at the same table with her husband in almost three years and tension rose as to just what she might do or say . . . .;

"I always thought that Elizabeth had large eyes" *P'u-yi* informed his guests, "but my brother's new wife is certainly her rival." The tension was momentarilly broken by the gush of laughter that followed the Emperor's remark and as dinner progressed, the guests relaxed and almost began to enjoy themselves, when without warning Elizabeth reached across the table and wrenched a huge turkey leg from the massive bird that had been placed there moments before, and began to devour it with the messy avarice of a starving man; everyone sat stock still as she reached out and clawed more of the birds flesh with her long nails, covering her costume with grease and gravy, totally oblivious to the shocked guests, around her. Needless to say *P'u-yi* was furious and when Elizabeth's brother in an effort to distract attention from his wolfish sister, started to do the same *P'u-yi* nearly expired with pentup rage.

P'u-chieh's young wife found not only Elizabeth, but the whole household a mystery to her; a drug addicted Empress, a totally ignored secondary consort, an Emperor who kept to his private apartment where no women were allowed. She was completely puzzled; but even in her innocence was soon aware that the servants referred to a particular attendant of the Emperor, a boy of fifteen or sixteen as the 'male concubine', at which she was at first incredulous then shocked; true she had read of such things, especially among nobles and Emperors, but she never thought to be part of such a family but, she determined to accept the situation and never mentioned the fact, not even to her husband.

P'u-chieh (P'u-yi's brother), with his wife Hiro Saga on their wedding day 1937.

P'u-yi's 'confinement' within the walls of the claustrophobic Palace was slowly eating away his will and sense of purpose, and without Johnston's rational advice and company he felt himself sinking into a well of self-destruction. He was allowed no political voice by the Japanese, and in the early days, when he had dutifully gone to his office early each morning, where he had sat waiting to 'rule', or at least be consulted; he had left by noon having seen no one, slowly realizing that he was not needed, and returned disheartened to his apartments. During the latter years in Manchukuo he became gradually more religious and in accordance with the laws of Buddhism, vegetarian and instructed his attendants not to kill even a fly, the reality around him was too painful to bear, he turned inward upon himself in an effort to preserve his sanity.

On 7th July 1937, the first sparks were kindled of what would certainly become the flames of the second world war. It happened a few miles outside *Peking* when the Chinese and Japanese forces confronted each other in a prelude to a full scale Japanese invasion of China. Japanese forces and supplies poured across the Manchukuo-Chinese border in ever increasing torrents, flooding the north, to make the Japanese masters of *Peking*.

The government of Manchukuo put the Empire on a war-footing; *"Live or die with Japan and, united in heart and virtue, smash the power of Britain and America!"* Was Lieutenant-General Yasunori's commands to both the country and the palace.

> "Every time Youshioka reported to me that the Japanese had occupied a major Chinese city he would make me get up with him and bow low in the direction of the battlefield as a mark of mourning for the Japanese soldiers killed in the fighting. After he had made me do this a number of times I needed no prompting to make my bow when he told me of the capture of Wuhan. . . . . he suggested to me that I should write a congratulatory letter to the butcher Okamura who had taken the city and send a telegram to the Japanese Emperor." [2]

Before the fateful 7th, the *Kwantung* Army had interfered little in *P'u-yi's* domestic and private arrangements, but after that, policy changed dramatically. Visitors were restricted to the palace and were not allowed to talk privately with him; all his mail was strictly censored and he found himself under constant scrutiny. Yoshioda would make frequent visits to the palace during the day, stay for ten minutes and then without explanation return five minutes later, giving ridiculous reasons for his constant comings and goings. It quite unnerved the already anxious Emperor when the squat uniformed figure appeared even in the middle of a meal for no apparent reason, the speech he grunted over and over again was: "Japan is the equivalent of Your Majesty's father, and the Kwantung Army represents Japan, so, the commander of the Kwantung Army is really the equivalent of Your Majesty's father! Is that not so?" And on another occassion;

"Buddhism came from abroad, a foreign religion! As Japan and Manchukuo share the same spirit they should also share the same religions beliefs. His Imperial Majesty the Emperor of Japan is the divine descendant of Ama-terasu-o-mi-kami, (the Japanese Sun Goddess who forms part of the Shinto religion), every Emperor is a reincarnation of the great god; all Japanese who die for the Emperor become gods themselves!" With this shower of 'cultured' pearls he left the room, although *P'u-yi* was in no doubt that he would soon return.

The young man, whose whole life had always been in the hands of others, never his own, realized that he must do as he was told and agree with everything, he had no other safe choice, he was left in no doubt of that.

Before he was forced to undertake another State visit to Japan in May 1940, *P'u-yi* received the belated news of Reginald Johnston's death; it was a severe shock and as he tearfully reflected, in the silence of his private room, on the years they had spent together, first as pupil and tutor, then as close and intimate friends, he could not believe that Johnston was not somewhere waiting for him as he had always been. How different both their lives would have been if he had been able to go with him to England, how different . . . .

303

There can have been no momentous event in the history of the twentieth century than occured at this time, sparked off by the Sino-Japanese war, followed quickly by the Pacific war, and in consequence the destruction of the British, French and Dutch Empires in South East Asia, followed by the birth of the People's Republic of China.

A declaration of war was handed to the Japanese Ambassador in Moscow on the evening of 8th August 1945, and hostilities commenced the next day as the Russian Communist armies flooded over the Manchukuo border. Early the next morning the Russian air force bombed *Hsinking*, narrowly missing the palace and hitting the gaol which was opposite. There is no doubt that the Emperor was their target; the Privy Council met at first light and *P'u-yi* soon learned to his horror, that not only were they under attack from the skies, but that a large well equiped land force was even now advancing deeper into his 'Empire'.

Much had been reported in recent months of the massive American bombing of Japan and news was beginning to filter through concerning the fate of Hiroshima; early in the meeting, the Japanese representatives proposed that the government should forthwith move to an inaccessable region near the Korean border. The Japanese forces were holding the Red Army at bay, but with the likelihood of future air raids, the Emperor's safety could not be assured if he stayed in *Hsinking*.

From that moment onwards, *P'u-yi* slept in his clothes with a pistol always by him, martial law was ordered throughout the palace. The next morning he was informed by Yamata, the Chief of staff, that the Japanese army was going to withdraw and hold southern Manchuria, the new Capital would be established at *Tunghua*, and that he must be ready to move that same day! *P'u-yi* was taken aback and asked for two extra days to organize his large household and pack what they would need; this was grudgingly granted, and as the harrassed officer left the room he paused, turning to the Emperor and said in harsh tones; "Do not take too long with your preparations Your Majesty, if the Soviets come you will be the first to be butchered, they are very experienced at killing Emperors." *P'u-yi* collapsed into his chair, his whole body cold and wet with the perspiration of fear . . . .then an even more chilling thought arose in his mind, 'might not his present captors, the Japanese, kill him first, rather than let him fall into the hands of the Russians?" It was too blood-curdling to contemplate. At nine on the evening of the 11th, only *P'u-yi* and his two wives were left in the palace, the rest of the family had already been taken to the railway station; Yoshioka arrived looking ill and tired; "Everything is ready, you will go in the second car, whilst the sacred objects will be transported in the first by Hashimoto Toranosuke, if anyone should pass them either riding or on foot they must make a ninety degree bow." He turned and motioned to Hashimoto and the President of the Bureau of Worship who took their place in the first car carrying the bundle of Shinto shrine objects. As the little convoy drove out into the road, *P'u-yi* could see flames coming from the deserted shrine.

The train journey to Talitzukou took three days and two nights; the original plan had been to go via *Shenyang*, but the train was rerouted along the *Kirin-Meihokuo* line to avoid the Russian air raids, which were hourly becoming more severe. When the train stopped at *Meiokuo*, Yamata the Commander of the *Kwantung* Army came on board and reported to *P'u-yi* that the Japanese army was winning many victories and that the situation was now quite stable. The Emperor knew this was said without any real conviction, and he could judge for himself as he gazed from the frosted windows of his compartment; military vehicles abandoned along the route, the men, who now looked more like refugees than soldiers, disorder everywhere. It was an uncomfortable and tedious journey, cold, cramped, and with very little food, only two warm meals in three days and a quantity of hard tasteless Japanese 'biscuits'. When the train at last arrived at *Kirin* station, the approaching Japanese defeat was obvious, the platform was crowded with women and children screaming and begging to be allowed on board with a cordon of Japanese troops between them and the train; fighting began at one end of the platform and chaos ensued.

305

On August 13th, they finally arrived at Talitzukuo, which was little more than a coal-mining settlement nestling among high craggy mountains. Two days later the Japanese surrender was announced.

Yoshioka had informed the Emperor. "His Imperial Majesty has proclaimed our surrender and the American Government has given guarantees of his safety and position" then falling to his knees he intoned as he bowed, "I thank heaven for protecting His Imperial Majesty", he glared at the still standing *P'u-yi* who quickly realized what was expected of him, and assumed a like posture intoning his less than enthusiastic 'thanks to heaven'. "But," Yoshioka cautioned, still kneeling, "His Imperial Majesty cannot assume unconditional responsibility for Your Majesty's safety. This will be decided by the Allies."
Once again *P'u-yi* felt the chill fingers of death pluck at his sleeve, he had experienced them many times in the past, but now they seemed colder and nearer.

That evening *P'u-yi* signed his second Abdication Rescript. He was then informed that he was to be flown to Tokyo on the 17th; "The plane is small and you must decide who to take with you", Yoshioka informed him, "be ready to leave tomorrow."

P'u-yi's heart was beating fast, it seemed that he would be saved from the 'Emperor-killing Soviets' just in time.

The small aircraft took the ex-Imperial party to *Shenyang* where they had to change planes for the flight to Japan. They were ushered into the airport waiting room to await its arrival. Before long the sound of a large plane could be heard, it landed and taxied almost up to the edge of the runway close to the waiting lounge. Then, its doors bust open and Soviet troops armed with submachine guns poured out and surrounded the terminal disarming the Japanese soldiers and advanced into the waiting room to face a terrified young ex-Emperor.

The next day *P'u-yi* was taken to the USSR aboard the same plane, there he was certain that only one fate awaited him.

CHAPTER ELEVEN

Siberian Winter

When the Soviet plane carrying the "Manchukuo War Criminals" landed at Chita airport in Siberia it was almost nightfall. They were escorted from the airport into a waiting Soviet army car which drove them across what appeared to *P'u-yi* as "A plain that stretched out black and immense on either side". Soon they entered woodland and began slowly climbing, the road began to narrow and twist, finally they came to a complete halt. Everything was quiet for a moment, then a voice shouted from the gloom in Chinese; "Get out and piss those who want to piss!" *P'u-yi*, at the sound of this Chinese voice, crouched lower in his seat, he was sure they had been ambushed by a band of Nationalists who had been sent to murder him. "During the whole of the first half of my life, I suffered from apprehensive fear almost all the time, it was an ever present torment to me. At this time, my greatest fear was of falling into the hands of the Chinese, which I believed would mean certain death. If I remained in the hands of foreigners I felt I had a much better chance of survival."[1] However, his terror subsided when the speaker, a Russian of Chinese origin, stepped forward and peering into the car repeated his somewhat basic invitation.

After this twofold relief, the journey was resumed. Two hours later the car drew up outside a large, not unhandsome building; the Soviet officer in the front seat turned half around and said; "This is your hotel and restaurant." *P'u-yi* could hardly believe his ears, "Hotel and restaurant?",this was not what he had expected. As the tired and bedraggled little party entered the hotel lobby they were greeted, if not welcomed, by a man in his mid-forties in civilian colthes, flanked by Soviet officers. "The Soviet Government has ordered that you are to be detained here until a decision is made how to deal with you" informed the out-of-uniform

Major-general in command of the Chita garrison. Then pointing to a bottle he said, "we are famous for our mineral water in the region, it is a great health-giving tonic. I recommend it to you."

After a few days things settled down to a routine, they were served three large Russian meals a day; there were attendants to wait on them, a resident doctor and nurses; radios, books, papers and other recreational facilities, it was more comfortable than the Palace of Manchukuo had ever been. *P'u-yi* began to relax for the first time in years, he was warm, well-fed and secure, and judging by the attentiveness of his captors, it seemed he was in no immediate danger. He even began to entertain hopes that he might be handed over to either Britain or America where he could really begin the 'new life' he had always hungered for; it seemed possible, after all these two countries were Russia's allies. "After a while, I started to dream, Russia, who was an ally of both the United States of America and Great Britain,......perhaps......perhaps if I asked they would allow me to move into a private apartment of my own, I still had enough jewelry to support myself, if I was careful, for the rest of my life. If I wanted to make this dream come true, first, I must secure my stay in Russia; so, during my five long years in Russia, besides speaking to the authorities on every possible occasion, I wrote a number of times requesting them to allow me to stay in Russia permanently. I never received a reply."[2]

At the end of the war the armistice had caught the Chinese National Government without troops in any part of Manchuria and due to Soviet non-cooperation, ports in the area were denied them. It was not until towards the end of November that *Chiang Kai-shek's* forces, transported by American ships, landed at *Chinwangtao*, south of the Great Wall, to reclaim an area of China that had now been out of their control for many years. Before the Russians had released their grip they had welcomed the Chinese Communist forces into the north-eastern provinces where 'People's governments' sprang up like mushrooms after a downpour. The ensuing civil war drove *Chiang Kai-shek* from the mainland of China forever, leaving him to sulk, comforted only by his 'borrowed treasures' for the rest of his life, exiled on an island, that until 1945 had been under Japanese control for many years. The last of the war-lords had been driven from the ravaged Middle Kingdom and soon China was to end her long march into the twentieth century, after almost fifty years of bloodshed and terror.

A few days later more 'Manchukuo detainees' arrived at the hotel-cum-sanatorium; *Chang Ching-hui, Tsang Shih-yi, Hsi Hsia* and others of the civil ex-administration. They came to pay their respects to *P'u-yi* and ask his help in persuading the Russinas to allow them to return to their families in China. *Chang Ching-hui* was the first to speak: "I have heard that you are quite willing to stay in Russia, how can that be? Our families are still in the North East and need our care and protection, besides we have much unfinished business there and we all want to return as soon as possible. Could you talk to the Russians for us and ask them if we can go back?" *P'u-yi* was amazed at the directness of *Chang's* request, he felt it more than inappropriate in the present circumstances and as far as their "unfinished business" was concerned he neither knew nor cared what this might be. "How can I possibly manage to do this for you? I am a prisoner like you, whether I remain here or not does not alter the situation; you will have to ask the Russians for yourselves, there is nothing I can do". On hearing this their attitude changed from requesting to pleading; "We are sure that if you tried just a little you could do it for us. This is the considered opinion of us all, we must have a representative, if we can not ask our 'Master' for help, who can we ask?" "Master", fell on *P'u-yi's* ear with a leaden thud, they no longer called him 'Your Majesty', even in private, not even; 'My Lord'; dispossession and eviction had been hard enough to bear but not to have the common courtesy extended to him from his former officials represented the final insufferable loss of face. However, he relented and became in essence a middle man between the "itching officials" and the Soviet authorities, although, in common with his own requests they fell on rocky ground.

Nevertheless, in the long empty days of his confinement *P'u-yi* mused on their situation, although he did not fully understand their Kuo-min tang politics and their meaningful hints about "unfinished business". It seemed that the Kuo-min tang government had "Great need" of these men and from what he was able to gather from their guarded conversations there was the promise of "much gold" if they returned. For some, the temptation seemed almost too much to bear; on one occasion an ex-Manchukuo official, who was acting as a cleaner within the detention camp, suffered a convulsive fit and fell screaming on the floor uttering all manner of "strange words"; one of his companions who was deeply religious interpreted this as a direct message from the gods and declared that the writhing ex-official was in fact one of the gods transformed into human shape, he fell to his knees and began to kowtow mumbling as he did, "Oh, great god please tell your servants your decision, when can we leave Russia and return home?" Others joined in hoping vainly for the news they longed for, but the ceremony came to an abrupt end when the Soviet guards entered and carted off the 'god' to the sick bay.

During the early part of their Siberian detention a Russian translator would, once a week read them news of current affairs with particular reference to the war in China. In the beginning *P'u-yi* fained interest in who was the eventual victor, both would want only one thing from him, his life and, as he had made up his mind to stay in Russia, the outcome seemed irrelevant to him. The other inmates were full of speculation believing that *Chiang Kai-shek*, with the military assistance of America could easily gain ascendance over the Chinese Communists. When the news finally came that the Communists had scored a resounding victory, they refused to believe it. Later as this truth became an accepted reality they were deeply despondent, their China had vanished forever, it was bitter medicine and hard to swallow. One of the number, who reckoned himself to be an "experienced politican" suggested that they should send a telegram to the new People's Republic expressing congratulations and hoping for a paternal response, all enthusiastically agreed, all that is but *P'u-yi*, who felt they were merely deluding themselves.

The seasons changed and the years dragged on relentlessly. They were moved to a 'reception centre' at Khabarovsk, but this was staffed and administered in much the same style and the inner-family members remianed together, and to all intents and purposes were well treated. *P'u-yi* became increasingly occupied by Buddhism

312

and spent a great deal of the time reciting scriptures and reading religious works. His devotions were interrupted when members of his family were transferred to another 'reception centre' on the far side of the town, for the first time in his life he was actually alone with no one to attend him. His father-in-law volunteered, but *P'u-yi* felt it was hardly the same as being surrounded by his host of willing helpers. A plot in the exercise yard was given over to the growing of vegetables and this seems to have engaged his attention, for even as a child he had been fascinated by growing plants; he now spent many a happy hour, tending to the small plot which he called, *the Imperial garden*, the name was not without its pathos.

The authorities at the reception centre handed out two books which the unenthusiastic inmates were obliged to read aloud to each other at set times each day, *Problems of Leninism* and the *History of the Communist Party of the Soviet Union*, both were boring and did not gain much from being translated into indifferent Chinese. However they endured the tedium, although none if any of the readers or listeners, understood a word of the "depressing and irrelevant" works.

After the evening meal came the high-spot of the day, the *mah-jong* tables were prepared and everyone settled down to the evening's entertainment with obvious enjoyment. From above, where the Japanese War Criminals were quartered, wafted the discordant strains of Japanese Opera, but it could seldom penetrate the rattle and clatter that arose from the *mah-jong* tables.

At this time, *P'u-yi* was 'advised' by one of the visiting commissars, that he should study hard, and "Learn to admit your guilt and your crimes against the people". He was incredulous, "What crimes?" he thought to himself "surely, the 'crimes' have not been committed by me, but against me!" And although he tried to come to terms with this strange communist ideology, he could make little sense out of the books he had been given.

He had managed to carry, undetected with him into exile, a quantity of jewels and small valuables, and it seemed quite natural to him that if he was to get on better terms with his Soviet gaolers,

313

he might offer them a portion towards their 'post-war reconstruction', that is what had been always done in China, and he had no reason to think it would not work here. With the help of one of his nephews he hid his treasures, concealing them in every imaginable nook and cranny of his bedroom, the major portion was secreted in the false bottom of a suitcase. Unfortunately he ran out of hiding places for the remainder, every bar of soap contained gems, no possible safe hiding place was over-looked; satisified with the new disposition of 'treasure' he left his nephew to clear up whilst he retired to his make-shift study to continue his Buddhist readings.

A few days later when they were all at recreation in the large down-stairs hall a Soviet officer appeared with an interpreter and held up a bright object and asked through his companion; "Who does this belong to? One of my men found it hidden in a radiator. Who does it belong to?" Everyone crowded around and peered at the bright piece of jewellery. "Its not mine" one said "let me see" asked another, "it has the mark of a Peking silversmith on it" he informed; "Who can have lost such a valuable thing?" *P'u-yi* recognized it at once, it was of the pieces he had left to his nephew to hide. The officer advanced on *P'u-yi* and held the piece of jewellery almost under his nose. "Does this belong to you?" he asked sternly. "No, no. . . . . it is very odd, I wonder who put it there" he protested. "I know that this belongs to you" said the officer producing a comb from his pocket, "these two things were found together, do they both belong to you?" the questioner menaced. "No, only the comb. . . . . . . .I know nothing about the other item" the trembling ex-Emperor protested. Far from convinced, the officer looked at his companion, then long and hard at *P'u-yi*, who was trying to stop his legs from shaking, then, with a look of disbelief they turned and left the room.

It was at this time that the interrogations began; everyone was questioned time and time again about their part in the 'Japanese war-crimes in the North-east', *P'u-yi* was no exception; finally after a long series of questioning, and to him quite terrifying 'interviews', he was summoned to appear before the International Military Tribunal for the Far East in August 1946. He found himself in a nightmare that seemed to have no end, his testimony and the cross-examination was mercilesss.

The Empress Elizabeth had died just two months earlier in June in a prison cell at *T'umen* on the Korean border, driven mad by her craving for opium and lack of food and the bitter cold of the Manchurian winter. Her agony ended at last in the fortieth year of her life, and in the twenty-fourth year of her marriage.

P'u-yi's Siberian confinement was temporarily broken, when he was taken to Tokyo to give evidence at the International Military Tribunal for the Far East against the Japanese War Criminals. His evidence lasted eight gruelling days and gave the press all the sensation it desired. He vehemently denounced the Japanese for their invasion of China and forcing him to become "puppet Emperor" of Manchukuo, and if his testimony was not wholly believed by the court, his reasons in giving it were preceptibly clear, it was his only public opportunity of stating his side of the story so that the new Chinese authorities might be disposed to treat him more leniently, should he finally fall into their hands. There were several emotional exchanges during the eight days *P'u-yi* stood in the witness box trying desperately to extricate himself from the web of Sino-Japanese politics that enmeshed him. He protested at the Japanese having introduce the cult of the 'Heaven Shining Bright Deity' into the North-east. Immediately the Japanese lawyer jumped to his feet; "How can you defend such a statement", he shouted, "How can you attack the very ancestor of the Emperor of Japan in this courtroom? Is that your example of Oriental morality?" "I did not force him to adopt my ancestor, why should he force me to adopt his" *P'u-yi* shouted in reply. A ripple of laughter broke over the court and the Japanese lawyer was forced to grunt and sulkily resume his seat. Then later, the sad fate of *P'u-yi's* wife was introduced, the Japanese lawyer tried to lay it at his feet, *P'u-yi* retaliated; "Even she was murdered by the Japanese!" It was in this vein that his evidence continued, whilst the Japanese lawyer tried every ruse to shake the tirade of devestating anti-Japanese testimony that poured from the fighting ex-Emperor. He even suggested that *P'u-yi* was not a qualified witness, which brought forth another surge of nervous laughter from the tribunal. During this brief time in Japan he was kept incommunicado at the Russian Embassy. Perhaps the last word in the tribunal's stacks of 'evidence' frightened *P'u-yi* the most; an American lawyer had shouted at him in his best courtroom denunciation manner; "You have put all the blame on the Japanese!" He accused, "but, sooner or later you will have to face the Chinese Government! And when you do they will surely condemn you for your crimes!" After he had given his evidence he was returned to the relative calm Siberia, to wait.

P'u-chieh's wife Hiro had shared Elizabeth's imprisonment. When the Japanese troops had been defeated by the Chinese Communists, although she had changed into Chinese costume and denied her relationship with the deposed Manchukuo Imperial family, her plight was heightened by Elizabeth's death. With a good deal of luck and fortitude she and her daughter finally arrived in Shanghai, and managed to be repatriated to Japan early in 1947. The secondary consort Jade Years had died of meningitis in the summer of 1944 at the age of twenty-two, five years after her marriage to *P'u-yi*. Her replacement 'Jade Lute' was gazetted as a concubine in the spring of 1944 (*Li Yu-ch'in*), she had found her way south of the Great Wall after the Manchukuo situation had exploded and finally reached nationalist territory where she was sheltered as an Imperial refugee by one of *P'u-yi* cousins. When the Chinese Communists took over she returned to her native city and obtained a position in a children's nursery and began to study the works of Marx and Lenin, with far greater enthusiasm than her former lord could ever muster.

In July 1950, the moment that *P'u-yi* had been dreading arrived; he was informed that he was to be handed over to the Chinese Communist authorities. His pleadings to remain in Russia were ignored. On July 31st the Soviet train carrying the 'Manchukuo War-Criminals' arrived at the station of *Suifenho* on the Sino-Soviet border. *P'u-yi* and his fellow prisoners were informed by a grinning Soviet officer that they were to be handed over to the Chinese Communist authorities the next morning, then, smiling even more broadly, advised the apprehensive 'criminals' to "sleep peacefully, you will need your strength now".

316

CHAPTER TWELVE

"Re-moulding and Citizenship"

On boarding the train at Khabarovsk *P'u-yi* had been separated from the other members of his household and shared a carriage with Soviet Army officers. They seemed relaxed and quite good humoured and offered to share their beer and sweets with him, which he politely refused. They even tried to cheer him up by telling humurous stories which they acted out, but they were unsuccessful. *P'u-yi* sat impassively, convinced he was going to his death, if not at the hands of these soldiers, then the moment he set foot on Chinese soil. He sat all night huddled in his corner silently reciting Buddhist scriptures his eyes wide open, unable to sleep, he felt the spirit of death circling around him. He was startled by the voice of an officer who was seated opposite; "At dawn you will see your Motherland; to return to your own country after so long should be an occasion for celebration." *P'u-yi* looked at him apprehensively, "You must not worry, Communist party and people have great generosity, so, do not worry." *P'u-yi* was in no way reassured by this ideological speech. He had been hearing of the "raging floods of wild beasts", as the communists were called in China. How could they now be so 'civilized'? The reason why he had not been killed in Russia was because it was one of the allies and restricted by international agreements he reasoned; China, he knew would be a very different matter. These same 'civilized' communists had overthrown *Chiang Kai-shek* and presumably they would hate him even more bitterly than *Chiang* had done. No, there could be little doubt that he was to meet a cruel and humiliating death at their hands. These terrifying visions allowed him no rest or peace and he determined that if he was to die he would shout at the last moment "Long Live the Emperor", and prayed to the great Buddha that he might have enough strength at the last to do so.

Early next morning a Russian officer pushed back the compartment door and told *P'u-yi* to accompany him as a representative of the Chinese Government wished to see him. He felt numb with fear as he followed the officer to another compartment where two Chinese officials were seated, one wearing blue civilian clothes whilst the other was dressed in khaki military uniform without any badges or rank except for a patch which read; 'Chinese People's Liberation Army' across his chest. They exchanged a few hushed words with the Soviet officer and then turned and looked *P'u-yi* up and down, then the civilian said, "I have come to receive you on the orders of premier *Chou En-lai*. You have now returned to your Motherland."

P'u-yi stood, head bowed waiting any moment to be handcuffed, but none were produced. An hour later he was escorted to another waiting train, on entering the carriage he saw he had been placed with officials and members of his household. They were all sitting straight-backed and pale, he caught sight of the soldiers carrying submachine guns stationed at intervals, his heart sank, this was surely going to be the execution ground, he took his appointed place among his companions and waited.

Some little time later the door at the far end of the carriage opened and a short unarmed man walked to the middle of the hushed carriage; "Good, now that you have all returned to you Homeland." He said as he looked from one to another.

"The Central People's Government has made arrangements for you all and you have nothing to worry about. There are medical personnel on board the train, so, if any of you are ill you may ask to see the doctor."

A moment after he had left, soldiers came in and issued bowls and chopsticks "this must mean" thought *P'u-yi* to himself, "that the journey to the execution ground will be a long one and this is to be our last meal." He tried to look out of the windows but they were papered over, no one spoke. Food was served, which helped to break some of the tension, a typical Chinese breakfast which consisted of congee, (a rice porridge) pickled vegetables, salted eggs, the prisoners ate ravenously, partly out of sheer hunger heightened by fear, and partly encouraged by the flavour of home cooking which they had not tasted for so many years. After the meal some of the faces regained their colour and most did not look quite so worried as before, food being regarded by the Chinese as the best possible medicine for all ailments. Some temporarily contented passengers even dozed after their feast, although *P'u-yi* could not, his mind was too active, assessing all the elements that surrounded him, slowly his one reliable companion, despair, took possession of him again.

Next morning the train slowed down and finally came to a halt. Someone murmured, *"Changchun"*. *P'u-yi* searched in vain for a break in the paper that covered the window. The distant sound of people singing filtered into the carriage and he felt sure that this would be his place of execution, for here he had been Emperor; suddenly two soldiers entered the carriage and for a moment he felt sure that they had come for him, but no, they were merely bringing around the morning rice congee, nothing more, slowly the train started to move again.

The next stop was *Shenyang*, the home of his ancestors, this time he convinced himself that this indeed would be his final resting place. An official entered with some papers, mopping his brow he complained, "Ah, its so hot today, now" consulting his list he continued, "the older ones among you are to follow me and come for a rest," then he started reading out the names from his list. *P'u-yi* was convinced that this was a ruse to separate them and as they disembarked, they were directed into a large car which was accompanied by troops armed with submachine guns, he whispered to his nephew 'little *Hsiu*', "This is the end, don't worry, we can go together to meet our ancestors." *Hsiu* looked at the ashen face of his Emperor but before he could answer, a soldier who had heard the pronouncement said, "What are you all afraid of? Haven't you been told that you are coming here to rest? Rest, that is all." The word "rest" had a disquieting finality and only heightened *P'u-yi's* forebodings. The car at last drew up in front of a large building with armed guards at the main entrance, they alighted and were unceremoniously escorted upstairs where they were shown into a large room plainly furnished with chairs and tables laid with fruit, cakes, cigarettes and hot tea.

When they had almost cleared the table of eatables and were sitting smoking and talking quietly among themselves, a man in his forties dressed in blue civilian cothes came in and tried to explain the situation to the apprehensive group; "Rest and relax yourselves after your long journey, there is no hurry, when you arrive at *Fushun* you can rest again before getting down to some serious study." *Fushun*? The military prison? Were they not to be executed after all? Then a familiar face entered the room, it was *Chang Ching-hui's* son who had arrived before them with an earlier group of 'war-criminals', he was able to quieten some of their fears, everyone was alive and well and the young children were either working or studying and were perfectly alright. Tears welled up in *P'u-yi's* eyes and he relaxed for the first time in five days, the spirit of death, who had been his constant companion for so long, now seemed to withdraw, just when he had felt himself slipping into madness.

For the hour or so it took the train to get from *Shenyang* to *Fushun* the atmosphere had changed considerably, the prisoners expressed, for the first time, a hint of optimism, even *P'u-yi* was infected by the faint rays of hope that began to shine around him, but the long trial was not over yet, nor was it to be for many years. The smiles of anticipation vanished when the little group got down from the train to find themselves circled by armed sentries with stern faces. They were bundled into waiting army lorries, and at this stage *P'u-yi* lost consciousness. When he had recovered he observed:

> "I was surrounded by a high, dark brick wall surmounted with barbed-wire and with watch-towers at each corner. I followed the others until we stopped in front of a row of single storied buildings. All the windows were barred. I realized that this was a prison. The soldiers hurried us along a narrow passage into a large room where we were searched. We were then led away along another passage until we stopped at a cell . . . . . . the sound of the heavy iron bolt being pulled across the outside of the door jarred on my ears. The cell contained a low wooden bed, a table and two benches . . . . . . I did not know the former Manchukuo officers who were in the cell with me at all well, and I did not speak to them, so I

322

did not know whether they too were frightened or whether they were just inhibited by my presence. They stood to one side with their heads lowered and did not make a sound. Then I heard the sound of the bolt being pulled, the door opened and a warder came in to take me to another cell, there, I was surprised to see my three nephews, my brother P'u-chieh and my father-in-law Jung Yuan. We had been allowed to stay together. They had already been issued with quilts, mattresses, and washing things. and a new set had been left for me." [1]

"This is a military prison", *P'u-yi's* father-in-law said, "everyone here wears army uniform. It does not seem that we are. . . . for the moment in any real danger, otherwise they would not have given us towels and tooth brushes. Do you remember when we were searched just now? They took our valuables, but gave us receipts, that is not the way ordinary criminals are treated . . . What's more, the food isn't bad either."

P'u-yi was deriving some comfort from this his when little nephew, *Ku* bluntly said; "Perhaps the food is only good because it is our execution banquet!" This had the immediate effect of cancelling out the former reassurance and *Jung Yuan* countered it at once; "No, that sort of last meal always includes wine . . . . . we have had no wine. We must just wait and see if the next meal is as good. If it is, then we will know for sure it is not what you think; I've never heard of a condemned man being allowed more than one banquet, have you?"

Little *Ku* hung his head and made no reply in the face of the irrefutable logic of *Jung's* statement. Even *P'u-yi* was beginning to believe the reasoning of his father-in-law; the food was just as good the next day, the only slight tremor was caused by a medical examination. Once this was over, they were issued with prison clothes, and, as if to confirm *Jung Yuan's* conclusions, a packet of cigarettes . . . . certainly this was not the way condemned men were treated.

Within a few days the first of the "study" books arrived, three in number; 'On New Democracy', 'The History of Modern China', and 'The History of the New Democratic Revolution'.

The immediate reaction to these hastily compiled volumes was, as might be expected, not enthusiastic. The first member of the ex-Imperial family to take any interest in them was 'little *Ku*' who, when he asked for explanations of some of the political terms, was answered by *Jung Yuan*; "Don't get the idea that this is a school . . . . it's a prison."

"But, didn't the governor tell us that we must study these books?" Protested little *Ku*.

"Whether you study or not, this is still a prsion, books or no books. A prison is a prison, you would be far better advised to study the Buddhist scriptures than waste your time trying to learn that stuff." *Jung Yuan* concluded, and to make his point, closed his eyes and began intoning scriptures in a low voice.

A few days later the family group was separated, much to *P'u-yi's* distress. He was at first put into a cell with eight strangers who clearly knew who he was and were inhibited by his presence, the atmosphere became more tense as the day progressed until he felt he could not bear the constrained silence any longer. He crossed the narrow cell and knocked loudly on the heavy wooden door; "What is it?" Came the voice from the warder outside.

"May I ask please to see the governor, I want to talk with him" *P'u-yi* pleaded.

"What about?" Came back the gruff reply.

"I, I want to explain to him that I have never before been separated from my family and, and I cannot settle down without them." This explanation was apparently greeted by silence; however, some short time later the cell door opened, the governor had sent back the message that *P'u-yi* might return to his former family cell. Delighted at this news he gathered up his bedding and taking hold of his small battered suitcase he emerged into the corridor where he met the approaching governor.

"Out of consideration for you older men the authorities have decided to give you food of a higher standard. We thought that if you were living with your relations but receiving different food it might have had a bad effect on them, so we . . . . . . "

"Oh that doesn't matter," *P'u-yi* interrupted, "I can assure you that it will have no bad effects on them." he just stopped himself in time for saying ("They have always had to accept that.").

The Governor looked closely at the ex-Emperor in his crumpled prison uniform clutching his threadbare bedding roll and smiling slightly said:

"Your ideas are far too simple, has it never occured to you that you must now learn to look after yourself?"

"Yes, yes, I realize I must . . .I shall learn step by step I assure . . ."

"Then start learning now!" the governor shouted.

On returning to his family cell he was warmly greeted and when he told them what the governor had said, they looked down without answer for they knew, as difficult as it might be, the imprisoned 'Son of Heaven' had no choice but to comply.

Ten days later *P'u-yi* was moved again to another cell.

> "My cell-mates were all former Manchukuo officers who would never have dared to raise their heads to me in former times; now I found their sniggers very hard to bare. Now that I had to look after myself I found it very difficult; when I was washing myself in the morning they would tell me that I must first fold my bed roll; but by the time I had managed to make an untidy mess of that they were all finished washing and there was no more water and by the time I had finished cleaning my teeth there would be no breakfast left. So it went on all day. But the worst thing of all was the rota of duties under which everyone had to take turns in sweeping the floor and cleaning and emptying the 'night-buckets'. Was I to empty the chamber-pots of others? The very thought of it made me feel sick, luckily I was saved from this horror by a cell-mate who insisted in taking my turn, I was so grateful. But as one danger passed another appeared." [2]

A few days later whilst the prisoners were taking exercise in the yard the governor walked slowly towards *P'u-yi* looking sternly at him all the while.

"*P'u-yi!*" He called in a stern voice.

The sound of his personal name came on his ears like a whip-lash; the use of it had always been forbidden and in prison he had always referred to by his number 981. He gave the governor a bewildered stare.

"*P'u-yi!*"The governor repeated walking up to him.

"Yes . . . . .governor"

"*P'u-yi*, were you not issued with the same clothes as all the others?"
The ex-Emperor nodded.

"Then why have you let them get into such a terrible state, look at yourself." By now the other inmates were all looking at him as he stood dejectedly before the governor. All the drab coarse clothes around him were at least neat and clean, whilst his were creased and grimy, one pocket was half torn off, buttons were missing from his jacket, it was inkstained, his trouser legs seemed to be of different lengths and his shoes had only one divided lace between them.

"How did your clothes get in such a state?" The governor questioned, "you must pay attention to the way others do things. If you can learn from the good points of others only then will you be able to make progress." This said the governor turned and left the exercise yard leaving 981 standing head bowed before the scornful gaze of the other inmates. There were audible sniggers, and the odd word of ridicule assaulted him from the crowd. He turned away for them in anguish, tears coming into his downcast eyes. "They want to ridicule me for their own amusement." He thought to himself. He looked up at the high grey walls; all his life he had been surrounded by walls of one kind or another, but at this moment of misery these seemed the cruellest and highest.

Two months later he was transferred to *Harbin* prison, it was towards the end of October and when *P'u-yi* first saw this former "Manchukuo" prison his heart sank. It had been built by the Japanese for the express purpose of confining the worst of the 'anti-Japanese-Manchukuo' dissidents and had gained the reputation of being a 'death camp'. It consisted of two fan-shaped two storey cell-blocks with a high watch-tower in the centre. There were iron bars an inch thick in front and behind each cell, separated from each other by thick concrete walls, each cell capable of holding seven or eight prisoners. There was no furniture and inmates were forced to sleep on the stone floor. This was to be *P'u-yi's* home for two years. This 'Japanese' torture-house has since been demolished on the grounds that it was too "severe", even for condemned murderers, but it was here in this bleak grey world that *P'u-yi* strove to survive.

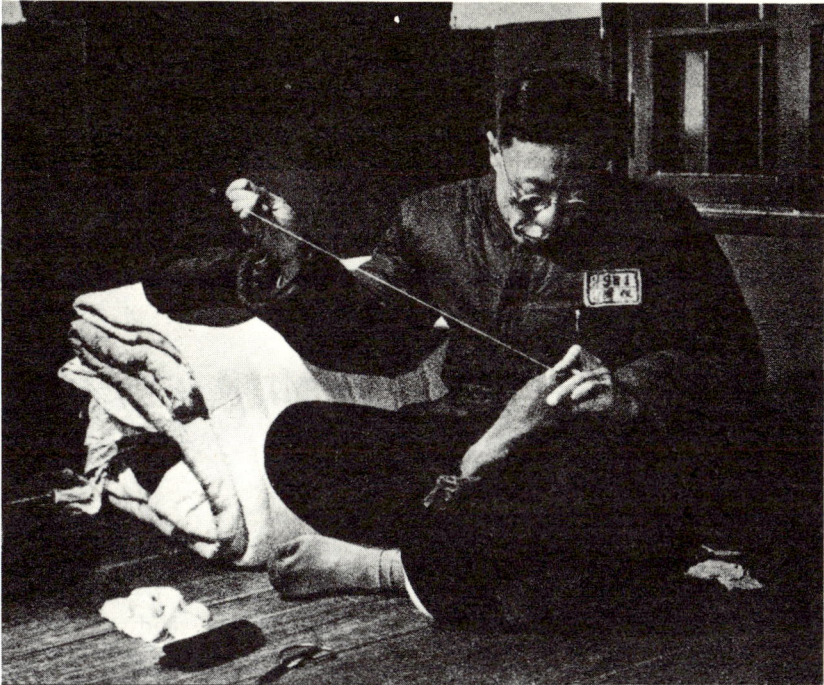

*P'u-yi in Fushun War Criminals Prison mending
and washing his clothes.*

After New Year 1951 the "Regulations for the Punishment of Counter-Revolutionaries" were announced in the Chinese press, and although the papers containing the actual details were denied the inmates, news soon seaped, it now seemed certain that their hour of judgement and death was near at hand. Anxiety was not confined to *P'u-yi*, all the inmates shared it, the arrival of army lorries, the sound of soldiers, the opening and closing of cell-doors and the clanging of the main gates struck terror into the whole prison population, their appetites and moral shrank with each passing day.

One morning the prisoners were informed that a high ranking Security officer was coming to talk to them, his speech would be followed by one from the governor, this had the immediate effect of creating even deeper gloom.

"First, I am here to tell you that the Chinese Government has no intention of killing you," the voice boomed over the crackling loud-speaker system;

"You are here to examine your consciences, to study and thus remould yourselves. The Chinese Communist Party of the People's Government firmly believe that under the People's political power the majority of you criminals will remould yourselves into new men! The Communist ideal is to remake the world! But first, it is necessary to remould all humanity! Ask yourselves, why is the People's Government making you study if it plans to kill you?"

Then the governor's voice took over;

"You have only one thought in your minds, 'death', you imagine that everything that happens to you here is a preparation for only one thing, your death! Perhaps some of you would say that if we are not going to kill you why do we not just let you go? No, that would not be possible! If we were to release you before you had been remoulded, you would surely commit other ideological crimes; besides, the poeple would never approve or forgive you if they saw you as you are now, criminals! You must study, study! And remould yourself, The Chinese Communist Party's policy of remoulding criminals will definitely succeed and facts have proved that the Chinese Communist Party never makes empty claims!"

The crackling stopped and the 'criminals' look furtively at each other, what did it all mean?

The answer was not long in coming; up to this time 'study' had been a somewhat haphazard business now, it was administered by a special political cadre from the central government. His first lecture was on the evils of feudalism and the inmates were ordered to discuss the topic and make notes. A few days later he addressed them again:

"As I have already told you, before you can reform your thought you have to understand the sort of person you are and what your present ideology is. Your ideology is inseparable from your personal background and history; so, you must start by examining them. For the sake of your 'thought-reform' each of you must write his autobiography!"

There was a stunned silence from the inmates; it sounded like a trick by the Communist Authorities to obtain a damning confession from everyone.

> "I regarded the writing of my autobiography as the prelude to my trial and I determined to make the most of this opporutnity to save my life. I knew the line I must take." [3]

> "After I had made many careful revisions I handed it in. I felt sure that it would convince any reader that I had thoroughly repented." [4]

The greatest problem was of course the comparing of the different 'biographical-confessions', for although *P'u-yi* might have edited his own version to perfection and expressed his 'remoulding' in glowing terms, he was sure to be compromised by the facts that other members of his family and ex-officials recorded.

At this time the Chinese Communist Government was preparing to deal with the cases of the Japanese war-criminals and the inmates were ordered to write down all they knew on this touchy subject. *P'u-yi's* fears were immediately rekindled, he had after all been the "puppet Emperor" of Japanese Manchuria and his visits to Japan could not easily be explained away.

By the spring of 1953 a period of "corrective-labour" began at *Harbin*; making cardboard boxes for the local pencil factory. Four hours a day in the factory and four hours of studying became the new never ending routine.

The prison authorities had arranged with the *Harbin* pencil factory that the prisoners should undertake the making of card-board boxes. The warders informed the inmates that, not only would this vary their routine, but manual labour would be good for them and helpful to the factory workers. These words had special significance for *P'u-yi*:

> "I had, of course, never made a pencil box in my life, for that matter I have never even sharpened a pencil! All I knew about pencils was what I could remember from the trade-labels on them . . . . . Venus pencils had an armless woman on them, German ones had clocks and I had never noticed the boxes they came in and therefore I had no idea that making these boxes would cause me so much trouble. Before I had been pasting them for long the novelty wore off, I seemed to be covered in the sticky mess, even my mind felt glued up. By the time I had finished my first, the others had made several, mine did not even look much like a box, or anything else for that matter." [5]

"How on earth did you manage to make that?" Old *Hsien* asked in astonishment, taking the box in his hands. "Why won't it open? What in the name of all the gods is it?"

Hsien had been brought up in Japan and was the former head of the Manchukuo Military Hospital, he had studied medicine and was the brother of the notorious female spy *Pi-hui*, (Kawashima Yoshiko), and son of Prince *Su*. The whole family had been fiercely pro-Japanese and now that the Japanese war-crimes against China trials were soon to begin, the old man seemed to pick on the ex-Emperor of Manchukuo at every possible occasion.

P'u-yi hated being mocked, especially by the bad-tempered old *Hsien* and now that attention had been drawn to his unsuccessful attempt at box-making the others gathered around giggling and pointing at the newly created "disaster". *P'u-yi* jumped to his feet and threw the offending box on to the waste pile.

"What? . . . . . Have you deliberately thrown away your wonderful box?" Old *Hsien* questioned his eyes popping with feigned amazement.

330

"I .. I am not throwing it away." *P'u-yi* murmured as he retrieved it from the waste pile, "I suppose its not so bad as to be completely useless", he added as he placed the offending box on the heap of already finished ones. Then as he turned back to his bench old *Hsien* confronted him.

"Rejects are rejects wherever they are put!"

The ambiguity of the insult was not lost on either *P'u-yi* or his scornful fellow inmates, unable to control himself, trembling with rage he turned on his tormentor;

"How brave you are when it comes to insulting me, like all bullies you show yourself to be a coward when you are faced with the strong, you . . . ."

"Me a bully? Who am I aftaid of? You still think that you are Emperor and that everyone has to wait on you and flatter you. . . . you . . . ."

"Quiet! Quiet you prisoners get on with your work" came the admonishing shout of the warder. Old *Hsien* shuffled away, but *P'u-yi* realized that he had no intention of letting the matter end there.

The next day the old antagonist sat himself next to *P'u-yi* and tutted and clicked his tongue as he scrutinized his victim's box-making. *P'u-yi* moved his chair and sat with his back to him, determined not to lose his temper again with this foolish old trouble maker.

That evening the prison authorities sent in some sweets to reward the Box-mokers;

"Well, Mr *P'u-yi*, you did a little better today, didn't you?" Old *Hsien* pronounced.

"Yes, a little better, no rejects today", *P'u-yi* parried.

"Hm, it seemes to be you would do a lot better if you were more humble." Old *Hsien* jibed smiling coldly.

"What is there to be proud about in making boxes", *P'u-yi* demanded his temper rising, it seemed that old *Hsien* always struck when he saw his victim relaxed and at ease.

"If I make any more reject boxes I am sure that you will point out the fact to me, you are worse than a Japanese fish-seller." Old *Hsien* snapped at the bate; "Look" he exclaimed holding one of *P'u-yi's* boxes aloft for all to see; *P'u-yi* almost choked on his sweet, the label was upside down, "Look", repeated the old tormentor, "even the label is a reject!"

P'u-yi could stand it no longer, he reached up, took the box from the gloating old man and hit him squarely on the head with it. This had the opposite to the desired effect, old *Hsien* merely increased his attack, hoping about holding his supposedly injured head; "Temper. Temper . . . . still acting the Emperor are you? What are you going to do? Chop off my head?" Just then the sound of the warders approaching tempted him to shout even louder, "Still dreaming about being Emperor again are you? You must be criticized for your own good, don't you know that is the people's way?"

"You are talking nonsense," *P'u-yi* answered, "I have never been trained to make boxes or anything else, that perhaps is my loss, I am slower than all of you, all this is new to me, can you criticise me for being born to the life I was? I am trying to adjust but you do not help me with your cruel behaviour. . . ."He was now almost sobbing, "there, will that satisfy you?". The others crowded around and separated the two protagonists and tried to smooth over the argument.

It was a large room and apart from *P'u-yi* and old *Hsien* there were sixteen others, two former Manchukuo officials and fourteen ex-officers. The prison warders entered and after a few hushed words with some of the inmates one picked up the offending box and walked over to where *P'u-yi* was standing, "Why quarrel over such a trifle? This is a very fair box, so, the label is upside down, why not just stick another on the right way up?"

The incident was closed, but not forgotten, for soon after this they were organized into a production line, each attending to one process. All were in agreement, it made the work easier and lighter and *P'u-yi* felt that he would be able to eradicate his former shortcomings under this new system. But, before long a bottle neck built up on his section and of course the first to notice it was, old *Hsien*, "One person's incompetence is affecting the work of all of us. Something MUST be done about it!"

P'u-yi was moved back to work on his own, much to his embarrassment.

"Once again I knew the total misery of loneliness. I was rejected by my fellow prisoners, I felt as though I had been standing naked before them, unable to clothe my incompetence. Old Hsien had won, he even coughed in a disgusting fashion every time he passed my table, his deeply pitted face revealing his delight in my misfortunes. How I needed just one sympathetic soul to talk to, everyone ignored me. That night I had a terrible nightmare, old Hsien's face was enormous and gazing evilly down on me, "You are a reject! You have always been a reject! And a reject you shall remain to the end of your miserable days!" It boomed. Then I saw myself squatting by a bridge like one of the monkey's guarding the bridge that the eunuchs had told me about when I was a boy. Then, I felt a cool hand on my head and awoke with a start. There was a figure in white standing beside me, my heart almost stopped, then the figure spoke, "You are running a very high fever, don't worry, you are quite safe the nurse is here to give you an injection, you will be well again soon." Then I drifted back into sleep.

I was ill for over two weeks but gradually recovered as I remained in bed doing neither any work nor study. I thought, thought more than I had during the previous two years; these ranged from imagining mountians of cardboard boxes with old Hsien enthroned on top to the terrifying face of the old Empress Dowager Tz'u-hsi from the mists of my childhood memories. Why had she chosen me to be Emperor? I who had been an innocent ignorant child, taken and enclosed behind the high walls of the 'Great Within'. There I had not been taught even the most basic of practical knowledge, with the result that now, I was almost completely inadequate. My real knowledge and skills were really less than a child's. I was now mocked and bullied by creatures like old Hsien, even if I was allowed to live by myself I knew that I would be incapable of surviving. Tz'u-hsi was alone responsible for my present pathetic state and I hated her for it. Whenever I had been laughed at previously or been shown to be incompetent I had presented it bitterly, hating those who found fault with me, and the People's Government that was incarcerating me. Now I began to think that some of the wrong was with myself. I really was laughable, ignorant and incapable. Previously I had resented the disrespect in which my nephews and the others held me, but now I saw that there was really no reason why they should respect me. . . . . . what after all, was so divine about me?

The Mongol old Cheng had once told me, that when his father Babojab rebelled in the early years of the republic the whole family had sworn to be prepared to die for the sake of my restoration; his mother had worshipped me as god. He had then added bitterly that it was a thousand pities that she was now dead otherwise, 'I would have told her that the Hsüan-t'ung Emperor was now no more than a piece of rubbish, a reject!''

I had been deeply hurt by this, now I realized I could not blame them, all of them, for saying what they did.

In turn I blamed the old Empress Dowager and her ministers of making me Emperor and I hated the Forbidden City with a new intensity.'' [6]

From the end of 1953 onwards the inmates studied 'Imperialism' in all its forms for some three months and the subsequent discussion and self-criticism sessions that this generated were painful in the extreme for prisoner 981.

In March 1954, most of the prisoners were moved back to *Fushun* prison so that the 'investigating organization' could begin its work which commenced with the 'investigation of Manchukuo war-criminals' towards the end of that month. The People's Government had made thorough preparations for this investigation and a batch of Japanese war-criminals were transferred to *Fushun*. The Government had been collecting and colating material for several years and some two hundred investigators were involved, all of whom had undergone special political and legal training.

The investigations proper commenced at the end of March. As far as the prisoners were concerned the investigations consisted of reporting the alleged crimes of others and admitting their own. By the end of the year the investigations were basically finished.

A meeting was called at which the prisoners were informed that now, after the past few years of reflection it was time for them to openly acknowledge their personal guilt. The Government would now examine all the 'confessions' and reports of the crimes committed by the Japanese war-criminals, and the cases of Chinese traitors. They were further informed that whatever decision the Government finally made would be dependent on the nature of the crimes and the attitude of the prisoners; leniency to those who confessed and severity to those who resisted. Another nightmare was beginning, not just for *P'u-yi*, but for all the inmates. Again *P'u-yi* was obliged to write his life history for the investigators. One key aspect caused him much deliberation and worry;

"When writing about the end of the Manchukuo period I came to the declaration of war against Japan by the Soviet Union. I had, at the time, been terrified that the Japanese might push me aside at this time of crisis, and had thought of any way that I might ingratiate myself with them. On the night after hearing of the Soviet declaration of war on Japan I had sent for Chang Ching-hui and Takebe (the head of the 'General Affairs Office of the State Council of Manchukuo'), on my own initiative. I gave them an oral edict ordering them to mobilize speedily and do everything possible to support Japan against the attacks of the Soviet Red Army. What was I going to say about this now? I had to mention it as there was always the possibility that others knew of it; but if I did mention it, then would not this one action I took without prompting from the Japanese, make the investigators suspect that I had not, after all, been completely under the control of Yoshioka? If they did, the whole of my story would be invalidated. I therefore decided not to say too much on the subject, a little reticence could surely do me no real harm. I put the blame for this edict on Yoshioka, then rewrote the confession out again, going into more detail citing the things that I dared mention and concentrating on the crimes of others. Finally I handed all this in and waited to be summoned by the investigators. Then my mind filled with dark mist; I wondered what form the questioning would take, would the interrogator be an ordinary human or a monster? Would they use torture on me as the old Board of Punishments had? I was sure, whatever it was it would be cruel. I spent ten uneasy days tortured by such thoughts, then, the dreaded moment arrived and I was told by the warders that the investigators wanted to see me. I was taken to a room that was about ten metres square; in the middle was a large desk behind which sat two men. . . they indicated for me to sit on a chair beside the desk.

The older of the two men than asked my name, age, place of origin and oddly enough my sex; the younger man's pen scratched across a pile of papers as he wrote down my answers. 'We have read your confession,' said the older man 'and now we are going to talk with you.'

They asked me many things about my childhood up to the time of my capture and seemed satisfied with my answers, 'Very well, that will do for the moment, interrogator Chao may have some further questions to put to you later.' "[7]

P'u-yi returned to his cell a little reassured, he had not been tortured, and apparently his answers had been accepted. Next day he was taken again to the small square room, this time only *Chao* was present and *P'u-yi* wondered if this young man could discern the truth or would he be hot-tempered and aggressive. "There is one question I would like to ask you" *Chao* began, "What was the procedure for issuing Imperial decrees and rescripts in Manchukuo?"

P'u-yi answered directly, then *Chao* mentioned one decree in particular,

"How long before this particular decree was promulgated, did you see it?"

"Probably one or two days beforehand," *P'u-yi* answered, "but it could have been three or even four."

"There is no need for you to reply at once. You can tell me when you remember clearly. Now, let us go on to another question."

P'u-yi could not answer this satisfactorily either and the young interrogator said,

"Well, let us put that one aside too until you can remember. Now," producing a pile of material *P'u-yi* had written, "You have written here that the Japanese invaders took sixteen million tons of grain from the Northeast in one year, following a plan made by Furumi Tadayuki, the war-criminal who had been deputy chief of the 'General Affairs Office of the State of Manchukuo'. This is far too vague. Which year was this? How can you be sure that the figure was sixteen million tons? You must give me more details! Do you know the annual grain production figures of the Northeast?" *P'u-yi* remained silent.

"Then, on what evidence did you base the statement in your written material?" The question was greeted by more silence, "Was your only authority gossip? Do you yourself believe what you have written?"

"I . . . . .I don't know" *P'u-yi* replied at last.

"You don't know? . . . . If you do not believe it yourself, why did you write it? . . . . . If you do not tell the truth about yourself and others what is the point of writing anything?"

P'u-yi left the room realizing that he could not escape from the truth of the interrogator's last statement, but whose view of the truth, theirs or his? Soon after this *P'u-yi* attended a study meeting on the crimes of the Japanese in the Northeast, it came as a severe shock to him and left a lasting impression.

The most striking testimony came Furumi Tadayuki who participated in the proceedings himself. He told how both he and his superior Takebe Rokuzo had planned and carried out the Japanese policy of "looting" the Northeast. He spoke in great detail about the policy of forcibly seizing the land of the peasants for the resettlement of Japanese immigrants; about the detailed policy of the 'Five year plan for Developing Production' that was wholly designed to plunder the natural resources of the area; about the official use of opium for the common people and of consolidating supplies for Japan's war in the Pacific. One incident in 1944, when fifteen thousand labourers were conscripted from the Northeast for military construction at *Wangyemiao* in *Khingan* Mountains. The conditions under which these unfortunate men were forced to work were so bad that more than six thousand died. He told how the 'Japanese Opium Policy' was initiated early in 1933, at a time when the Japanese Army was in need of funds for its invasion of *Jehol*. As production of the "evil Poppy" was not then under Japanese control they imported over two million ounces and dropped leaflets by air all over the area encouraging the cultivation of the plant. By 1936 the Japanese had extended the area under Opium Cultivation, expanded production and gave themselves the legal monopoly of its sale. Opium-dens sprang up everywhere and young people were especially encouraged to use the drug. In 1942 the Japanese 'Asia Rival Council' held a 'Conference on the Opium Needs and Production of China', which passed a resolution stating that, "Manchukuo and the Mongolian border regions are to meet the opium requirements of the Greater East Asian Co-Prosperity Sphere"; the area under cultivation was then increased to three thousand hectares. It was calculated that Manchukuo, before its collapse, produced over three hundred million ounces. There were said to be three hundred thousand addicts in *Jehol* alone.

This, disgusting though it was, was nothing to what was to come when the catalogue of brutality and murder was exposed. The Japanese Police were directly responsible for countless atrocities and apart from the confessions of the officers involved a number of eye-witness accounts were read; one came from a sixty-one year old peasant *Hung Yung-hung* who had been arrested for sending a letter to the Allied Army and had been a witness to a mass murder:

> *"On the 26th day of the second month the police took over thirty of us prisoners to dig a pit outside the western gate of Chaoyuan. We returned to the prison after nightfall. On the 27th I and Wang Ya-min, Kao Shou-san and Liu Cheng-fa were taken in one group and twenty others were taken in a second group to outside the west gate, there a group of twenty men had been shot. Then, another batch of twenty-two men were brought and shot. The police then poured petrol over their bodies and set them on fire. One of the men was not yet dead and he tried to run away, his clothes were on fire, they shot him. When all the bodies had been burned we were told to bury them. This grave of forty-two men is still there outside the walls of Chaoyuan, I could find the place easily again."*[8]

By the end of the meeting the hall was in uproar;

"We demand that the People's Government avenge the Chinese people!" "The Japanese and Chinese traitors must pay this debt with their blood!"

These and many other shouted protests echoed around the room and *P'u-yi* felt that they were all aimed at him, he had been Emperor of this barbarous State, he must be the biggest criminal of them all, his punishment the most severe.

One of the rules during this lengthy investigation was that every report had to be read by the person accused in it, if they agreed with the facts they had to sign it. This, as far as the Japanese ex-Manchukuo officials were concerned, presented few problems to *P'u-yi* as they had mainly stuck to the facts and had avoided any elaborations, he willingly signed them. But, when it came to the written testimony of his relations it was not quite so straightforward. One part of his brother-in-law's report contained the following:

> *"On the evening of August 8th, 1946 I went to the palace to see P'u-yi. He was writing something, Chang Ching-hui and Takebe were waiting outside for an audience. P'u-yi showed me what he had written had its general import was that all the Manchukuo armed forces were to fight alongside the Imperial Japanese Army to help defeat the invading Soviets. He said that he was going to give this order to Chang Ching-hui and Takebe, and he wanted to know if I had any suggestions to make. I said that there was no alternative."* [9]

This *P'u-yi* saw as disastrous to his own credibility having, in his confession laid all the blame on Yoshioda. Piece by piece uncompromising details of daily life were coming to the surface and though innocent enough at the time, now, taken out of context and scrutinized they became more than unflattering to the demoralized ex-Emperor.

Another excerpt from his brother-in-law's report which described and episode already chronicled shows just how differently it reads out of context:

"When films were shown in the palace we had to stand up if the Japanese Emperor came on the screen, and clap any shots of Japanese soldiers making an attack. This was because the projectionists were Japanese.

There was a drive to economise on coal in 1944, P'u-yi gave orders that there were to be no more fires in the Yi Hsi Lou (a building within the palace complex), in order to impress Yoshioka, but he used an electric fire in his own bedroom without letting Yoshioka know. When P'u-yi fled to Talitzukuo he put the Japanese goddess and the picture of Hirohito's mother in his carriage on the train, and he made a ninety degree bow whenever he passed them. He ordered everyone to do the same." [10]

This general disaffection seemed to run through almost the whole of the ex-Imperial family, especially among the younger members, *P'u-yi's* nephews; time and time again it was their testimony that caused him the greatest angusih. The accuracy of these statements is questionable but their effectiveness at this crucial time was undeniable. The following is part of such a statement made by 'little *Jui'*:

"This person P'u-yi was cruel, frightened to death and extremely suspicious; he was also very cunning and thoroughly hypocritical. His treatment of his servants was inhuman. When he was in a bad temper he cursed them and had them beaten, even if they had done nothing wrong. If he was feeling at all unwell or tired the servants suffered for it, and they were lucky if they got away with just a cuff or kicks. But when he was with strangers, especially foreigners he behaved as if he were the kindest man on earth. . . . .
In Tientsin he used to have people beaten with wooden rods or horse-whipped; in the Manchukuo era, many other new kinds of floggings and tortures were added . . . .
He made everyone act as his accomplice. When he wanted someone beaten he suspected collusion if anyone refused to do the beating for him or did not hit hard enough. If that happened, the beater would be beaten himself, and much harder. All of his nephews and attendants flogged people for

him at some time or other. One page of twelve or thirteen years old, (Chou Po-jen, an orphan), was once beaten so badly that he had wounds a foot long on his thighs which took two or three months to heal, even under the attention of a doctor. While this boy was recovering P'u-yi told me to take milk and other things to him and say, 'How kind His Majesty is to you! Did you ever have such good things to eat in the orphanage?' " [11]

After reading this and similar denunciations he almost gave up hope of ever justifying himself to the Communist authorities, true or false these statements had been made and he realized that denial would only add to the morass of 'evidence' that was growing daily around him.

> "In the past few years I had learnt something of my true worth from my pitiful attempts at washing clothes and making boxes, now, I had a clear indication of what others thought of me, even the members of my own household. I saw myself reflected in all the mirrors that surrounded me, I saw the image of a guilty man, completely lacking in glory with no possible justification for my past conduct. I signed the last accusation against me, neither knowing nor caring if it was true or false and walked away down the long corridor my mind full of sorrow and despair." [12]

After the mass denunciations, followed inevitably by the self-criticism session, *P'u-yi* found himself more isolated than ever, he felt that the authorities' determination to make him a "new man", was doomed to failure. Preparations for May Day were announced and the prisoners were allotted various tasks, that chosen for *P'u-yi*, whose general health and eye-sight were failing, was in the prison garden. He had only been at work a short time in the flower beds when old *Chang* approached him and snatched the plant he had just uprooted from his hand and shouted:

"What is this? What is this that you have pulled up? Eh?"

"A weed, I was told to weed the flower beds, wasn't I?" *P'u-yi* answered quietly.

"Do you call this a weed?" Old *Chang* continued at the same accusing volume, "Can't you tell the difference between a weed and a flower? Can't you see that all the plants you have uprooted are flowers?"

The kneeling ex-Emperor and the red-faced Mongol had became the centre of attention and the others pressed forward to see what all the noise was about. *P'u-yi* remained on his knees, head bowed wishing that all the flowers or weeds would disappear.

"You really are a reject, look at this!" Old *Chang* shouted to the others snatching a pile of flower plants from the pile in front of the embarrassed *P'u-yi* and scattering soil over him,

"He can't even tell the difference between flowers and weeds! I suppose he had pots of weeds in his palace . . . . "

A warder interrupted the tirade by taking the plants from the angry old man's hand,

"Do you have to behave like that? What good does such behaviour do? You should be helping and teaching him who to weed properly, not shouting at him, if he is shown he will not make a mistake the next time. Now, all of you, go back to your work."

"I just never imagined that there were still people who did not know the difference between weeds and flowers, that's all . . . . . . "
Old *Chang* self-consciously protested.

"Well, now you know differently, we must help him, shouting helps no one." Admonished the warder as *Chang* skulked away, then, turning to *P'u-yi* he helped him to his feet and noticed that his cheeks were stained with a mixture of tears and earth,

"Now, you go and clean yourself up and then report back to me and I will try to help you." *P'u-yi* nodded and walked slowly across the yard to the wash sheds, the warder watching him as he almost stumbled across the uneven ground, "this man was the Son of Heaven", he thought to himself, "now he is a sad old wretched man unable to look after himself and always making mistakes, who could believe it."

Another nightmare began as *P'u-yi* had to fight his way through accusations made against him from all sides, but mainly from his ex-officials who were also trying desperately to extricate themselves from the crushing burden of guilt. Somehow he survived. One evening after one of the more harrassing interrogations he opened his small suitcase to find a particular article and as he fumbled in the semi-darkness his fingers touched the leather photograph wallet he had kept hidden away, taking it out he opened it, Johnston's face smiled back at him, he shut it quickly and replaced it in the safety of the case and wept for a long time.

Soon after the Chinese New Year of 1956 the prison Governor announced at the end of a lecture on the 'Growth of the National Economy':

> *"You have already studied the documents on the First Five Year Plan, agricultural co-operation, and the socialist transformation of handicrafts and privately owned industry and commerce. You have also read in the papers about the appearence of joint state-private enterprises in some of the big cities. But all you know about socialist reconstruction is what you have learnt from books. You need to see the present state of the country with your own eyes to be able to link your studies with reality. For this reason the Government will arrange for you to make visits to the outside in the near future. You will see Fushun first, and later you will go to other cities."* [13]

The atmosphere this generated amongst the inmates was cheerful and expectant, they interpreted it as meaning that the day of their final release must be near at hand. All that is, except *P'u-yi*, who knew that even if some were released their number would certainly not include him. The thought of trips 'outside' filled him with dread for he had no way of knowing what reception would await him, if it was anything like that inside the prison, then, it was to be strenuously avoided.

> "During the first day of our visit we all tried to make ourselves inconspicuous. When we reached Taishanpao, (a village on the outskirts of Fushun), none of us dared to raise his head. In this uneasy state we listened to the leader of the co-operative talking about their past and present. Everyone we met was kind to us and I congratulated myself on going unrecognized for so long. But when I was in the

house of a member of the co-operative at the very end of our visit something happened, and I was unable to conceal my identity any longer.

The house that we visited belonged to a family named Liu. The parents worked in the fields, the eldest son was a book-keeper, the second son was at middle school, and the daughter worked at a local hydro-electric plant. When we arrived only Mrs Liu was at home. She was cooking, and when she saw the commune cadre leading us in she took off her apron and invited us to sit in the north-room which was newly built. She treated us as guests, inviting us in and to sit; there was a chest of draws by the wall, on it stood a large clock, a tea service, a number of vases and a tea caddy.

The cadre did not tell her who we were and asked her to talk to us. Although she was not a good talker she told us in her own simple way that she came from a family of seven who lived by tilling the soil, seven 'mou' (a little over an acre), and that during the Manchukuo period they had lived like beggars. "We grew rice, but we had to eat acron-flower as we had to hand all our rice to the government officials. We all dressed in rags, some families were even worse off than us. One New Year the children had nothing to eat and it was very cold, my husband said that we should have a secret meal of rice to honour the New Year. That night, very late the police raided the village, and we were very frightened; but in fact they had come to take men for forced labour, my husband was taken and we wept for everyone knew that few men ever returned from these forced labour camps. . . . ." She then showed us the rice barrel in the corner which was full, "These days its a different story but how often did we see it in the time of Kang-te?" (*P'u-yi's* title as Emperor of Manchukuo.) This last remark stung me to the quick. [14]

P'u-yi had been apprehensive since entering the house, without thinking he stood up and said: "The Kang-te of whom you speak is me, I was the Emperor of Manchukuo, I owe you my apologies." Even before he had finished speaking the other ex-Manchukuo officials were on their feet. The old lady was dumbfounded, she had guessed that they were prisoners but this revelation was almost too much for her and she buried her face in her hands. Then looking up she said after a deep sigh; "It is all long over now, let us not say anymore about it," and wiping away a tear she added, "as long as you are good men now and help our country and people, you will be alright." At these quiet words the embarrassed men, almost without exception, were deeply moved, some sobbing to themselves. The attitude at the end of their three day visit was in sharp contrast to the beginning, and when they arrived back at prison there was much to think about and discuss.

On 10th March, three days after he had returned from the first outside trip a warder told *P'u-yi*, his brother *P'u-chieh*, his two brothers-in-law and his three nephews to go to the Governor's office. They were all puzzled but on entering the reception room they could not believe their eyes; there to their astonishment stood *P'u-yi's* uncle *Tsai Tao*, with his third and fifth sister. They had been separated for over ten years. His uncle was looking fit and well and when he looked at his sisters in their cotton-padded clothes he thought he was dreaming.

Tsai Tao was *P'u-yi's* only surviving relation from the previous generation. In 1954, he had been elected to the National People's Conference as the representative of China's two million Manchus. He was also a member of the National Committee of the Chinese People's Political Consultative Conference. He confided to *P'u-yi* that he had even met Chairman *Mao* a few days ago at the second meeting of the congress. He said that the premier *Chou En-lai* had introduced him to the Chairman as Mr *Tsai Tao*, the uncle of *P'u-yi*. *Mao* had shaken him by the hand and said, "I have heard that *P'u-yi's* studies are progressing very well; why don't you go and visit him?" It was a joyous reunion for all concerned and the news that most of the *Aisin-Gioro* clan were safe and that Manchu nationality had been recognized filled *P'u-yi* with more happiness than he had known for many years.

Many of the members of the ex-Imperial clan had changed their names to *Chin*, *Chao* or *Lo*; his fathers family in *Tientsin* for example, had taken the name of *Chin* and after the proclamation of the Communist Constitution there were over 2,400,000

Manchus registered throughout the country. This change affected not only the young members of the *Aisin-Gioro* clan but also the *beileh* (Manchu nobles), such as *P'u-yi's* uncle *Tsia Tao* and the ex-Emperor's sisters. *Tsai Tao* was now 69, but neither his mental nor physical vigour was in any way impaired, he treated his ex-Imperial nephew with the same mixture of charm and deference he had always shown. He explained that after the communist takeover he had worked for a department of the People's Liberation army in charge of horses and, it was with a twinkle in his eye, that he related the fact that he had spent some time in the steppes of the Northeast, their old homeland. At present he was about to undertake a trip to inspect the work of the national minorities as part of his duty as a member of the National People's Conference. When the People's Liberation Army had entered *Peking* many of the old Manchus had been very apprehensive, especially those of the Imperial clan but in April 1949 the new authorities published an eight-point covenant promising, among other things, to protect the lives and property of all except counter-revolutionaries and saboteurs; this seems to have calmed their worst fears. Most of the Manchu old guard had not been involved in the "Manchukuo puppet regime", as it was now termed, and almost all retained their old reverence for the 'Lord of Ten Thousand Years'; when they learned that their Emperor was in prison their worst fears resurfaced.

> "In Peking all the descendants in my generation from my great-grandfather the Tao-kuang Emperor and of Prince Tun, Prince Kung and Prince Ch'un were all over sixty, excpet for a few cousins of mine who were a little younger. My second cousin P'u-chin, (*P'u Hsueh-chai*), an outstanding artist, calligrapher and player of the 'ku Chin' (an ancient Chinese stringed instrument), was now over sixty . . . . . . He had been elected president of the Calligraphy Research Association and had become a teacher at the Academy of Chinese Painting where his brother P'u-chien also taught. His cousin P'u-hsiu who had been a 'Companion of the Chien Ching Gate' in the Forbidden City and who had looked after my property at Tientsin whilst I was in Changchun, had now lost his eyesight and had been unable to earn a living. (After the establishment

of the People's Republic he had been invited to become a member of the Institute of Classical and Historical Studies. (Similar institutes had been brought into being all over China and many of the old Manchu Guard found their intimate knowledge of former times in demand).

What made the deepest impression on me was the change I could see in my sisters. Some six months before I had exchanged letters with my brothers and sisters in Peking. I had gleaned from what they wrote that sweeping changes had taken place in society but I had never given the matter any serious thought. During the 'Manchukuo' days all my brothers and sisters with the exception of fourth brother and sixth sister had lived with me in Changchun and accompanied me on my flight to Tunghua. After my capture I was very worried that they might be treated as traitors. Second sister's husband was the grand-son of the Manchukuo premier Cheng Hsiao-hsu, third sister was married to the son of the Chief of Staff to Chang Hsun, the monarchist general who had planned my restoration in 1917. The father-in-law of my fourth sister had been the Manchu official who had become notorious for killing the woman revolutionary Chiu Chin in 1907. All my sisters' husbands had been either military or civil officers of the 'Manchukuo regime'. Only sixth and seventh sisters had been regular students, but I was still greatly worried in case they were all punished because of me. Later my correspondence with my family proved to me that my worst fears were in fact groundless. Fourth brother and seventh sister were both now primary school teachers, sixth sister a freelance artist, fifth sister a seamstress whilst sixth sister had become a 'social activist'.

Third sister had been through a very hard time. Her son had been ill and she had not returned to Peking after the Japanese surrender but had stayed in Tunghua. She had no property and as she was afraid of attracting unwelcome attention because of her origin and fine clothes she had set up a cigarette stall in the Tunghua market place. She was very nearly discovered by the Kuo-min tang agents and forced to leave; she was also swindled by a local merchant who sold her matches that would not strike. After a few years of this wretched life she finally returned to Peking in 1949. She now had a new job which she spoke about with great enthusiasm, explaining the new marriage law to her neighbours. It gave me quite a surprise; she had always been a very refined young lady and always asking me for presents. Who would have expected that this spoilt lazy girl was now a social activist? I once made a calculation on the basis of the 'Jade Register' of the Imperial family compiled in 1937, this provided information about the rate of infant mortality in my branch of the Aisin-Gioro clan. Thirty-four per cent of the children had died in the Ch'ing Dynasty, ten per cent during the republic, but none in the ten years since the 'People's Liberation'. The figures for the whole Aisin-Gioro clan were staggering, almost forty-five per cent of the boys and girls of both my and my father's generation had died in childhood, almost all under the age of two. My brothers and sisters in Peking now had twenty-seven children between them. My uncle Tsai Tao had sixteen grandchildren and great-grandchildren. P'u-chieh's wife had written to him from Japan telling him that their elder daughter, a girl of eighteen, had killed herself in a suicide pact with a young man because of a love affair; there were different versions of the story none seemed satifactory." [15]

From that year onwards the family continued to visit *P'u-yi* in prison.

During June and July 1956, *P'u-yi* was called as a witness in the military tribunal hearing the cases against the Japanese war-criminals at *Shenyang*. At this time there were over a thousand Japanese in captivity in China, some in *Fushun*, and others at *Taiyuan*, all charged with crimes during the Japanese invasion of China. Forty-five were put on trial at this time, one was Furumi Tadayuki the former vice-head of the 'General Affairs Office of the Manchukuo State Council'. It was against him and his superior Takebe Rokuzo that *P'u-yi* was called to give evidence. (Furumi was sentenced to eighteen years imprisonment and released in February of 1963).

P'u-yi giving evidence at the Military War Criminals Tribunal of the Supreme People's Court. To the far right is Furumi Tadayaki.

"As I went into the court-room I thought of the victory in the Korean war, the successful signing of the Geneva Agreement, and China's position in the world since the founding of the People's Republic. The trial of Japanese war-criminals on Chinese soil was unprecedented." [16]

It was a harrowing experience for *P'u-yi*, balanced as he was between the end of the old life and the possible beginning of a new, not knowing how far the pendulum of fate would swing and if it would ultimately be in his favour.

Part of Furumi's speech before sentence was passed upon him is worthy of notice:

"There is not a square inch of land in the whole of the Northeast that bears no trace of the barbarity of Japanese

349

Imperialism, and these crimes of Imperialism were my crimes. I most deeply acknowledge that I am a war-criminal who had openly violated international law and humanitarian principals by committing the gravest crimes against the Chinese people, and I sincerely ask their forgiveness for this. Over the past six years the Chinese people have treated me with kindness, although I was so terrible a criminal, they have given me a chance to reflect upon my crimes. Thanks to this I have recovered my conscience and reason, I have learnt which road men should take. I do not know know I can possibly repay my debt to the Chinese People." [17]

After *P'u-yi* had given his evidence, the principal judge had turned to Furumi and asked him what comments he had to make. He bowed deeply and said that every word of the ex-Emperor's testimony was true.

The Japanese war-criminals after finally returning to their own country contributed to a book entitled, 'The three-all Policy', (burn all, loot all and kill all), the policy of the Japanese invaders of China. In it they described how they had exterminated whole regional populations, used poor Chinese peasants for experiments in bacteriological warfare, dissected people alive, together with many other bloodchilling revelations. The book was reported to have sold fifty thousand copies in the first week in Tokyo, much to the annoyance of the American occupying authorities.

As Chinese New Year approached in 1957 prison discipline relaxed and among the celebrations some theatrical presentations were planned by the inmates. Most of the Japanese war-criminals had been sentenced and transferred and their place was taken by a new set, the *Chiang Kai-shek* war-criminals. The prison authorities and their political masters, made sure that the content of the proposed plays should be in keeping with the new ideology. Two plays were outlined, one a form of documentary or 'living-newspaper' called, 'The defeat of the Aggressors', about the British invasion of Egypt; the other about the 'transformation' of the Manchukuo traitors.

In previous years *P'u-yi* had not really taken part in these festivities except for singing occasionally in the choir, and he was startled when old *Wan*, the chairman of the study committee approached him.

"*P'u-yi*, there is part for you in the first play. It won't be very difficult and there aren't many lines to learn. You can even improvise if you want to. It would do you good as part of your re-education . . . . what do you think?"

"Well . . . " *P'u-yi* replied hesitantly, "if you think I could do it . . . I am willing to try."

"Of course you can do it, " grinned old *Wan* with delight, "You have a good clear voice, a good presence . . . . . . "

"You don't have to flatter me, I have already agreed. What sort of part do you want me to play?" Enquired *P'u-yi* with a half-smile.

"The play is called, 'The Defeat of the Aggressors', its about the Brtitsh invasion of Egypt and all the rumpus it caused. Its all based on newspaper reports, old *Jun* is playing the leading role, the foreign secretary Selwyn Lloyd, you will be playing a left wing Labour MP."

Later *P'u-yi* went to see his brother *P'u-chieh* who had written the script to hear his explanation of it and copy out his lines. As he was to play a foreigner he had naturally to wear Western costume, these he borrowed from the prison clothes store and hurried back to his cell to try them on. He had just put on the rather tight white shirt when old *Yuan* came in.

"What on earth are you doing *P'u-yi*?" He enquired in astonishment.

"I'm going to be in a play," he half coughed, "please help me loosen this collar its choking me," this achieved, he next tried on the waistcoat which was also too tight, "can you loosen the belt on the back for me?" *P'u-yi* asked, "I must have put on some weight, can you pass me the shoes." He added perching on the side of the table.

"Ugh, these English leather shoes are too tight, do I really need to wear them, after all I am only playing an MP?"

"Of course you must, why I've heard that British Labout MP's even wear scent, how can you wear Chinese padded boots with your costume? Don't worry after you have worn them for a while they

351

won't pinch and you can soon get the waistcoat altered. You just relax and learn your lines", he encouranged, then turning at the door he added smiling, "Its great news to hear that you are going to be in the play, I shall tell all the others" and with a shrill crackling laugh he scampered away down the corridor.

Although his part was small and there were few lines, he recited them incessantly in order not to let either himself or the others down. Towards the end of this play Selwyn Lloyd was making a speech in the House of Commons trying to justify the failure of the invasion, when some opposition members started to question and then attack him. This was *P'u-yi's* cue, he had to stand up and say to the foreign secretary, "There is no need for you to continue to defend your actions! They are disgraceful, disgraceful . . . . I say it again, disgraceful!!" The chamber was then supposed to break into uproar and demand his resignation, at which tumult *P'u-yi* was to shout "Get out . . . . get out!!"

The night before the play was to be performed, *P'u-yi*, who had never suffered from insomnia lay awake, tossing and repeating his lines over and over. The next day was New Year, and the prison hall was full to overflowing as a delighted audience enthusiastically applauded the choral and solo singing, Mongol songs and dances, conjuring; all leading up to *P'u-yi's* big moment. The interval finally arrived and the 'Defeat of the Aggressors' opened the second half. Old *Jun* strode onto the stage looking to the audience every bit as real as the misty impression they had of what Selwyn Lloyd actually looked like, old *Jun's* big nose and wide eyes suited the part admirably. He raged and thundered to the delight of his captive audience, then ten minutes in old *Yuan* nudged the already petrified *P'u-yi* and whispered to him, "Now, don't be too wooden, put some go into it, come on, its your turn" pushing the terrified MP into the centre of the stage; he gazed at the audience and felt his legs trembling, "Go on, say your lines, argue with him!" Old *Yuan* hissed . . . . *P'u-yi* stiffened, took a step towards the posturing foreign secretary, pointed an accusing finger at him, and realized in panic, that he had forgotten his lines! "No. . . . No, No. . . . No. No. No!!" He heard himself shouting in English, even old *Jun* under all his makeup turned pale.

"No. . . No . . ." *P'u-yi* continued, then suddenly remembering his lines, he delivered them point blank into the startled face of his fellow actor, who promply forgot his lines, but *P'u-yi* was now in control of the situation;

"Get out . . . . . .get out! Get out!!" He roared, and the bewildered foreign secretary did just that. The audience went wild, shouting and cheering for to them it appeared as a great feat of realistic acting.

When he rejoined his fellow inmates in the hall for the second play, he was congratulated from all sides, for the first time in many years he was popular with his fellows, not a "reject", not shunned, but applauded.

He resumed his seat with a light heart, hardly able to believe in the change his brief performance had made to the attitude of his fellows.

During the second half of 1957 more trips into the surrounding country were organized for selected prisoners and *P'u-yi* visited *Shenyan*, *Anshan*, *Changchun* and *Harbin*, slowly his understanding of·this "New China" began to grow:

> "During the previous forty years I had forgotten that I too was really Chinese. I had joined the Japanese in praising their nation as the most splendid on earth; I had believed that everything foreign was best; I had always thought the Chinese stupid compared with the white races. Even during my time in prison I was unconvinced that this new China could take its place in world affairs . . . . After the Korean armistice was signed and China played a new role in world affairs at the Geneva Conference I had thought about China's international relations since the Opium Wars; from the time of my great grandfather the Tao-kuang Emperor to the Kuo-min tang and Chiang Kai-shek there had been a continues attitude of self-depreciation. During those 109 years the bringers of cannons and opium, the destructive pseudo-missionaries, the foreigners who thought themselves civilized and superior . . . . all had come to China and burned, killed, plundered and cheated. These foreign powers had stationed their troops on Chinese soil, cities, ports, whole tracts of land became

353

theirs and they had regarded the Chinese as little better than slaves, savages in need of their cruel god. They had caused China many years of disgrace, forced her to sign unequal treaties and turned her people into slaves. They had stolen railway-building rights, mining rights, river transport rights; demanded 'equal opportunity', 'the open door', 'most favoured nation treatment', 'leased territories', 'mortgaged tarriffs', 'consular jurisdiction', the list seemed endless. But this shameful period had gone forever. The Chinese people were now rebuilding their own country, a country in which foreigners could no longer demand but only wait to be invited." [18]

1958 began full of hope for *P'u-yi*. During most of the past autumn he had been engaged in the annual coal-moving, instigated by the prison authorities against the long cold winter, although in no way used to this sort of heavy manual labour, he was determined to keep up with the other inmates and not let himself down in their eyes. Of course he still made mistakes but the laughter that greeted them was no longer directed at him, but rather with him, this made all the difference.

As the year dragged on with its endless 'study sessions', 'self-criticism' and the allotted tasks of manual labour, *P'u-yi's* high hopes began to grow tired, as tired as his weak body, he could see no end to his captivity and the letters he received from his sisters only brought his despair into darker relief. On September 14th 1959, a special resolution was passed by the standing committee of the National People's Congress entitled:

SPECIAL PARDON

Proposal of the Central Committee of the Communist Party of China to the Standing Committee of the National People's Congress

The Central Committee of the Communist Party of China proposes to the Standing Committee of the National People's Congress that in celebration of the tenth anniversary of the foundation of the great People's Republic of China a number of reformed war criminals, counter-revolutionaries and common criminals should be granted special pardons.

We have won a great victory in the socialist revolution and the socialist construction of our country. Our motherland is flourishing, production and construction are forging ahead, and the living standards of the people are being steadily raised. The government of the people's democratic dictatorship is unprecedentedly consolidated and strong. The people of the whole country are more politically conscious and better organized than ever before. The political and economic state of the nation is excellent. The policy of the Party and the People's Government of combining punishment with leniency in dealing with counter-revolutionaries and other criminals, and the policy of combining reform through labour with ideological education have achieved great successes. The majority of the prisoners now under detention have been remoulded to a greater or lesser extent, and a considerable number of them have genuinely reformed.

In these circumstances the Central Committee of the Communist Party of China believes that at this time, when we are celebrating the tenth anniversary of the founding of the People's Republic of China, it would be fitting to announce and put into effect a special pardon for a number of war criminals, counter-revolutionaries and common criminals who have really reformed. The adoption of this measure will help to change negative factors into positive ones and be of great assistance to their further remoulding, as well as to that of the other criminals still in captivity. It will enable them to realize that under our great socialist system their future lies in reform.

The Central Committee of the Communist Party of China requests that the Standing Committee of the National People's Congress will consider this proposal and reach an appropriate decision.

Mao Tse-tung
Chairman of the Central Committee
of the Communist Party of China

September 14, 1959

This was heard first by the prisoners over the radio and was greeted with much enthusiasm, this was on September 18th, from that time onwards the inmates talked of little else. They were informed by the governor that they would, if included in the pardon, be released in batches providing that they had been sufficiently "remoulded" ideologically. For most of the prisoners it meant reunion with their families, but it was not so for *P'u-yi*. After the general hysteria had subsided, he realized that he really did not belong in this "New China", any more than he had really belonged in the Old. His mother has been dead these many years, his father had died in 1951, his wives were either dead or had divorced him. The prospect of living alone filled him with dread and he reasoned that he might as well end his days in prison, at least he was fed and housed after a fashion.

Some weeks later the inmates were summoned to the assembly hall. Draped across the platform was a large red banner on which was written, "Fushun War Criminals Prison Special Pardon Meeting", the sight took his breath away. Sitting on the platform were the two prison governors, a representative of the Supreme People's Court and other officials. After a few words of preamble the governor introduced the representative from the Supreme People's Court, he rose and walked to the centre of the platform, consulted a sheaf of papers and said in a loud clear voice; *"Aisin-Gioro P'u-yi"*. *P'u-yi's* heart leapt, a warder escorted him to the front of the platform where he stood shaking, head bowed, listening intently as a voice read out:

Notice of a Special Pardon
from the Supreme People's Court of
the People's Republic of China

In accordance with the Special Pardon Order issued by the Chairman of the People's·Republic of China on September 17th, 1959 this Court has investigated the case of the "Manchukuo" war criminal Aisin-Gioro P'u-yi.
The war criminal Aisin-Gioro P'u-yi, male, 54 years old, of the Manchu nationality, and from Peking, has now served ten years' detention. As a result of remoulding through

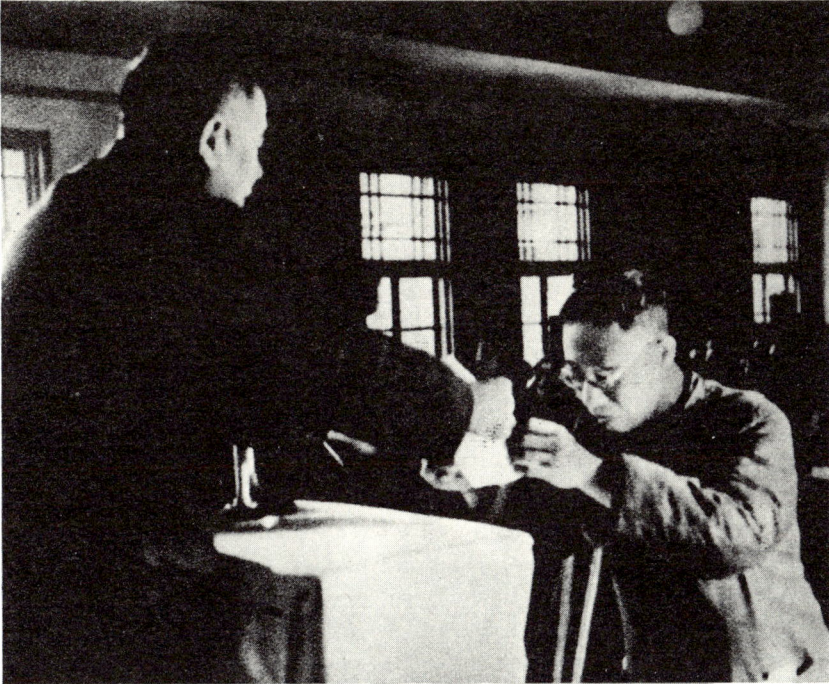

中華人民共和國最高人民法院
特赦通知書

1959年度赦字第 C11号

遵照一九五九年九月十七日中华人民共和国主席特赦令，本院对
在押的伪满洲国战争罪犯爱新觉罗·溥仪进行了审查。

罪犯爱新觉罗·溥仪，男性，五十四岁，满族，北京市

人。该犯关押已经满十年，在关押期间，经过劳动改造和思想教育，

已经有确实改恶从善的表现，符合特赦令第一条的规定，予以释放。

P'u-yi receiving his 'Special Pardon' on 4th
December 1959 and the document itself.

labour and ideological education during his captivity he has shown that he has genuinely reformed. In accordance with the stipulations of Clause I of the Special Pardon Order he is therefore to be released.

Supreme People's Court of
the People's Republic of China

December 4th 1959

Before the speaker could finish *P'u-yi* had burst into tears, sobbing as though his poor tired heart would break. Someone shook his hand, the sound of clapping surrounded him and he wept as never before.

> "I was on a train. Outside was a snow-covered plain, bright and vast, unfolding before me like my own future. Inside the train I was surrounded with ordinary workers. This was the first time in my life that I had sat with them or shared a train compartment with them. Now, I was one of them." [19]

On December 9th he arrived in *Peking*, his former capital that he had left thirty-five years before. As the train steamed to a halt, he peered out of the carriage window along the platform, then taking his one battered case he alighted, there waiting for him were his fifth sister and fourth brother whom he had not seen for four and twenty years respectively. They shook hands warmly and addressed him in the old familiar form of 'Elder Brother', the sound of which brought the old lost days flooding back. They walked down the long platform arm in arm then, as *P'u-yi* approached the station clock he stopped and took out his pocket watch, the prison governor had insisted he take with him, it was the French gold watch which Reginald Johnston had given him in 1924 at the Foreign Legation, in the case lid was a faded photograph of his 'English Tutor'; he gazed at it for a moment, checked the time with the station clock, replaced it carefully in his pocket, both he and it had come home.

He stayed with his fifth sister and her family in their small home. The next morning she asked him what he would like to do, "Now that you are back in the old city you should have a good look around, after all, you were never free to see the outside city in the old days. Where is the first place you would like to see?" She enquired.

"The *Tien An Men*, (the Gate of Heavenly Peace)" , *P'u-yi* answered at once.

"Very well, 'Elder Brother' that is where we shall go."

When they arrived *P'u-yi* gazed at the majestic *Tien An Men* Gate which stood before him, on his left stood the imposing Hall of the People, on his right the Revolutionary Museum, behind him the Monument to the Revolutionary Heroes. In company with fifth sister and his cousin *P'u-chien* he strolled west towards the Cultural Palace of the Nationalities with its white walls and blue roof.

"Elder Brother, are you tired? This must be the first time you have walked so far."

"No, no I'm not at all tired," *P'u-yi* replied, "for a very good reason, this is the first time I have ever walked so far." he added with a teasing smile.

> "The first time I rode on a bus I gave my cousin P'u-chien a fright. As I was waiting in the bus que I saw other people standing aside for old people and children to get on first, so I did the same for a woman who was standing next to me. I did not realize that she was the conductress. Seeing that I was not getting on, she jumped aboard, the door closed behind her and the bus moved off. A few moments later my cousin came rushing back from the next stop, and even before he reached me we were both laughing." [20]

In March 1960, he was sent to the Peking Botanical Gardens where he spent half of his day studying Communist ideology and the other half working in the greenhouses, learning how to transplant and care for seedlings.

The Peking Municipal Authorities organized a number of visits around the city for the newly released prisoners so that they might get to know and use the city better. All the usual places were included, factories, school, libaries and finally the *Forbidden City*. His former inmates insisted that *P'u-yi* become their unofficial guide and after some coaxing he agreed.

P'u-yi at work in a green house.

His voters card issued in 1960.

He was more than a little apprehensive as they entered his former home, it was different, changed; gone was the stale air of decay he had known. All the hangings at the doors, windows, bed covers, cushions, all were new, made by the Palace Museum's own work shops from the original patterns.

As he passed through the various courtyards and palaces where he had once been the 'Son of Heaven', 'The Lord of Ten Thousand Years' the present seemed to slip away from him, his companions merged into the long shadows that surrounded him; the sounds of their voices ebbed into silence, he stood there alone in the *Purple Forbidden City*, a lonely bewildered little boy;

"Whenever I think of my childhood my head fills with a yellow mist, the glazed tiles were yellow, my sedan chair was yellow, my chair cushions were yellow, the linings of my hats and gowns were yellow, the dishes and bowls from which I ate and drank, the material in which my books were covered, all, were yellow . . . . yellow . . . . yellow . . . ."

Epilogue

After his release from prison in late 1959 *P'u-yi* was obliged to continue his 're-moulding', and in March 1960 he was sent to the Peking Botanical Gardens of the Institute of Bontany of the Chinese Academy of Sciences. There he spent half his time working, whilst the other half was given over to study. Under the watchful eye of the staff he learnt to plant seeds, tend them and transplant them in hot-houses, this time without digging them up in mistake for weeds.

On 26th November 1960 he was issued with a voters card. In March of 1961 having completed the preparatory stage in his ideological re-education he became an assistant library attendant for the Historical Materials Commission of the National Committee of the Chinese People's Political Consultative Conference.

In 1962 he was invited to sit on the National Committee of the Chinese People's Consultative Committee to hear reports of 'Construction of the Motherland'. He died quietly in his sleep early in 1967, a little over seven years after being released from prison.

Reginald Fleming Johnston, K.C.M.G., C.B.E., Hon. LL.D., M.A. (Oxon) F.R.G.S., died in Edinburgh on the 6th March 1938 at the age of 64. This remarkable and modest man perhaps contributed more to Anglo-Chinese understanding than any other Britain of his generation. He was the author of many books of which the most outstanding was 'Twilight of the Forbidden City', (Gollancz 1934).

On returning to England he became Professor of Chinese at the University of London. To the end of his life he remained staunchly pro-Chinese and devoted to his 'Imperial pupil', who was still 'Emperor of Manchukuo' when Johnston died; he did not live to see the downfall and humiliation of his beloved *P'u-yi*. The only items Johnston mentioned in his will were his 'sable coat' and some of the other presents *P'u-yi* had given him, they seemed all he really cared about. To the end he remained fiercely anti-christian and left clear instruction that "No religious service of any kind is to be carried out in connection with my person". His ashes were scattered over the waters of Loch Cranignish.

List of Illustrations

Notes

Chapter 2

1   Johnston R F, The Nineteenth Century and after, (trans) July 1912.
2   Wilhem Richard, A Short History of Chinese Civilization, London 1929.
3   Lattimore Owen, Manchuria, Cradle of Conflict, New York 1932.
4   Hart Sir Robert, These from the land of Sinim, 1900.
5   Giles Dr H A, China and the Chinese, New York 1902.
6   Sun Dr Yat-sen, The Principals of the People. (San-min-chu-i). An English version which was published in the North China Daily News in 1927.
7   Ibid.
8   Johnston R F, Twilight in the Forbidden City, London 1934.
9   Ibid.
10 Aisin-Gioro P'u-yi, Journals (edited extracts) Peking 1964.
11 Ibid.
12 Ibid.

Chapter 3

1   Yuan Ming Yuan (Summer Palace) is not as usually assumed one building but a collection of palaces and pavilions, a number of which were designed in the European baroque style by the Jesuits and destroyed by the French and English expeditionary forces in 1860.
2   Ting Dr V K, Saving China, Tientsin Press 1922.
3   Aisin-Gioro P'u-yi, Journals (edited extracts) Peking 1964.
4   Cheng Shih-gung, Modern China 1919.
5   Bigelow P, Prussian Memories, New York 1915.
6   Aisin-Gioro P'u-yi, Journals (edited extracts) Peking 1964.
7   Ibid.
8   Ibid.
9   Ibid.
10 Escarra Jean.

Chapter 4

1   Irons N J, Fans of Imperial China, Hong Kong 1982.
2   Ellis Haverlock, Psychology of sex.
3   Aisin-Gioro P'u-yi, Journals (edited extracts) Peking 1964.

Chapter 5

1   Li Chi, Records of rites and ceremonies, Da Tai edition.
2   Giles Dr H A, Chinese Biographical Dictionary.
3   Johnston R F, Twilight of the Forbidden City, London 1934.
4   Not to be confused with Ch'en Pao-chen, who was governor of Hunnan in 1898. Bland in his 'China, Japan and Korea' confused the two, as have a number of Western Writers.
5   Aisin-Gioro P'u-yi, Journals (edited extracts) Peking 1964.
6 to 12 Ibid.
13 Johnston R F, Twilight in the Forbidden City, London 1934.
14 Ibid.
15 Ibid.
16 Aisin-Gioro P'u-yi, Journals (edited extracts) Peking 1964.

Chapter 6
1   *Aisin-Gioro P'u-yi, Journals (edited extracts) Peking 1964.*
2   *Johnston R F, Twilight in the Forbidden City, London 1934.*
3   *Ibid.*
4   *Aisin-Gioro P'u-yi, Journals (edited extracts) Peking 1964.*
5   *Ibid.*

Chapter 7
1   *Johnston R F, Twilight in the Forbidden City, London 1934.*
2   *Ibid.*
3   *Ibid.*

Chapter 8
1   *Johnston R F, Twilight in the Forbidden City, London 1934.*
2   *Ibid.*
3   *Johnston R F, A Chinese Appeal to Christendom Concerning Christian Missions, 1911.*
4   *Kotenov, New Lamps for Old, 1931.*
5   *Chin Leang, Private Journals.*
6   *Johnston R F Twilight in the Forbidden City, London 1934.*

Chapter 9
1   *Li Lien-ying, Private Diary.*
2   *Aisin-Gioro P'u-yi, Journals (edited extracts) Peking 1964.*
2   *Ibid.*

Chapter 10
1   *Aisin-Gioro P'u-yi, Journals (edited extracts) Peking 1964.*
2   *Ibid.*

Chapter 11
1   *Aisin-Gioro P'u-yi, Journals (edited extracts) Peking 1964.*
2   *Ibid.*

Chapter 12
1   *Aisin-Gioro P'u-yi, Journals (edited extracts) Peking 1964.*
2   *Ibid.*
3   *This forced autobiography was published in Chinese in a heavily edited form in 1964 and extracts from it were used to promote the Chinese "Communist ideology" although lurking behina this "remoulded" attitude much of P'u-yi's real attitude is disearnable.*
4   *Ibid.*
5   *Aisin-Gioro P'u-yi, Journals (edited extracts) Peking 1964.*
6 to 20   Ibid.

Bibliography

P'an Chi-chiung, Mo-tai huang-ti ch'uan-ch'i, Peking 1957.

Ch'in Han-ts'ai, Man-kung ts'an-chao, Shanghai 1946.

P'u-Chieh Mrs, Ruten no Ohi (Memoirs of Hiro Ashinkarkura), Tokyo 1959.

Yamada Seiichiro, Kotei Fugi, Tokyo 1960.

Umemoto Sutezo, Sen-un Ajia no Joo, Tokyo 1957.

Ts'ai Tung-fan, Tz'u-hsi, Shanghai 1918.

Tsebg P'u, Nieh Hai hua, Shanghai 1906.

Ch'ai Q, Fan-t'ien-lu ts'ung-lu, Shanghai 1926.

Aisin-Gioro P'u-yi, Journals (edited extracts), Peking 1964.

Hummell, Eminent Chinese of the Ch'ing Period, Washington 1942.

Young C W, The International Relations of Manchuria, Cambridge 1929.

Cameron M E, The Reform Movement in China 1898-1912, Stanford 1931.

Wen Ching, The Chinese Crisis from Within, London 1901.

Der Ling, Two Years in the Forbidden City, New York 1924.

Cheng Shih-gung, Modern China, London 1919.

Fa Ling Ta Ch'uan, Law and ordances of the Republic of China, Shanghai 1924.

Bland J O P, China, Japan and Korea, 1921.

Lattimore O, Manchuria Cradle of Conflict, New York 1932.

Bland & Blackhouse, Annals and Memoirs of the Court of Peking, London 1914.

Bland & Blackhouse, China Under the Dowager Empress, London 1910.

Johnston R F, Twilight in the Forbidden City, Gollancz, London 1934.

Johnston RF, Lion and Dragon in Northern China, London 1910.

Sun Dr Yat-sen, San-min Chu-i (North China Daily News)1927.

Hsiung S I, The Life of Chiang Kai-shek, London 1948.

Tong Hollingtion, Chiang Kai-shek, London 1930.

Lord Brooke, An Eye-witness in Manchuria, London 1905.

Mcaleavy H, A Dream of Tartary, London 1963.

Asakawa K, The Russo-Japanese Conflict, Cambridge, Mass. 1904.

Ching-shan, Diary, Leyden 1924.

Ken Shen Weigh. Russo-Chinese Diplomacy, Shanghai 1928.

Wu Yung, The Flight of an Empress, London 1937.

Tsou Jung. The Revolutionary Army.

Liang Ch'i-ch'ao, Intellectual Trends in the Ch'ing Period.

Weng T'ung-ho, Diaries, Shanghai 1883.

Chinese Political & Social Review, Peking 1926, Vol X No 4.

North China Herald, 1900-1926.

North China Standard, Peking.

The North China Daily News. 1927.

The Times Literary Supplement, August 1933.

The Observer, August 1933.

China Illustrated News, Tientsin.

Peking Gazette.

Peking and Tientsin Times.

New China Review.

Journals of the North China Branch of the Royal Asiatic Society, 1933.

International Jounral of Ethics, April 1922.

Daily Telegraph, February 6th 1924.

The Fortnightly Review, October 1933.

The Peking Leader, March 1919.

The New China Review, 1921.

Shun-t'ien Shih Pao, July 1923.

Ching Pao, Shanghai.

Yu-hsi shih-chieh and Hung mei-kuei.

Press cutting in the Mainichi Shimbun collection, Tokyo.

London Illustrated news, 1900-1927.

Hsin Ch'ing Nien (New Youth), May 1917.

Shih Pao, Peking.

Pei-Ching Jih Pao, Peking October 1919.

Yu-hsi Jih Pao, Peking 1921-1922.

Imperial Court Gazette 1900-1924.

Far Eastern Times, November 1917.

Min Pao, Peking August 1925.

Index

369

370

Acknowledgements

First, I must express my heartfelt thanks to my Chinese friends, many of whom I cannot name for obvious reasons, they have helped in the long research in so many ways, often, at risk to themselves, supplying invaluable documents and evidence. To Anson Wong, who has assisted me at every stage, and who has accompanied me on many of my quests for information, I owe a debt of gratitude that these few lines can not begin to repay. Andrew Derbyshire, who undertook the arduous task of proof-reading. David Frost for the excellent cover photo and the reproduction of the many, historic illustrations. To all those who have given of their time, advice and enthusiasm, thank you. This book must be my offering to them all.

月該所開幕瓏寶雜陳奇珍備具中外瞻仰俵

為巨觀此該所成立之實在情形也惟此項古物係

屬清皇室私產本擬由政府備價收歸國有徒以財

政支絀迄未實行現值大局少定清皇室待款甚亟

沿格對於民國及清皇室均買有保存之責朝少

維護常用兢兢竊以國粹重要為中外觀瞻所係

自未便由清皇室收回而未經付價以前究未能屬

諸國有常此懸置珠非永久辦法亟應從速解決